KENSHO

A Modern Awakening

*Instigating Change
in an Era of Global Renewal*

SUSAN STEINBRECHER
with JOANNE MOYLE

ISBN: 1461094682
ISBN-13: 9781461094685
LCCN: 2011906006

Published by
Kensho Press

DEDICATION

I would like to dedicate this book to my wonderful siblings. Each one is unique and extraordinary in their own way.

To Patrick, who represents strength and grace —
a difficult combination to master.

To Betty, who truly understands the bigger picture —
that all there is in this world is love.

To Ethel, who is a real God-sent angel to many on this earth.

To Mike, who has a contagious spirit of fun and optimism.

To Jim — there is not a man with a bigger heart than he.

To Julie, who possesses a deep sense of care and compassion
for others.

I am inspired by each of you!

DISCLAIMER

The information contained herein is not intended to provide specific physical or mental health advice or any other advice whatsoever for any individual and should not be relied upon in that regard. It is not intended to be, nor should it be, a substitute for direct, personal, professional physical or mental health care and diagnosis from a qualified, licensed practitioner. The author is not a medical professional and nothing herein should be misconstrued to mean otherwise.

CONTENTS

Preface	Kensho: A Modern Awakening *. . . Just a Little Dust on Their Eyes*	xi
Introduction		xv
Chapter 1	Shift Happens	1
Chapter 2	Towers in the Sky	13
Chapter 3	Why This Works	29
Chapter 4	A Sense of Community	53
Chapter 5	Conscious Optimism	69
Chapter 6	The Collective Global Brain	89
Chapter 7	Benevolent Revolution	103
Chapter 8	What's Wrong With This Picture?	117

Chapter 9   Making the Connection   139

Chapter 10   Euro-Sense   153

Chapter 11   Flower Logic   169

Chapter 12   A New Vintage   183

Chapter 13   Follow the Yellow Brick Road   211

Chapter 14   Neuro-What?   233

Chapter 15   Distractions and Dogma   251

Chapter 16   A Giving Spirit   263

Chapter 17   Life: A Love Story   275

Chapter 18   Going Mental   297

Chapter 19   Mindful Mastery   325

Chapter 20   The Age of Imagination   351

Epilogue   371

Notes and Sources   375

ACKNOWLEDGEMENTS

I love the phrase "It takes a village", and this book is a perfect illustration of it. The words "thank you" are completely inadequate to express how I feel about the numerous people who helped with this project. Every person who touched this book provided their love, skill, and spirit. First and foremost, I want to thank Joanne Moyle. This book would have been utterly impossible without her deep sense of caring, perseverance, expert skill, and love. This planet is a better place because of her. Joanne's work is truly magical.

Secondly, I would like to thank Jill Armstrong for her hard work as well as her humor and light, which were so welcome and critically necessary during those times when it looked like we would never finish.

A special note of thanks is owed to Mark Sebanc, who made a promising draft come to life with his exceptional editing skills, as well as to my team of associates, Robert Schaefer and Lorinda Bailey, who contributed in numerous ways, whether it was editing, contributing text, or attending the numerous planning meetings and conference calls that helped take the message of the book off the page.

Last but not least, I am deeply grateful to every person who provided us with their time and expertise by granting us the interviews for this project. Whatever substance and depth are to be found in this book can surely be attributed to their peerless insight and wisdom.

PREFACE

Kensho: A Modern Awakening

...Just a Little Dust on Their Eyes

A great being (Brahmā) appeared to Prince Vipassi, urging him to share his good news and enlightenment with the world. The prince declined the advice remarking that, if he were to teach his wisdom to others, they wouldn't be able to receive or grasp it anyway. He fretted that communicating the simple message of awakening to the hapless masses was like "wading upstream". Awakening seemed to him a fruitless endeavor and an effort largely wasted.

But the great Brahmā was persistent in asking Buddha Vipassi to share the hopeful news of awakening. After all, Brahmā maintained, people merely have "a little dust on their eyes", which prevents their ability to be free.

Scholars and masters of Zen Buddhism have described the word "Kensho" as being the "heart of Zen", and it literally means "awakening". The Japanese Zen Master Dogen referred to the gentle realization of *Kensho* as the awakening to one's true nature:

Learning the way of enlightenment is learning selfhood.
Learning selfhood is forgetting oneself.
Forgetting oneself is being enlightened by all things.

Although this book is not an investigation of ancient Zen Buddhist wisdom or awakening, it is inspired by the archetypal message of *Kensho*.

I believe that to become enlightened by the world around us is to ultimately discover oneself along the way. This can be difficult and challenging at times, and it is easy for us to focus instead on our inner fears and anxieties, allowing skepticism to inform our orientation to the world. Our news media drives this message on a daily basis and leads people toward a world that focuses on the "uncommon ground" of humanity, with stories about what separates us from one other.

I have learned, throughout my career as an executive coach and organizational consultant, that cynicism exists whenever "a little dust on our eyes" blocks our ability to awaken to what is truly possible within ourselves, hindering us from seeing past our problems and our fears with a brave and open heart. Awakening to the joy and beauty of life requires courage, if we are to grow beyond the constraints of pessimism and angst and thus be transformed by the wonder and beauty of the world around us.

This book presents some of the many "awakenings" that surround us and the myriad reasons for harnessing optimism. Many of the voices presented here offer a bold and optimistic vision for our future, casting a golden light upon the shadow of fear and revealing the great potential for humanity in the 21st century. I am thrilled to have unearthed the stories of some of the many remarkable people around us today who impart their transformative vision. Their lives – and their life's work – provide a clear sense of purpose and boundless promise, allowing us to look toward our future with a sense of awe and gratitude. My hope is that they may inspire you to discover what is at the heart of the true meaning of Kensho: a joyful awakening to the interconnectedness of all beings in the world, not to mention the marvels that lie within our very selves, so that we may walk with buoyant steps as we proceed on our life's journey.

We are not an island; we are nothing less than "the stuff of stars".

INTRODUCTION

The times are strange and out of joint. It's in the air. We can sense with disquiet that the balance of things is shifting. Even the weather seems disordered and in flux. The old order is faltering, and we look at the world around us with alarm and confusion. Many of us feel weary and overwhelmed, unsure of how to cope with everything that's happening.

We are tired of being lied to and manipulated by our government, by corporations, by Wall Street, by the institutions that for so long have given structure and meaning to our society. Along with our disillusionment comes a feeling of being untethered and cast adrift. As human beings, we feel deprived and incomplete, inasmuch as we crave meaningful connections in our lives and in our relationship to the world.

A few years ago, we saw the end of a decade of more opulent times. We had chased the dream and felt that, because we had worked so hard, we bloody well deserved "it". And so we got "it" whether or not we had the money in the first place. "It" included everything bigger: cars, TVs, and especially our homes, together with the luxurious accoutrements that went along with them.

In the end, the problem is that, the more you own, the more it owns you. We have to insure, preserve, and secure all of these possessions, and that's an enterprise that becomes complicated and exhausting. The

excitement begins to wear thin. We begin to reel from the debt burden that we assume to purchase more… and more. Even though we
wanted bigger and better "stuff", we are not any better off for it.
Many believe that it is this seductive, dynamic acquisitiveness that
played a large role in getting us into the financial troubles that came
to a head a few short years ago.

Maybe the best thing to come out of this dilemma is that it has
prompted us at length to question the whole framework within which
we have built our lives. What's important to us now? Why aren't we
happy? And why does everything seem so hard?

In business, more and more people have become disenchanted
with corporate life as it is. They long to do something that has meaning and value, something by which they can make a difference in the
world. They are struggling to create more balance in their work and
especially in their personal lives. This sense of inner conflict has left
many of us asking, *Where do we go from here?*

Often the path to enlightenment comes through a crisis. When
our lives are spinning out of control, we finally pay attention. While
no one wants to endure these hardships, if we use this time as one of
learning and awaken to the clear realization of what's truly important
in life, maybe we can get back on track.

I believe that it's critically important as well for us to change our
perspective every once in a while, in order to see ourselves and the
world in a new light. By adopting this frame of mind, some of us are
actually embracing this time of upheaval. We've come to be grateful
for the challenge, seeing it as an opportunity for growth and learning
and developing new talents and skills. We've begun, in fact, to live life
like it's a momentous occasion of wonder.

Current trends seem to confirm that this hankering for a change
in perspective has a natural appeal for us. Thus, in recent years, we

have become more focused on personal transformation, spending over 11 billion dollars a year on self-improvement products and services, eschewing some of our former, more flamboyant purchases in order to embark afresh on our emotional, mental, and spiritual paths.

Major scientific discoveries, astounding new modes of communication and the exchange of ideas are moving at lightning speed, adding to the pace of change and renewal, speeding the transformation of us and our world. At the same time, personal initiatives like volunteerism have become commonplace, as many of us are putting our minds, our hearts, and our backs into improving the lives of others in our communities, our country, and even the far-reaching corners of the planet.

As well, corporate social responsibility is coming to the forefront of our consciousness. This is mirrored in our asset strategies, with 2.7 trillion dollars going into socially responsible investments. Business is becoming more aware too of the science behind authentic incentives to productivity. A new breed of forward-thinking companies that embrace the concept of "purpose motives"[1] is flourishing, putting people before profits. It is, indeed, an intimidating, awe-inspiring, white-knuckle-ride era we are living in. And sometimes it feels like it's hard to keep up.

Despite the fact that things continue to move so very rapidly, I undertook this project, because I felt myself prompted to gain a deeper, more intimate sense of where we are headed as a global society. So it was that I began researching and interviewing fascinating people who were forward-thinking trailblazers, champions of brilliant ideas. I learned that so much more can be achieved than I ever dreamed possible. It's all a matter of simply shifting our perspective and becoming willing to listen to the wake up call. The days of blinkered, compartmentalized thinking are long gone. All countries, all citizens of this miraculous planet are in this together.

So, what does the future hold? While I don't have the answer, I do know that we are moving into a new frontier, a new way of thinking and being. Join me in discovering some of the most brilliant men, women — and kids! — of our day, minds brimming with exciting new ideas, people who will surely be of inestimable help to you on this journey. Some will be familiar to you, others will not. But all of them will shed the light of their courage and wisdom onto these pages for you. My sincerest wish is that you might draw on their messages of inspiration and hope to buoy your spirit, so that you too may act as a catalyst for change and awakening in your own life and community.

Be strong and bold-spirited, as you engage this wonderful, mysterious world of ours with renewed joy.

One of the core teachings in Buddhism, is impermanence (*anicca*). Nothing lasts forever; nothing is static; nothing remains in a fixed state. The awakened state is connected with an ability to accept the impermanence of everything in our midst, including ourselves. We therefore can fully appreciate the beauty and delicate wonder of all transient phenomena around us.

Everything changes, nothing remains without change.
~ *The Buddha*

I

SHIFT HAPPENS

Imagine how the world has changed in just the last 150 years.

A horse-and-buggy society has given way to the telegraph, the telephone, cell phone technology, and the age of the internet.

In a matter of seconds, you can call a person across the globe just as easily as dialing a friend living next door.

Human achievement has brought us to an unprecedented point on Planet Earth, a point where there are no restraints, not in terms of time, distance, or place, when it comes to our reaching out and connecting with one another.

It is as though the magic that the world's first astronauts felt, when they saw the whole of Earth from far above, has triggered a new reality. Thanks to technology, now we too can view the entirety of our planet in extraordinary ways.

Just look around. Our world in the year 2011 *is* a global village, not some vast, unconquerable, inhospitable mystery for mankind to fantasize about. Global connectedness is the here, the now, and it's the driving, pulsing heart of human history, as we gaze ahead at 2020 and beyond.

Where all this will lead no one knows. But one thing is certain. We, as a global society, stand on the brink of enormous change in the next 20 years.

In fact, experts such as the renowned futurist David Houle believe that there will be as much change on Earth in the next decade as humanity has seen in the past 20 years.

I asked Houle to provide some clarity and bring us up to speed on where we are at this incredible, troublesome, exhilarating juncture in mankind's history and what we might expect in the future. What I learned was that we need to get ready for a few surprises.

The decade ahead, says Houle, is poised to become the single most important and most transformative period in human history in terms of breakthroughs in alternative energy, health, and medicine, as well as economic and political evolution and practice around the world.

Many moral dilemmas will most certainly be faced in this time of change. Turmoil will most certainly follow, as 20th century models of business and government give way to 21st century alternatives.

The landscape of our lives, says Houle, will change profoundly, as technologies that once aided a quadriplegic to connect with a wheelchair or made Twitter possible will morph into the beginning of 'the global brain' and brain wave interface.

That new reality might be frightening to some and exhilarating to others. After all, we humans resist change. It's as true now as it was when early man fastened together the first wheel.

There is uncertainty ahead, to be sure, as we 21st century citizens struggle to find our way by trial and error.

But the future is coming. The time has come to embrace change now and turn the great unknown that lies ahead into what Houle predicts will be a golden era of transformation.

When David Houle's book, *The Shift Age*, was published in 2008, it made huge headlines because of this author's strong, surprising insights into the future of our planet. Houle is ranked as one of the top futurists in the world. He is also frequently called "the CEO's Futurist," having consulted with more than 1,500 CEOs and business owners in the past two years.

Houle has earned such high public regard after 20 years of active leadership in the media and entertainment industries, working with NBC and CBS. He was part of the senior executive team that created and launched MTV, Nickelodeon, VH1, and CNN Headline News. An Academy Award nominee, Houle won two Emmys and acted as Co-Executive Producer for a nationally syndicated kids' program called "Energy Express." He also won the prestigious George Foster Peabody Award and the Heartland Award for "Hank Aaron: Chasing the Dream".

Houle's highly-acclaimed semi-annual "Shift Age Trend Report" is required reading for CEOs and business innovators around the world (found at www.davidhoule.com).

Houle also writes the highly regarded futurist blog, www.evolutionshift.com, with the tag line, "A Future Look At Today".

In February 2010, he became a featured contributor to Oprah.com. He is currently working on a book about transforming K-12 education in America.

You have said and written that one of the main forces today is "the Flow to Global". What do you mean?

We are entering the global stage of human evolution. Humanity has moved from family to tribe to village to city-state to nation state, and now our only real boundary is planetary — at least for the foreseeable future. This means that we are in a real, powerful flow to a global orientation of humanity.

Just think about the word global. It was not a word most of us used 10-15 years ago. Maybe we said we were international travelers or had an international business. Now we talk about participating in the global economy. Think about the major problems that we face as humans and they all have the word global in front of them: global recession, global financial meltdown, global climate change, global water scarcity, global overpopulation.

Another way to think about it is that up to now the word globalization was solely used as an economic term. It is now no longer just that. Today it describes the force that is and will course through all aspects of human endeavor and society.

In the next decade we will begin to realize that this is the global stage of human evolution and there is no turning back.

What would you say is the most significant force today that is moving humanity to this "Flow to Global" and this next global evolutionary step?

I think that it is the accelerating electronic connectedness of humanity. We are becoming ever more connected and it is changing our consciousness.

Our current evolutionary stage – Modern Man – has been on this planet for 150,000 years. As recently as 160 years ago the speed of human communication was a horse day – how far a horse could travel in a day. For example, if something happened in Chicago on a Monday, no one in New York would know about it for a few days. In 1859 the U.S. Postal Service created the Pony Express, as it was determined that a horse could go at a relative gallop for 30 miles. So every 30 miles there was a new horse and rider to carry the mail. That lasted for 2 years, and in 1861 the telegraph was invented – and human communication has sped up ever since.

Today there are more than 4 billion cell phone subscribers in the world, and the global population is 6.8 billion. That means that anyone can communicate with anyone at any time from anywhere. If

I was in a room 15 feet from another person and called them from my cell phone to theirs, it might take 4-5 seconds for their phone to ring. If, standing in that same room, I called someone on the other side of the world, it might take — due to extra relay times through communications satellites — 9 to 10 seconds for their phone to ring. That means that the difference between 15 feet and 12,000 miles is 5 seconds.

For the first time in human history it can therefore be said that there is no time, distance or place limiting human communication. That is a transformative reality that truly connects us all in a brand new, globally-oriented way.

You just used the word "transformative". You have spoken about "the Transformation Decade". Would you please explain what you mean by that?

We have entered the Shift Age, and the first full decade of the Shift Age is the Transformation Decade, 2010-2020. The dictionary definition of transformation is a change in the nature, shape, character, or form of an individual or entity. When you think about that definition it is pretty clear that most things in our lives are being transformed. Just think about how you communicate today versus even three years ago. You probably text, use social media, and think nothing of calling someone in the world no matter where they might be.

The Transformation Decade will be a decade of incredible change. There will be as much change in these ten years as in the past twenty years. This decade will be known for being the decade when humanity fully starts to reorganize around a new global construct. It will also be the single most transformative decade in the history of health and medicine, as we will be confronted with moral dilemmas we have never had to face and for which we are ill-prepared. It will be the most transformative decade in the history of energy, and the energy landscape in 2020 will be noticeably and profoundly different than the current one of 2011.

Transformation and change are often accompanied by turmoil. Will this be a difficult time for many?

Yes, of course it will. Turmoil will occur, as people are largely resistant to change. As the great Marshall McLuhan said: 'Most of the people drive down the freeway of life looking in the rear view mirror'. Everyone can tell you where they have been, what their story is, what has been important to them and what they like. Ask them where they are going, what changes they will embrace, and they struggle to answer. Most people don't live with a forward-facing vision and are anchored in the known, the familiar, and the past.

We are entering the 'creative destruction' phase of many businesses. This means that old business and social models must give way to new models. Whenever that happens, there are casualties, there are institutions we have grown up with that all of a sudden seem to fall apart. One hundred years ago it was the horse and buggy business. Today, it is modern media, old manufacturing models, and institutions in general. This is a natural cycle of life and of human progress and evolution.

A simple way to think about all this is through the filter of centuries. What is something that is 20th century? What is something that is 21st century? Newspapers were 20th century; the Internet is 21st century. General Motors is 20th century; Tesla is 21st century. Petroleum is the 20th century energy source. Wind, solar, biomass and space based solar power is 21st century.

Another way of thinking about where we are in history is to realize that society always has a rear-facing sense of itself. In other words, what we think of when we think of the term '20th century' didn't really start until WWI. Prior to that, the developed countries of the world were living with 19th century sensibilities. The dominant country in the world, Great Britain, was still in the Victorian Age. In the U.S. we still thought of ourselves as an agricultural country, and New York was ruled and socially dominated by the 400 families of the social register. WWI forced humanity into the 20th century, and most of what we think of about this century flowed forth after that war.

We are in a similar situation today. Most of the institutional thinking is still from the 20th century, particularly in government and politics. There is a vast and growing number of people on the planet, however, who feel this is a limitation, a negative force that is holding us back. So the way I see it, this Transformation Decade of 2010-2020 will be the decade when humanity will be letting go of the past, the legacies from the last century, and begin to face the issues and opportunities of the 21st century.

The energy equation, crumbling infrastructures, national debt…do you feel that some of the actions to solve these major global issues will be addressed over the next 10 years?

Yes, these will all be addressed in the Transformation Decade. Alternative energy, the need for 21st century infrastructures in the United States, and the global problems with debt will all be fully faced in the next ten years. The degree to which they will be successful is what is in doubt.

The United States and most countries of the world will go through significant changes in the political and governmental landscapes in the coming years, with varying success. If the United States wants to remain the great country we all think that it is – or can be – we must make transformative changes. This is one of the key issues I speak to when addressing audiences.

The United States has a 'vision vacuum' today. When I was growing up and a young man observing the 'space race', the vision of putting men on the moon and bringing them home safely was a unifying vision for our country. It not only provided this unified vision, it also created many unexpected developments and discoveries that have greatly improved our lives. The first photograph of the 'whole earth' was the trigger for launching the global environmental movement that has now changed human thinking about our precious spaceship, earth. The technologies that were developed as necessary for our space successes have had benefits to this day. The new gadgets we now revere such as the iPad®, netbooks, and smart phones all have in them technologies that can, to some degree, be traced back to the space race and the discoveries and innovations that came from that vision.

Today I have been calling for a new vision, a 'vision for America for the 21ˢᵗ century'. I think that much of the fractious debate in America these past few years comes directly from not having a unifying national vision that we can all, to varying degrees, buy into. I think that there is a clear vision for America for the next 20 years that can not only keep the country foremost in the world but can also bring about transformative change that will improve all our lives.

This vision is:

A complete rebuilding of the energy, communications, and transportation infrastructures of the United States. As a country we have some of the oldest infrastructures that exist today. By committing to completely rebuild our infrastructures, we will create the foundation for the 21ˢᵗ century economy, we will change our energy habits, we will become more efficient, and we will lessen the congestion, pollution, and education problems that negatively affect us. We must create a large, all-encompassing vision that will stimulate young people to be great, to live in creative innovation, and to embrace the highest possibilities imaginable. Anything less will be failing to build upon our record as one of the greatest countries in history.

Please explain how technology (and the Neurosphere) is driving transformation at a constantly accelerating rate and why it is the propelling force behind the evolution of the global brain/consciousness.

The accelerating electronic connectedness of the world is one of the three forces of the Shift Age that is and will transform humanity. The other two are 'the Flow to Global' and 'the Flow to the Individual', both of which are amplified by this connectedness.

I said earlier that there is no longer any time, distance, or place limiting human communication. That changes everything.

The ever rapidly growing electronic connectedness is becoming a Neurosphere that is already an alternative reality, the new screen reality, if you will. Just think about the word 'friend'. Until a few years ago, that usually meant kids we grew up with, kids we went to school with, or people we physically met. Now, via Facebook, Twitter, and other social networks, there is a definition of 'friend' that is not place-based. In fact it is a verb.

This Neurosphere is truly a technological model for a coming change in consciousness. When that consciousness begins, I cannot say. I do think that it could start to happen in the 2020s. That is why the decade 2010-2020 will be the Transformation Decade, as we will be going through the preparations for this coming ascendant consciousness.

We are fast entering a new global connectedness where smart chips communicate with one another, where we can know anything about almost anything in a matter of seconds. The phenomenon of Twitter I see as the beginning of the global brain. It is an intelligent human search engine where we can share immediately with people we have never met.

Currently we are quickly moving to having the human technology interface become almost completely based on touch and voice. How do we check into airports? How do we use Bluetooth-enabled cars? How do we use our touch screen phones? All of this is just preparation for the next interface, which will become widely used in the Transformation Decade: brain wave interface.

Brain wave interface comes from research done with quadriplegics, where first with embedded chips, then with brainwave sensors, quadriplegics could be integrated with their wheelchairs. This technology will now be coming to the consumer marketplace, so that in the next few years we will have the first brainwave interfacing with our computers. Just think about how we will teach our young when they are using brainwave technology at home!

This is a signpost pointing toward a new, higher level of direct global consciousness to come. It might come in the 2020s or a bit later, but we are certainly moving in that direction.

Any final futuristic thoughts or visions?

We have left the Information Age and entered the Shift Age. This new Age, the global stage of human evolution, will rapidly leave our history behind. Place is no longer something that limits us. Time is no longer something that limits us. We are transcending our national boundaries. We are entering the Global Economy 2.0, where we will move toward a more integrated whole economy that is cooperative, collaborative, incredibly interconnected, and therefore much more dynamic.

All of this change will thrust us rapidly into a future that, even 20 years ago, would have been unimaginable.

How long will the Shift Age last? I don't know, but would suggest 20-30 years. What will succeed it? I am not sure, but it will be an Age or an elevated state of change based upon this new emerging consciousness. It is this transformation that will allow us to successfully deal with all the problems that today seem almost insurmountable.

We are moving toward a new golden age of humanity. It is one of the most exciting times to be alive in human history!

The Buddhist principle of interdependence teaches us that all things in this world are connected. When we behold the sunflower, we also behold the sun itself. The awakened mind calls us to act in stewardship of precious resources, including the resources of our time and our labor. All things are inseparable from this amazing existence.

I shall teach you the Dharma: When this exists, that comes to be; with the arising of this, that arises.
~ From the Majjhima Nikaya

2

TOWERS IN THE SKY

A stick figure with briefcase and a business suit and tie
He walks across the perfect lawn
And he stands there at the foot of the golden office tower
He says — "I must get to work today, I have to get inside somehow"
But the golden office tower was just a cliff the sun was setting on
So he ran up along the cliff and was gone forever...
~ Jane Siberry (Map of the World, Part ll)

What is a city skyline without its skyscrapers? For decades the ubiquitous, glittering towers in the sky have symbolized North America's reach for prosperity and economic dominance in the world market. These architectural wonders have also come to symbolize the career "arrival" of newly minted business professionals from around the world.

We all recognize the image and know the impact these symbols of success have on our psyches. From the iconic and aspirational TV show *Mad Men* to the modernist Emirates Towers of Dubai, we intuit great power and high-art glamour when we gaze upon these imposing structures, and we imagine the same to hold true for the well-heeled workers within. Awe-struck as we are by the arresting beauty of these architectural wonders, we envision that to work in an office with an eagle-eye view from the heights must be the ultimate measure of success in the urban age.

Over the decades, dreams such as these have driven workers to aspire to and achieve great things. But the office tower work model has begun to take its toll on our environment, as well as our personal lives.

Telecommuting offers a new way to work — a new model for employers and new opportunities for freelancers and entrepreneurs. But the impact of e-work goes well beyond individual or corporate benefits; it will impact our nation and the world. A strong national e-work program can dramatically reduce our fossil fuel dependence and slow global warming. It can increase productivity. It can provide new employment opportunities for at-home caregivers, the disabled, and the underemployed. It can offer rural and economically disadvantaged populations access to better jobs.

It can improve family life and emancipate latchkey kids. It can bolster pandemic and disaster preparedness. It can reduce traffic jams and the carnage on our highways. It can alleviate the strain on our crumbling transportation infrastructure. It can help reclaim many of the jobs that have been lost to offshoring. And the billions of dollars saved by companies and individuals could fuel economic growth and bolster retirement savings.
~ Kate Lister & Tom Harnish[2]

Day in, day out, we commute from the suburbs, often adding more than two or three hours of travel time to our busy days — a fact that wreaks havoc on a worker's productivity and their quality of life.

Businesses lose $600 billion a year in workplace distractions.[3]

Today's commuting workforce rushes into city centers and up banks of elevators to their work stations each day. Popping Tylenols and Tums, they deal with the stress of deadline time-crunches and unrealistic expectations, as well as other distractions that diminish their state of mind and their overall productivity. In between the daily barrage of assignments, they attempt to carve out a few moments to juggle family responsibilities with texts, emails, and phone calls. This is the emerging reality of many in the corporate office tower archetype.

Yet, just as the Industrial Revolution changed the world and re-placed the pastoral, horse-and-buggy lifestyle with the buzz of ma-chinery and cars, the age of the Internet has the global workforce standing at the brink of change once more.

According to futurist Frank Feather, the Internet Revolution is unwinding most of what the Industrial Revolution put into place. Thanks to ever-evolving computer technology, today's workers are digitally managing information in urban centers around the world. Armed with smartphones and laptops, legions of employees can deal with demands and deadlines on a subway car. They can make project revisions or dialogue with colleagues remotely to share information and implement new ideas.

We now live in a world where digital exchanges have replaced the traditional paper shuffle in our towers in the sky. But this new way of life, on the job or off, is causing our global society to experience some profound and fundamental shifts. Digital technology has not only made the workplace faster. It has freed it up, allowing people the opportunity to work anywhere and at any time.

Long commutes to work are bad for employee health and have a negative effect on corporate productivity. A recent study of over

3,000 employees showed that those with flexible schedules were less likely to have health problems that affect their job performance.

Best Buy's average productivity increased 35% through its flexible work program.[4]

It also takes a toll on the environment, adding more and more toxic fumes to the planet's ozone. In fact, traffic jams idle away 2.9 billion gallons of gas and release more than 58 million extra pounds of CO_2 every year.

As digital technologies continue to evolve and transform global cultures and economies, telecommuting will become the way of the future for a number of reasons.

"The word 'telecommuting,' by definition, lends itself to creating 'virtual workplace' portals, whether one works from home or the coffee shop down the block," says journalist Judy Martin.

In 2010, for example, Wikipedia estimated that as many as 50 million people work from home at least part-time. In fact, those who manage staffs today are likely to have at least one teleworker among the rank and file.

"In this Information Age, technological advances allow employees to work from just about anywhere, which spawned the term 'workshifting,' or the ability to shift one's working space from place to place," says Martin.

Workshifting via technology is leading a revolutionary movement, as sites like Workshifting.com can attest to.

"A Work+Life Fit" BDO Seidman survey of CFOs showed 75% agree that flexible work increases productivity.[5]

There are many factors that make the growth of this trend inevitable and enviable. Telecommuting can lead to a reduction in operating costs and dangerous greenhouse emissions. The flexibility of telecommuting makes life easier for working single parents or dual-income families, who often find themselves burnt out Monday to Friday from juggling family life with the 9 to 5 grind.

"Workers are striving for better balance," says Martin. And that modern-day desire applies to both men and women.

The time and needs of employees are, indeed, shifting. And while telecommuting offers many advantages, it may not be for everyone.

Telecommuting cannot work effectively, unless managers and employees dialogue better and more frequently. This off-site employment model also brings certain basic work ethics into review such as trust, competency, ingenuity, and adaptability.

Some employees may find the need to regulate their own schedules outside of an office too difficult. Others may miss the social interaction and the visibility that comes from being on site each day. Yet for those who can get past all this, telecommuting has the potential to ease the many stresses that affect families, global economies, and the planet.

First and foremost, telecommuting on a broader scale could greatly impact the quality of work around the world.

Dow Chemical estimates a 32.5% increase in productivity among its teleworkers.[6]

According to a 2010 report in *The Atlantic*, researchers led by Nobel Prize-winner Daniel Kahneman outlined which cities were the worst to commute in for IBM's Computer Pain Index. Beijing topped the list, followed by Mexico City, Johannesburg, Moscow, and New Delhi. London, Toronto and New York were also included among the 20 worst cities. Interestingly, Stockholm rated as the best commuter city for suburban employees.

This report also made one other clear assertion: "Commuting is a waste of energy and time, and carries with it enormous economic costs."

For example, researchers contributing to the annual Urban Mobility Report now believe that commuting costs America an estimated 90 billion dollars per year in terms of lost productivity and wasted energy. Research conducted by the Martin Prosperity Institute also estimates that every minute shaved off America's commuting time is worth approximately 19.5 billion dollars. That translates into 97.5 billion for five minutes, 195 billion for 10 minutes, and 292 billion for every 15 minutes saved nationally.

Sun Microsystems saves $68 million a year in real estate costs, $3 million a year in reduced power consumption, and $25 million a year in IT expenditures with flexible work options for 17,000 employees (2,000 primarily working at home, 15,000 up to 2 days a week).[7]

In this regard, the impact of the virtual workplace could be enormous in years to come. But in a world fraught with upheaval and unrest, the virtual workplace also offers many opportunities to adapt and evolve society for the better.

Tomorrow's telecommuting workforce may be healthier, happier, and far more productive. At the same time, the businesses of tomorrow may streamline corporate waste in a huge number of ways, thanks to a 21st century work model. This means that the greatest reward workshifting may offer in the future is its benefit to our planet.

Telecommuting: Freedom for the Future – An Interview with Judy Martin

Emmy award-winning broadcast journalist Judy Martin, walks between two worlds, covering the mainstream aspects of business news, while emerging as a writer and speaker on personal transformation, social consciousness, and work-life culture.

Martin spent nearly four years as a NYC Correspondent for American Public Media's *Marketplace Morning Report*, where she reported live from Ground Zero after 9/11. Her work has also been heard on CNBC Business Radio, NPR, BBC Radio 3, and the *World Vision Report.*

Martin's work can be best described in the words of East Indian poet and philosopher Rabindranath Tagore, "We gain our freedom when we attain our truest nature." Her belief is that the evolution of consciousness is influenced when personal passion and right livelihood intersect. She sees that as the seedbed that can transform the idea of work into a meaningful vocation.

For Martin, exalting the human experience at work and in business can fuel a radical shift in the way we approach global economic and social concerns. She's working with the Source of Synergy Foundation to jumpstart a collective conversation in the media on the infusion of a more conscious approach to our human capital.

From that commitment, Martin's blog was born: WorkLifeNation. com. With it, Martin covers breaking news on work-life culture and conscious business practices.

I spoke to her to get her take on today's virtual workplace and where it will lead employees from all walks of life in the years to come.

Telecommuting is often referred to as the "virtual workplace", "telework", "homeworking", and "workshifting". What exactly is telecommuting and why is it such a growing trend?

Telecommuting is simply working outside the traditional nine-to-five office space or workplace, using 'telecommunication' tools such as the phone and computer.

The term 'workshifting' has not in the past been as widely used as telecommuting, but it's truly leading a revolutionary movement, heralded by the Spring 2009 launch of Workshifting.com, a site dedicated to analysis and solutions for the mobile workforce population. That workforce is growing exponentially worldwide and especially in the United States. A recent whitepaper by global market intelligence firm, IDC, estimates that three-quarters of the workforce in the U.S. will be mobile by the year 2013.

Why is telecommuting a growing trend? One could write a book about the reasons: reduction in operating costs, avoiding growing transportation nightmares, reducing greenhouse emissions, side-stepping the expense of commercial real estate, and the urgent call for more workplace flexibility. On the socio-economic front, tele-commuting makes it easier for mothers to on-ramp back into the workforce and for single moms and dads to manage family and work related responsibilities better without burning out. In addition, there is a general dismay with the traditional nine-to-five office working environment for many folks who want to switch careers and do some-thing that they enjoy. You'll find this tone with everyone from Gen Y crowd to Gen X and the baby boomers. Workers are striving for better balance. But it's also important to mention that not every kind of job lends itself to telecommuting and not every kind of employee is well suited or interested enough in fostering the discipline required to work from home.

What are some of the less evident rewards of telecommuting for both the employer and employee?

Numerous studies show that telecommuting can increase pro-ductivity of employees, improve loyalty, help foster engagement, and provide for a better work-life balance or 'work life fit.' Researchers at Brigham Young University found, in a study of more than 24 thousand IBM workers worldwide, that telecommuters with flexible working options 'balanced work time and family life' up to 19 hours longer than typical office workers.

When a parent is granted the tools and responsibility to design their own work schedule and also take care of family concerns, there is a tendency for them to be a more effective employee by mere de-fault. They want to keep their job and appreciate the ability of a company to be flexible. Telecommuting is its own reward for both the employee and employer. When working in a telecommuting situation, the onus is often on the worker to be accountable for their work. This lays the groundwork for improved communication between both parties, or else it won't work.

Also, in an era of dual-income families where both parents are working, a situation that requires more flexible working arrangements, telecommuting can help retain highly skilled employees for longer periods of time. When you work with such employees on their schedules and how and when they should be working, they are likely to be more loyal and engaged. Also, it's in the best interest of employers to hold onto these workers instead of paying the cost of recruiting and on-boarding employees.

What skill sets do leaders need to adopt, in order to effectively manage remote teams?

The most important skill is communication. To effectively manage, a leader must be able to communicate with employees in a standardized and consistent way in order to articulate job descriptions and duties, appropriate checks and balances, the nature of interpersonal communication among workers, the shape of manager to employee communication and, when appropriate, how communication with the client is to take place. Leaders must also understand how communication styles might differ between remote team members and office workers.

Interest-based negotiation skills are also a critical part of that communication. A manager and employee must come to agreement on how and when workers will get their responsibilities done in an effective and efficient way. This requires managers to be open to myriad working scenarios that employees might suggest and doing their best to meet those desires, while balancing them with the needs of the organization. Without being contentious, both sides can broker a win/win scenario.

Overseeing flexible remote teams also requires a certain finesse to keep a harmonious relationship between the remote workers and those who are not telecommuters in one's department. Managers might need to adjust their focus and lens to adapt to the needs of two completely different work scenarios. Deadlines, communication face time, and equipment needs might differ in those two environments.

You have said that workplace flexibility is no longer a women's issue. It is now considered a "bottom line" issue. Please explain.

The tide has shifted around the need for work-life flexibility, because it's not perceived as just a women's issue anymore. Because of the economic crisis, high unemployment, and dual-income families, men are taking on more responsibilities in the home.

In the 2008 National Study of the Changing Workforce, for the first time, men were experiencing more work-life conflict than women as compared to past studies by the Families and Work Institute. The elevated levels of work-life conflict experienced by men increased from 34% in 1977 to 45% in 2008. The report attributes this to changing gender roles. Employed fathers are spending more time with their children than their similarly aged counterparts did three decades ago, and men are taking more overall responsibility for the care of their children.

It's in the best interest of a company to encourage and create more flexible working environments for retention purposes. With baby boomers retiring over the next decade, it will leave a huge hole in the workforce. Add to that the growing number of entrepreneurs in America and the talk of a talent crunch for skilled workers. With the growing number of women in the workforce, who are now more than half of the talent pool, companies will need to attract and retain workers as part of their bottom-line concern, so that it's in their best interest to keep engaged workers, no matter the gender.

You often refer to the "24/7 work life merge". What are some of the personal challenges one may confront in maintaining this sense of balance?

We're more connected because of the internet and technology in general. Our workplace is evolving, entrepreneurs abound, and many work from home. Be it baby boomer, Gen X or Gen Y, many thirst for more meaningful work, but demand more family and 'me' time. The lines have blurred in the quest for success, serenity, and significance in what I call the '24/7 work-life merge.'

Part of the shift has to do with crisis. Since 9/11, the economic meltdown, and the leveling out of the global marketplace due to technology, we're all scrambling for meaning and to make a living and retain a normalcy within our family lives. We're challenged with navigating the chaos of a decade of economic difficulties and furthering our careers, as we raise families.

The merging of the living and working experience is creating a desire for more meaningful and purpose driven work, because our human values are fighting the panic of our times and are rising to the surface. When chaos hits, there is inevitably a shift. In these radically changing times, people are clamoring for more humanity in work and in business.

More and more, we're redefining success in terms of values, passion, and profit. But to succeed, we have to keep the flame going, and that means cultivating serenity and resilience while navigating the sensory overload. The more flexible we are and the better we are at handling the shifts in a 24/7 world, the easier it will be to make a difference. And that's where significance comes in and working consciously toward a greater purpose. When we're happier in our work or careers, it helps to fuel more positive outcomes in our quest for work-life balance.

IBM's 80,000 teleworkers save the company $700 million a year in real estate costs.[8]

Future Forecast: Make Way for the Virtual Workplace

Frank Feather is a business futurist with a remarkably accurate 30-year forecasting track record that often defies conventional wisdom. He is ranked as one of the "Top 100 Futurists of All Time" by Macmillan's *Encyclopedia of the Future*. A best-selling author and dynamic keynote speaker, this U.K. transplant to Canada has consulted to companies including Ericsson, IBM, Ford, Nokia, and Shell. Since 1984, Feather has also been special adviser to China on economic modernization and market reforms. I talked to Feather to get his predictions on the impact of the virtual workplace on society in years to come.

Clearly, there is an underlying need for a "revision" of the way we work and live. Can we use this as an opportunity to be more productive and fulfilled?

Global society is undergoing two fundamental shifts about which most people are oblivious.

The same happened in the Industrial Revolution, in that people did not realize how life was being totally transformed from a rural and agricultural model to one based on urbanization and machine/time-driven life and work in centralized factories. But that long shift, which lasted several decades, transformed society, culture, economics, and politics.

The Internet Revolution is unraveling most of what the Industrial Revolution put in place. The vast majority of the urban population of North America, Europe, as well as Japan and other developed economies, are info-knowledge workers who can work from anywhere. Yet we persist with the absurdity of centralized workplaces and commuting. Skyscrapers now mimicked in China and major cities of the developing world are nothing more than paper shuffling factories in the sky, where even the paper is being digitized. Why do we continue with this insanity? Ninety percent of the people working downtown simply do not need to be there. In the Internet Age, you do not go to work. Work comes to you, wherever you elect to be. Everything gets reversed.

Simultaneously and relatedly, the global village brought about by easy communication has made us increasingly aware of the need to be better stewards of the planet's environment. It makes no sense to commute when it simply isn't required. Commuting destroys the environment, it destroys work-life balance, and it destroys families. Yet we persist.

I stopped commuting over 25 years ago, and there is no way that I would ever do it again. Life is too valuable, both personally and in terms of the planet.

TRY THIS

In order for a telecommuting relationship to work, there must be a relationship built on trust. If this is lacking, the relationship between the employee and employer will surely break down. Employers must screen carefully when selecting employees for this type of work. Finding the right person who can really manage this well, taking into account their personal style, preferences, and integrity, is key.

Telecommuting employees should keep in mind that work-life balance is important, but it's crucial to be open and honest about the situation at home. For example, if working from home, are you able to arrange for sufficient childcare assistance? Here are some other considerations.

Is Telecommuting Right for You?

Employer's perspective:

- Does the work that you are asking the employee to perform absolutely have to be performed in your office setting?

- Can you trust this employee to perform the task without a great deal of supervision?
- How social is this employee? If they are extremely extroverted, working alone may be very difficult.
- Can you provide some mechanism to allow for the team of employees to gather in person at least once in a while? This is important for alignment and relationship building.
- Do you have technological resources to support long distance connection? For example Skype, email access, and possibly a dedicated phone line?
- How often does the employee's work require a "just in time" in person gathering? If it is a lot of the time, can it still occur with technology?

Employee's perspective:

- Do you have the space in the home to set up a home office that is effective and efficient in nature? For example, a room big enough, with a door to close, that is also quiet enough to minimize outside distractions etc.?
- Are you good at working alone with minimal supervision and contact with others?
- Do you have good time management skills to help you with setting priorities? It is often very tempting to run a load of laundry and do chores around the house as you are moving in and out of the home office. This can all be distracting and create a lack of productivity.
- Do you have the family support to work in the home? Occasionally, family members see you at home and therefore assume that you are not in "work mode". You must be able to set boundaries with significant others in the household.

- Are you more introverted or extroverted? Extroverts in particular struggle with telecommuting, as they are suited to talk things out with co-workers and brainstorm with others. You can do some of this over the phone, but it's not as effective with "high extroverts".

Just as treasures are uncovered from the earth,
so virtue appears from good deeds,
and wisdom appears from a pure and peaceful mind.
To walk safely through the maze of human life,
one needs the light of wisdom and the guidance of virtue.
~ The Buddha

3

WHY THIS WORKS

There is no pillow so soft as a clear conscience.
~ *French Proverb*

When it comes to building successful businesses for this new century, most people would present the usual theories on how to get the job done. New ideas, bigger markets, cost-cutting and better implementation of technology would certainly top the "to-do" list.

But for those visionary leaders who look beyond the obvious, one fundamental necessity is key. Global businesses need a conscience. They also need to move far beyond the days of Wall Street's financial engineering, corporate mismanagement, and well-publicized waste. In the words of Jeffrey Hollender, a leader in socially and environmentally responsible communities and the co-founder and executive chairman of the green household product company, Seventh Generation, the successful businesses of tomorrow must "create new products and services that deliver a return on purpose, as well as a return on investment".

In response, a new generation of entrepreneurs has emerged, driven by one purpose. They want to use business as a powerful weapon for change. They are setting the ground rules, in order to transform their businesses into something that yields more authentic economic value and more awareness of social responsibility to our world.

That's a tall order to fill. In fact, many critics may say that these aspirations are too lofty and too broad to work within the realities of existing business models. But today's radical-thinking entrepreneurs are dauntless. They are ready to take on the challenge from the grass-roots up.

Of course, the need to turn a profit cannot be tossed out the window by these new thinkers. But for noteworthy groundbreakers like today's new "Certified B Corporations", something more compelling and meaningful is spearheading them on.

Touted as the next big thing in the global market, these new hybrid companies are making social responsibility their primary business mandate. As well, everything these companies do aspires to be ethical, accountable, environmentally-friendly, and financially transparent. That combination will certainly appeal to consumers. Tired of "old guard" companies that put bottom line profit above all else, today's consumers have higher expectations from the businesses that they want to associate with and support. Companies, however, that fail to recognize this fundamental shift may be left in the dust.

Becoming a B Corporation is by no means an easy feat. In fact, bearers of this title must pass a rigorous, standardized test by third-party evaluators. They must also live up to a mission statement that reflects an ethos of positive change in terms of their employees, local communities, and the environment. It can be daunting, and the kinks have yet to be fully worked out in these business models of the future, but most will agree that it is well worth the effort.

Corporate responsibility is like playing a game with no rules, on a field with no boundaries, with referees who can never agree on who actually won the game.
~ *Jeffrey Hollender*

While B Corps are a great start, Hollender says standards and metrics must be instituted and full disclosure must be required for every license that is granted for such new businesses. A sense of holistic nurturing must also be expressed by all parties, from the CEOs right on down to the mailroom for this new model to grow and thrive.

According to Hollender, tomorrow's companies must balance growth and profits with justice and equity. This process is a long-term one and certainly not without its challenges. But if these values become corporate cornerstones for the future, new purpose will be gained by consumers – and by investors in terms of their investment.

From building on corporate consciousness and sustainability practices to offering employees opportunities to fulfill higher goals, socially responsible companies can work. But they can only do so by assimilating this new culture of social responsibility and "giving back" into their corporate DNA.

Tim Sanders, author of *Saving the World at Work*, also maintains there is a "Responsibility Revolution" on the immediate horizon. Sanders believes that companies who adopt the "done the right way" point of reference for their product or service deliver a powerful benefit to their customers, as well as delivering a sense of purpose to their employees.

As Sanders and Hollender point out, America is a nation of employees, not a nation of owners. Businesses that continue to put politics and profit above the elevation of socially responsible practices will ultimately realize that they are losing ground, in the form of reduced profits and, in some cases, the loss of their best and brightest.

Companies like micro-lender Kiva.org swear by a mission statement that reflects the "Responsibility Revolution". Launched in

2005 by Jessica Jackley and Matt Flannery, Kiva.org offers entrepreneurs who are too poor to qualify for traditional loans an alternative funding arrangement with which to start or upgrade businesses. The applicants may be farmers in Cambodia or shopkeepers in Mongolia. The minimum loan is 25 dollars and the interest rate is 0%. Remarkably, the repayment rate for loans is more than 98%.

In fact, since Kiva.org was founded, almost 700,000 people have pledged 128 million dollars in loans to more than 325,000 people.[9] The company is looking ahead, determined to help small businesses in the United States access startup funding through community involvement with their new ProFounder plan.

Ted Ning, the Executive Director of the LOHAS (Lifestyles of Health and Sustainability) Conference in the United States and Executive Editor of the *LOHAS Journal*, says that a growing awareness from the media, combined with an interest in healthy living, spirituality, and social justice, moves consumers to become more informed and ultimately open their wallets to more "green" and ethically driven companies.

In Japan, members of the LOHAS Business Alliance (LBA) also dedicate themselves to stimulating business alliances that can bring more ethical standards to the economy. The non-profit organization currently has 100 business members who are committed to a business lifestyle made up of sustainable and eco-conscious practices, people like Asia's LOHAS co-chairperson, Toshi Ide, for example – whom I interview below.

More than just a pretty series of ad campaigns, LOHAS plays into the new paradigm shift among consumers who want to live healthier lifestyles and buy products that leave a lower carbon footprint on society.

No matter what place tomorrow's business leaders choose as their theater of operations, respect, reverence, and responsibility are the keys to making this new business model work in the years to come.

Tomorrow's captains of industry have a long list of matters to address. In all respects, the future's brightest, boldest business leaders must adhere to a new "triple" bottom line that favours the economy, the environment, and the world community. Once such an approach enters more and more into the mainstream, consumers will see big, traditional corporations like Walmart championing this new economic message. And it should be noted here that the train has already left the station.

In 2009, Walmart announced the creation of a *Sustainable Product Index* to "establish a single source of data for evaluating the sustainability of products." While the task has been criticized by pundits and is a long way from being perfected, Walmart's research has had some positive impact on consumers.

Imagine walking down the aisles at your local Walmart and seeing an "ecological impact" rating tag attached to everything from a Transformers action figure to a box of Kraft Dinner. Every manufacturer and processor, over 100,000 suppliers in all, will likely have to comply, revealing their products' ecological impact or else risk being dropped from Walmart's shelves. This is a scary proposition for some of Walmart's major suppliers, many of whom would be forced to close their doors if they were not able to meet such terms.

Also interesting to note is that it is estimated that over 20 percent of China's factories are involved in Walmart's supply chain. All this could have a striking impact on these, as well as many other off-shore suppliers to Walmart.

Walmart's actions and those of other large-scale businesses that are adopting socially and ecologically responsible models have the potential to catapult the ecological manufacturing initiatives and product "life cycle transparency" programs of their suppliers into warp speed zones.

According to reports from *Fast Company*, consumers shouldn't expect to see daily updates on Walmart's Index in stores until 2013 at least. But the landscape of the world's global economy will continue to change and shift, mirroring a new spirit on the part of consumers. Businesses that heed this call and choose to make social responsibility and meaningful corporate practices the new standard will usher in an era that transforms society in ways global citizens cannot even imagine.

Last year, the *Harvard Business Review* featured a cover story announcing that sustainability has become the key to successful corporate strategy.[10] The article, co-authored by Ram Nidumolu, C.K. Prahalad, and M.R. Rangaswami, boldly stated that, "There is no alternative to sustainable development". I whole-heartedly agree. The authors go on to say that:

> *Executives behave as though they have to choose between the largely social benefits of developing sustainable products or processes and the financial costs of doing so. But that's simply not true… Our research shows that sustainability is a mother lode of organizational and technological innovations that yield both bottom-line and top-line returns. Becoming environment-friendly lowers costs because companies end up reducing the inputs they use. In addition, the process generates additional revenues from better products or enables companies to create new businesses. In fact, because those are the goals of corporate innovation, we find that smart companies now treat sustainability as innovation's new frontier.*

It takes 20 years to build a reputation and five minutes to ruin it. If you think about that, you'll do things differently.
~ *Warren Edward Buffet*

Trends of Tomorrow: An Interview with Ted Ning

Looking into the decades ahead, entrepreneur Ted Ning sees a marketplace that is evolved and aware of its impact on the world. Known as "Mr. LOHAS", Ning, as mentioned above, is the Executive Director of the LOHAS Conference and Executive Editor of the *LOHAS Journal*. His "green" company and his business vision revolve around the idea of creating transformation in society and putting social responsibility on an equal footing with profitability. Involved in community outreach and nonprofit endeavors since his youth,

Ning walks the green sustainable talk even at his Boulder Colorado home where he recycles and composts to reduce waste, bikes to work, lives in a "green" home that is solar powered, and is a member of a community supported organic farm where he and his family get most of the food they consume.

How did you become involved in the LOHAS movement?

I grew up in the mountains of Colorado in a LOHAS oriented family. My parents were "hippies" and involved in nonprofit work. I have three adopted sisters from Vietnam and Korea. Growing up in the mountains gave me a powerful appreciation of nature. My journey with LOHAS began seven years ago, when I answered an ad in the paper for a LOHAS data entry analyst and worked my way up to running it.

How has LOHAS evolved over the years, from its initial stages, primarily as an acronym for a type of market research, to the thriving business community and social movement it has become?

The LOHAS movement has grown for a variety of reasons. I think people have gained awareness from the media, An Inconvenient Truth being a prime example. This has rendered them more educated and prompted them to seek change. LOHAS has evolved to be beyond just green. It is much broader, encompassing social justice, spirituality and healthy living.

Are consumers and companies confused by the varying definitions of sustainability? What does sustainability mean to you, and how does it apply to LOHAS principles?

There are many studies out there stating consumers are confused, and for good reason. There is a lot of information and greenwashing that make the market very difficult for laymen to understand. There are over 1000 certifications out there and a whole arena of unregulated marketing. This leads to major confusion. Hopefully the new FTC guidelines will help.

To me, sustainability means returning what is equal or more to any relationship you have. This can be relating to a person, the environment, or anything else.

According to your research and experience, what are some of the advantages of becoming a LOHAS-focused company?

Currently, many studies show that people are seeking to purchase from companies that have values similar to their own. Social responsibility is paramount in today's world. LOHAS consumers are seeking this transparency and authenticity and can smell out a rat. They can be your biggest fans or biggest enemies, depending on what you do and say. This is where I see the future going for companies and consumer relations.

What does LOHAS do to encourage companies to enter the green market segment?

Many companies come to us to understand the LOHAS market segment, particularly the early adopters and trendsetters. They are also the most educated and teach others about what they know. Hence they have a strong influence. Many companies don't know how to communicate effectively with this sector and want to develop relationships with other LOHAS companies, and we help connect them.

Unfortunately, we are often made aware of companies that are guilty of greenwashing, that is, falsely portraying their products and policies as environmentally friendly. How can concerned consumers determine which companies are "authentically green" and trust-worthy? A recent study revealed that consumers are also unsure of how to verify green claims such as "environmentally friendly" or "organic".[11] What actions are being taken to monitor and resolve these issues?

There are three principles to follow in determining if a company is greenwashing:

1. Is their claim based on a single attribute? If so, it can be misleading.
2. Is the claim vague? If there is no proof or specific details, the claim could also be misleading.
3. Is the claim a tradeoff from another aspect that is not green?

It would seem that the demand for green products, as well as ethical, transparent company practices and corporate philanthropic programs, is on the rise. Are we in the midst of a "Green Economic Revolution"?

Yes, I think that consumer awareness is driving this. Also, the economic downturn has companies scrambling for relevance and new ways to demonstrate their value.

What are some of the immediate challenges faced by the LOHAS business community? As a movement, what are LOHAS' goals for the future?

Immediate challenges include greenwashing and consumer confusion. I also feel that the LOHAS market is a relatively new, emerging market and a fragmented one at that, which is a challenge for many to get their head around. It certainly takes a conversation to help people arrive at an understanding of what LOHAS is. But I do feel the LOHAS movement will continue to expand, as consumer awareness of green shopping and sustainable lifestyles becomes more mainstream. Taking a shopping bag to a store or driving a hybrid gets social praise and is not looked at as odd. This was not the case 10 years ago, when these trends emerged.

The role of modern business: To provide ever better goods and services in a way that is profitable and ethical and that respects the environment, individuals, and the communities in which it operates.[12]

A New Business Lifestyle: An Interview with Toshe Ide

Toshe Ide has a vision. He sees a future ahead in which businesses of all kinds operate not only to produce goods, but to have and demonstrate meaning. That is the core ethic behind LOHAS Business Alliance in Japan, where Co-chairman Ide and others have united to create a business model encouraging a healthy lifestyle and sustainability. The idea is second nature to Ide. As president and CEO of gConscious, Inc, this maverick headed the first company to become a carbon offset provider in Japan. The best-selling author and former Silicon Valley software engineer has also developed best-selling desktop music applications. In all ways, Ide, like others in this new generation of socially responsible entrepreneurs, is using his talents and interests to create companies that benefit the world community.

I'd like to start with a general question about the purpose of LOHAS and what it means to be a part of the LOHAS community.

LOHAS is a community and a lifestyle made up of health and eco-conscious individuals and businesses. It started as a marketing keyword to describe the group's values and perceptions. Its primary purpose is to associate these individuals with the other members of LOHAS and LOHAS oriented businesses. Together, we can share information, principles, and best practices among the LOHAS community.

Many North American consumers are not familiar with the definition of LOHAS. You have said that approximately 70 percent of Japanese adults, at least, recognize the term and up to 40 percent can articulate its meaning. How is the LOHAS lifestyle interpreted in Japan? Why do you think the movement has been embraced so enthusiastically?

In Japan, LOHAS was first introduced by a green magazine called *Sotokoto*. They also worked with an ad agency to promote the LOHAS concept. As a result, several big corporations used LOHAS in their ads, which helped raise awareness with 'green' consumers. The main group that resonated with the concept initially was women ranging from their late 20s to 40 years of age. They bought into the concept as a 'cool' lifestyle. The images used in the campaign were of working women who practiced yoga, ate organic food, and were inclined to choose eco-products. So I would say that, initially, LOHAS Japan was media driven. But once the concept got out and the word spread through blogs, as well as editorial and social media, recognition of the integrity behind the image spread rapidly. In other words, LOHAS is certainly not just about 'pretty pictures'.

In terms of why people believe in the LOHAS concept, I think there are two factors at play. The first is the paradigm shift to a green and low carbon society. People are growing more and more sensitive to the magnitude and impact of their choices. They are becoming keenly aware that eco-friendly products and companies contribute to the green movement. Another factor is the trend toward health-conscious lifestyles. People spend more time and money to maintain optimum health, seeking out natural and organic methods and products that align with their beliefs. I think the combination of these two factors resonates with eco-conscious consumers worldwide.

Describe some of the ways in which companies and consumers are embracing the LOHAS way of life.

I'll use the clothing manufacturer Patagonia as a good example. They were one of the first companies to declare the use of 100%

organic cotton in the manufacturing of their apparel products. The company also donates 1% of their total annual sales to non-profit organizations that protect the environment. The "1% for the planet" concept is also spreading to other companies worldwide. Consumers buy into their concept. The interesting element here is that people actually choose to pay a premium price for these goods, because they identify with the mission and the message.

What are the 5 principles of a LOHAS company? How does your consultancy assist companies with the integration of these principles into their business culture?

LOHAS companies must be, 1. Vision oriented, 2. Health conscious, 3. Green, 4. Caring for their employees 5. Social contributors. Our consultancy assists companies, top management in particular, in truly understanding the LOHAS principles and making decisions that reflect them in accordance with their vision and business strategies. The action plan then follows the vision to ensure accountability on all levels.

Is the notion of the "triple bottom line" — economy, environment, and society — a common ideal for most Japanese organizations?

Yes. There is an adage by which the merchants of the Ohmi region in the Edo era lived more than 200 years ago and which still holds true today: A business will never achieve success, unless they incorporate honesty and integrity into their business transactions. And this must be followed on three levels: seller, buyer, and society. The 'triple bottom line' concept is at the heart of many Japanese companies. In harmony with this ancient belief is the fact that more and more Japanese companies have made the decision to include environmental declarations within their CSR agendas.

What are your thoughts on the challenges of achieving carbon neutrality in Japan? In your opinion, are there viable solutions that would facilitate the increase of carbon offsets in the rest of Asia?

Carbon offsets were first introduced in Japan in late 2007 as part of the effort to reduce greenhouse gases. My company, gConscious, Inc., was one of the first 'Carbon Offset Providers'. This program was synchronized to commence with the Kyoto Protocol in 2008. As a result, most of the sources of carbon offsetting fall under the category of a Kyoto credit, which is to say that they are CER (Carbon Emission Reduction) certified by the UN Framework Convention on Climate Change. There are more than 900 carbon offset products sold in Japan. So I would say that the carbon offset market in Japan has been flourishing. People recognize it is a positive means to contribute to CO2 reduction, and businesses also derive value as it is an eco-conscious marketing tool, appealing to like-minded LOHAS consumers.

Business as usual is dead. Green growth is the answer to both our climate and economic problems.
~ *Danish Prime Minister Anders Fogh Rasmussen*

Revolutionary Vision: An Interview with Jeffrey Hollender

Nowadays, Jeffrey Hollender is one of the world's most admired leaders when discussion arises about the new socially responsible business ethic. *Seventh Generation's* founder and Chief Inspired Protagonist (now retired from the company, though still an active board member) has motivated companies world-wide to jump on the socially and environmentally responsible bandwagon. When it comes to pioneering green businesses, few companies enjoy the standing that *Seventh Generation* has earned. For 20 years, the company has made green cleaning products a household item and has done much for building a market and a supply chain for green goods. In this article, originally published in *GreenBiz.com*, Hollender shares some of the lessons he's learned after two decades in the trenches.[13]

"10 Things I've Learned About Building a Revolutionary, Responsible Company," by Jeffrey Hollender

1. The only real brand of responsibility is holistic and systemic, not compartmentalized. Corporate responsibility only works when it is strategic, not programmatic, and is driven from both the top down and the bottom up. It balances concerns about justice and equity with efforts to enhance growth and profit. It pulls these values into every corner of a company to impact every process and decision. And it offers original sources of innovation and opportunities for new products and services that deliver a return on purpose, as well as a return on investment.

2. Authentic companies must build a collective corporate consciousness and embed it into every molecule of their DNA. As our own experience at Seventh Generation has shown, this is a long-term process. It starts by achieving collective clarity about what matters and constructing a communal view of what the company should be. Once this self-awareness is established, it can be brought to bear on decision-making to ensure that a company walks its talk in every way.

3. Our mission is our primary product. At Seventh Generation, we've come to understand that our purpose and values are far more important than our products. In our view, strategy is synonymous with advocacy. In standing for something that truly matters, we're sharply distinguishing ourselves in the marketplace and instigating changes that couldn't be made if we played the same game as everyone else.

4. Businesses must create meaning at work and unleash people's potential. We're dedicated to offering opportunities for our

employees to realize their deeper aspirations and providing work that fulfills higher goals in addition to traditional financial aims. We view our company as a community in which our employees are animated by a larger sense of purpose and as a result act more like the individual entrepreneurs our company needs them to be.

5. Radical transparency is required. Information technologies now let the public keep an eye on everything we do, and we invite this scrutiny. Publicly sharing all our activities preempts our critics, and more eyes on our behavior mean more advocates and friends. Radical transparency also creates new partnerships and in this way becomes the first step towards overcoming the deficiencies that ultimately harm our profitability.

6. Company culture is critical. It's almost impossible for most customers, investors, and other stakeholders to see, but it may matter more than anything else. A few traits of a responsible culture include a company's level of honesty, how well people are treated when no one's looking, acceptance of criticism and disagreement when directed toward senior management and the humility to know that no one has all the answers. When bad behavior occurs at BP, Goldman Sachs or Toyota, it almost always starts with a culture that allows or encourages irresponsible behavior.

7. Ownership is essential. America is a nation of employees, not a nation of owners. Business is one of the most effective ways in which wealth is transferred from employees to investors. Businesses that don't ensure that every one of their people is an owner and not just an employee will never be truly responsible.

8. Business, money and politics are a dangerous combination. We must get business money out of politics now. Seventh Generation will not make any donations to individual

candidates. No business should. Want to understand why the financial industry is driving the meltdown in our economy? Look at the almost half a billion dollars a year that they have been spending to influence policy in Washington. It's a game big business spends far too much money trying to rig.

According to the Center For Public Integrity, for example, companies and groups that lobbied against financial reform spent a total of $1.3 billion in 2009 and the first quarter of 2010 on all lobbying efforts. Just one trade group, the U.S Chamber of Commerce, spent nearly $31 million on lobbying in the first quarter of 2010 alone. Individuals, small businesses, and NGOs can't compete with that kind of overwhelming influence. When regulations are strong, they don't have to.

9. Full cost accounting is the only way to level the playing field. We urgently need new regulations requiring that companies account for and pay for the costs of their externalities, that is to say, those environmental and societal costs their operations and products create. Currently these very real, very private expenses are passed on to the public in the form of additional health care burdens, ecological remediation, other publicly financed solutions to problems, and the higher taxes needed to pay for them. The result is an economic system that does little to encourage good behavior and even punishes those trying to do better.

If cleaning product companies, for example, had to pay the real costs for using up nonrenewable, petroleum-based raw materials, i.e. for the impacts created when these materials are extracted from the earth (think BP), for the pollution the resulting products produce, and for the illness their formulas cause, retail prices would climb, and healthier alternatives would emerge as the most affordable option. As it stands now, safer and more sustainable products are forced to compete without assistance against those produced by companies receiving hidden, de facto government subsidies covering the more significant costs of their operations.

10. Standards and metrics are missing in action. Ask the CEOs of the Fortune 500 companies to raise their hands if they are running a responsible business. How many hands will go up? Well 500 of course. Corporate responsibility is like playing a game with no rules, on a field with no boundaries, with referees who can never agree on who actually won the game. We need standards and metrics now. B Corp is a great start, but social and environmental disclosure should be required for every license that is granted for a new business.

Quality means doing it right when no one is looking.
~Henry Ford

Changing Your World at Work: An Interview with Tim Sanders

Renowned author, speaker, and businessman, Tim Sanders, says that it's important to determine who your "Saver Soldiers" are in the workplace. These are the people in your workplace that are successfully driving green initiatives, involvement in the community, quality of life, safety, outreach, and charitable projects. The former Chief Solutions Officer at Yahoo, Tim Sanders' research savvy and deep understanding of the human condition make him an indispensable consultant to some of world's biggest brands. He is frequently featured in top tier media such as *The New York Times, Financial Times, The Wall Street Journal* and *Fast Company.*

In your book, "Saving the World at Work: What Companies and Individuals Can Do to Go Beyond Making a Profit to Making a Difference", you champion the message that no matter who you are, where you work, or your position in an organization, you can make a difference. You can shape your community, you can change the world at work. Could you give us some insight into how an individual can instigate this process?

Here's the thing to keep in mind: organizations are run by real people. They can be inspired, influenced, and incentivized to change any process or pursue a new direction. Mostly, leaders drive them, but in many cases field level 'soldiers' have been the agent of change. I call them 'Saver Soldiers.'

They first identify something broken or an opportunity that resonates with them at a personal level. This is where the passion comes from. They tie the required change to the success of the group, so they can make some friends 'at the bank.' They network kindred spirits together to create a group. They celebrate success and welcome the detractors. It's a process. In no way can one person change the status quo by him- or herself.

What is the "Responsibility Revolution"?

This is a shift in paradigm, where 'done the right way' is a winning feature for a product or a service. It delivers a powerful benefit to its customer, user, or the employees behind it. It's the result of several factors: urgency concerning the environment, an understanding that communities should have to pay for corporate profit-making, and a general lack of confidence that government can stop the bad guys.

Who are "ThemGeners"? How has this group triggered the Responsibility Revolution?

I call the upcoming group of leaders 'ThemGeners', because they always ask the inconvenient question: 'But what will this mean to them?' Which is to say that they're focused on others, i.e. 'them'. They vote with their dollars, take jobs at companies with a good track record, and use social media to 'change the world and alert the masses.'

I agree with your observation that a company is either a "nutrient, filler, or a toxin" to their community. What is the secret to effective community outreach? How can companies enrich their community relations?

In the case of Timberland, for example, community service is integrated into multiple parts of the business. They use it in evaluating a candidate for hiring. They give employees a week off every year to serve with the volunteer group, City Corp. They contribute copy in their ads and catalogues for causes and communities. When they have company meetings, one of the days is devoted to community service in the host-city community. This forms a culture and spurs social innovation.

In the case of two Figlio restaurant chain operations in Columbus, owner Peter Danis staked his claim on the concept of green business. He bought wind energy offsets and shared the news with clients, which gave them a fresh new reason to eat with him instead of a chain like Applebees. He adopted a thoughtful recycling program and eliminated paper-based or mail marketing. As well, he asked employees to make suggestions, which led to energy, water, and plastic conservations gains. Over the last few years, he has saved more money than he spent and has garnered state-wide awards, as well as *USA Today* coverage for his efforts.

Your book, "Saving the World at Work", was published in 2008. How has the Responsibility Revolution evolved over the last few years?

I released the book one day after Lehman Bros. declared sudden bankruptcy. At the time, the media thought I was 'late by about one year.' Meaning that they believed that the Great Recession would

spell the death of the hybrid car, organic foods, CFLs, Save Africa, all
of it. All companies would care about was survival – profits or death!

Of course, that wasn't how it worked out. Automakers are spew-
ing out hybrids and electric cars. Consumers are flocking to eco-
friendly products. Fueled by social media like Facebook, community
outreach programs are continuing to be the ultimate tie-breaker in the
war for young talent. If nothing else, a new generation lived through
a teachable moment that supports The Law Of Interdependence:
'That which happens on Wall Street will eventually ripple to Main
Street and vice versa.'

*Upon closing, I'd like to ask you: What key message would you like to share that
might inspire and encourage both companies and individuals to make the world
a better place?*

Do something. If not you, then who? You live in a unique
time in history, where you can take your values to work and create
a win/win/win. Find out what social opportunities exist at work
and join them, whether they touch on people, communities, or the
planet. Start a movement, if you find a glaring opportunity to help
your company or organization 'be less bad.' Read books like *Cradle To
Cradle*, so you can learn how to innovatively do away with all waste.

Finally, be good to the people that work with you and do business
with you. They are people, and they have as many rights to quality
of life as you do. Trust them. They will appreciate your efforts, and
your sweat will not be in vain. Expect nothing in return. Do the right
thing, not because of who they are, but because of who YOU ARE.

TRY THIS

Are you a Saver Soldier?

Through his experience and research, Tim Sanders has defined
the leadership DNA that Saver Soldiers possess.[14] Saver Soldiers are

the people in the workplace who are successfully driving eco-conscious efforts, community involvement, quality of life, safety, outreach, and philanthropy. Their impact often ripples all the way up to the company's mission statement.

The Six Laws of the Saver Soldier:

1. The Law Of The Ledger: The organization or company is a baby that we all look after. That means that we must always innovate our way to social synergy, which is the way that we can do well by doing good.

2. The Law Of Interdependence: Everything is connected, and everything we do has an external cost. ThemGen see it this way, raised as they've been on the web. Nothing is independent, and the opinion that 'we need to make profits to stay independent,' is socially repugnant. Companies must run in a way that helps customers, partners, and local communities and that doesn't steal from future generations.

3. The Law Of Abundance: There is enough to go around. In fact, when you give to others, the likelihood is that you are creating value for everyone. In point of truth, you have enough time, money, and respect to accomplish anything. Value is created by sharing, not scarcity.

4. The Law Of Reciprocity: People reciprocate when you invest in them, are kind to them, trust them, respect them, or join their value-systems. Free riders are actually rare (although they do sting your ego). When you help the world, you'll get credit for it.

5. The Law Of The Long View: When it comes to assessing your strategy, you must expand your time horizons. You must consider scenarios outside the financial reporting period. Otherwise, you'll never be able to account for the external costs you are creating. During the next few years, on

account of the Responsibility Revolution, the bill will come in and crush many companies and organizations.

6. The Law Of The Last Mile: Nothing is accomplished with the hoopla of an announcement or a launch. If the project does not achieve full execution, i.e. if the last mile isn't run, the race was all-for-nothing. In fact, it's better for you never to have tried than for you to have made a half-hearted attempt and then give up.

("The Six Laws of the Saver Soldier" reprinted with permission from Tim Sanders, "Saving the World at Work: What Companies and Individuals Can Do To Go Beyond Making A Profit to Making A Difference" DoubleDay, 2008)

Walking the path of awakening includes a heart filled with empathic joy for the world around us, and for the liberation of all beings.

We see that all other human beings exist in us and that we exist in all other human beings. We see that the past and the future are contained in the present moment, and we can penetrate and be completely liberated from the cycle of birth and death.
~ Thich Nhat Hanh, "The Sutra on the Eight Realizations of the Great Beings"

4

A SENSE OF COMMUNITY

A community is like a ship, everyone ought to be prepared to take the helm.
~ *Henrik Ibsen*

What does the word community mean to you?

Is it a global village free of any outdated barriers? A small-town neighborhood that can band together with seamless ease and coordination? From families to corporate CEOs, defining what community should mean in the 21st century is capturing our attention. This is because it is within our communities that we realize the power of conscious choice and the power of intention for the good of others.

At the most basic level, traditional definitions of community hinge on geographic, ethnic/political, and demographic points of reference. Besides this, there are also virtual communities and activity-based groups. But, if you take away the scientific classifications and organizational understanding, you'll find that, on the most basic level, communities exist because of a common identity and a common goal, encompassing a distinctive set of precepts bounded by a shared understanding. From this dynamic spring the secret and not-so-secret societies that provide us with a home for our ideas, our beliefs, and our highest potential.

I am more interested now in furthering the goals of our alliance for a new humanity. In getting people to commit to global communities, for peace consciousness, removal of poverty, social justice, and the healing of our eco-system...
~ *Deepak Chopra*

Community is about conversations, our communication with like-minded people, where we share insights with those whose worldview resonates with our own belief systems and interests. Our communities provide an invitation for us to join together in a forum of harmonious interaction.

Community is all about connections, our links to family, friends, neighbors, and others who are in need of our help.

What is... important is firstly that we learn to live with each other, and secondly that we try to bring out the best in each other, i.e. the best from the best, and the best from those who, perhaps, might not have the same endowment. And so this bespeaks an entirely different philosophy — a different way of life — a different kind of relationship — where the object is not to put down the other, but to raise up the other.
~ *Jonas Salk*[15]

Our world community is beginning to awaken to the fact that it is no longer about survival of the fittest. It is now, in the words of renowned scientist Jonas Salk, about "survival of the wisest."

We cannot truly create a modern expression of community without considering what the term has meant to humanity over the decades and also what no longer applies. In fact, I think that achieving the fullest expression of 21st century community compels us to do one thing: serve. Serving the community got me thinking about the idea of community and applying a "social purpose" model to the corporate world. It also got me asking myself whether compassion can coexist with profit.

I respect generosity in people and I respect it in companies too. I don't look at it as philanthropy. I see it as an investment in the community.
~ *Paul Newman*

How do we apply these honorable values to commerce? And why should we consider implementing these principles in our core business practices? How do companies and entrepreneurs begin to initiate, assess, and sustain more altruistic paradigms that benefit their communities?

While I don't profess to have all the answers to these questions, I believe in advocating that businesses of all sizes take on more community-oriented roles. By doing so both collectively and as individuals, we can rise above our limiting beliefs and create momentum for change. We all have the ability to make a difference by building a sense of community in our world and by sharing a message of compassion, support, and healing, along with the resources that will ensure success. By transforming our businesses, our communities, and our world in this way, we transform ourselves.

If you've been having a hard time achieving some positive momentum in the domain of business and commerce, it might be time to try something different, based on the philanthropic business models or community-minded corporate cultures of other successful companies.

Case in point: The Ineeka tea company.

We are a living example of how a company can create a very successful business model by leading from the heart.
~ *Shashank Goel of Ineeka*

Cultivating Consciousness: An Interview with Shashank Goel

In this interview I found a real measure of encouragement, as I discovered the innovative avenues Shashank Goel's company has taken toward social and economic progress as well as development both within the context of community and within a profitable business model. These concepts and business practices may not be practical to implement in all businesses – indeed they may not even be applicable to certain sectors – but many of his ideas and experiences offer up innovative "inspiration seed capital".

When you meet the Goel family, the founders of the Ineeka tea company in India, you will find a perfectly modern example of what companies can do when they put the needs of people and a responsibility to community before the proverbial bottom line.

Ineeka, which is the Sanskrit word for "Little Earth", was founded in 2005. What once was a ramshackle tea plantation is now home to 25,000 people, who live and work on the twelve tea farms under the Ineeka umbrella. And as a certified Fair Trade company, Ineeka provides its workers with higher than industry wages and bonuses. It offers access to specialized medical facilities, better housing, education for local children, scholarships, and much more.

The company also marries a concern for human welfare with a practical consideration for the planet. This "green" balance is the hallmark of Ineeka, which sustains itself, its employees, and their families in a self-contained ecosystem that is capable of growing prime crops without the use of chemical fertilizers or pesticides and without the exploitation of human lives for the mighty dollar.

This reconnection to grass-roots community spirit begs to be copied and adapted all around the world today. The bottom line of all this is that community spirit for the modern age is fluid and problem-solving. It's long on vision and social responsibility and short on selfish, profit-driven mandates. It begins with the power of one person and ends with the empowerment of all those around that one person, when the choice is made to act, grow, change, and give.

A society cannot flourish without some sense of shared purpose. The current pursuit of self-realization will not work. If your sole duty is to achieve the best for yourself, life just becomes too stressful, too lonely — you are set up to fail. Instead, you need to feel you exist in something larger and that very thought takes off some of the pressure. We desperately need a concept of the common good.
~*Richard Layard*

I wanted to start with your family history and what led you to acquire the tea farms in India and, eventually, to launch the Ineeka tea company.

The family history as it relates to our company goes back to the 1950s. When my parents got out of college in their early twenties, they moved from the northern part of India, where all the cities were, to this godforsaken place of Darjeeling, which was literally in the middle of nowhere. Darjeeling was where the British had set up the tea plantations. My parents found work there, starting off on the lowest rung of the management ladder within the tea farms and tea estates. My father began in an assistant management role.

The best of their lives was spent at a farm called *Ambootia* in the mountains of the Himalayas, which is truly one of the most beautiful, verdant places on earth. I was born there.

Over time they moved on, working on other tea farms, as they progressed within their profession. My father got to a point where he was managing a large number of tea estates, which was one of the top management roles within that community.

Then, in the early 1980s, Ambootia came to suffer a grave downturn. The owners of the farm at the time had let it lapse into serious disrepair and insolvency, as they had other business interests and so did not take care of the farm or the workers. To give you some background, the way the tea plantation communities are set up is very owner-dependent. If the owners don't have any interest in the farm, the people who have been living and working on the farm for generations can't just get up and leave, since they have nowhere else to go. It came to a point where the farm had to be shut down for a whole year. People were actually going hungry – it was just a total mess. There were 5,000 people who did not have jobs or income.

During that time, we were visiting the farm, because there is a temple there that is thousands of years old. Our family feels very spiritually tied to it. And while we were visiting, the people living on the estate approached us and said, 'We want to show you the state of our community.' They didn't have any food and it was in a terrible state. They pleaded for us to take over the farm.

This was in the early 1980s. This farm was also the site of the largest landslide in Asia, which occurred in the 1970s. It was up for sale at this point, and nobody wanted to touch it due to a number of factors. There was the aftermath of a landslide to deal with and many other concerns, as well as the fact that there were 5,000 people who had been out of work for a whole year, all of which served to create very problematic conditions. We looked at all of the issues, including the financials, and we looked at everything from all different angles. At length, we reached the conclusion that this was not a viable option financially or otherwise.

Typically, the tea farms in India are owned by families who have been generational owners, that is, business families who have had the funding and finances in place for generations. They are the archetypical farm owners. Contrary to that, we were not a typical business family. My father worked in the service environment, and we didn't have the money to buy the farm outright, so that it just didn't make sense financially. We kept thinking about it, even after we had made our decision not to purchase the property. Around the same time, we had a little farm that we had sold. Suddenly we thought, 'This doesn't make sense, but we have to do this.'

It was more of a heartfelt decision than anything else. And somehow we were able to pull together the resources to purchase the property.

How did you raise the funds? Was this through private funding?

It was personal funding. We just pulled together absolutely everything we had. From that day, and even today, we have not taken any outside funding from anybody. Ever since then, our goal has been to create a level of sustainability that has never been seen anywhere in the world and to do it through three different levels of sustainability: social sustainability, environmental sustainability, and, most importantly, economic sustainability. We set up our people to a point where they will never have to go through what they went through when we first acquired the property.

Our belief is that without economic sustainability nothing else matters. We decided that we were not going to take any funding from the outside, no grants or anything of that sort, because what happens then is dependence on others, and you don't become self-sustainable on your own. We also decided that, with the help of the people on the farm, we would convert it to organic and biodynamic agriculture. Everyone told us that this was not the thing to do and that we couldn't do it all at once. They said, 'Take your time and do it.' We said, 'No, that's the only hope we have.' The people on the farm supported us and truly believed that it was the only way to turn things around. Ever since then, our goal has been to create the best products in the world, in a sustainable manner, where the people are at the forefront of everything we do.

If you fast forward to the present day, we have been fortunate in that we have been able to achieve a lot of what we originally initiated. Today, our teas are positioned at the highest level in terms of quality and can be found, literally, all over the world. We are co-branded with *Harrods* in the U.K., *Mariage Frères* in Paris, and are positioned as the crème de la crème of teas throughout the world.

Give us a little insight into how all of this growth and success occurred over the years?

Until probably about three or four years ago, we had only two farms, but we had established such a recognition within our community and within the worldwide sustainable community that our customers came to us and said, 'We would like you to acquire more farms and take this model that you have created and expand it and we guarantee that we will support you through the purchase of your products.' Again, going back to our rule of thumb to never accept outside funding, we had to find a way to do this on our own. But it was only with our customers' support behind us that we were able to take that leap of faith. We are constantly sustained by our customers, who believe in what we do and are supporting us through the purchase of our products. This, and only this, makes our business sustainable. We still own all the farms. We went from two farms to twelve farms, from supporting 5,000 people to supporting 25,000 people.

How did you make that jump so quickly? You didn't have any outside funding. Was it simply these agreements with your customers that allowed you to do this?

Right. They were not even written agreements. They were basically verbal agreements. Also, we were fortunate that the people who were selling the farms went out of their way to choose us, and they gave us some very attractive financing terms, because they wanted us to have those farms over and above anybody else. So we were blessed on two levels. It was a huge jump for us, and we are still fine-tuning.

Literally, what we did was take one model that we had already created, and then we replicated that model twelve times. This is still an ongoing process, and buying the other farms was a huge risk for us, but we just took the jump and said once again, 'We have to do this.'

We also introduced the same model of social responsibility to these other farms. We took the same model of organics, biodynamics, and fair trade and replicated it, along with our strictest adherence to the highest level of quality.

We have come to the point today where we are the largest organic and biodynamic producer in India within the major tea-growing areas, which are Darjeeling and Assam, and we are also well-positioned in terms of our reputation for products of premier quality.

A couple of years ago we asked ourselves, 'How do we take this to the next level of sustainability?' We had, and still have, very solid and very strong partnerships within our tea-buying communities, but we thought we really needed to tell our own story. Interestingly, many of our customers pushed us on this and told us that we had to create our own brand, because we have such a fascinating history, not to mention that it would create another level of sustainability for us. You may say that we are competing with our customers, but really, they are the ones who pushed and encouraged us towards this! So our own brand, 'Ineeka', which actually means 'little earth' was born.

Our whole philosophy is based on the premise that we can't change the world, but that we can make a change and make a difference in our small corner of the world by making a difference in our own communities, in our own "Ineeka", that is, in our own little corner of the earth. We are hoping that other people see what we are doing and follow suit to amplify and extend this sense of community.

Ineeka is still a very small brand. It is currently only marketed in the U.S. and Canada. Our goal is to slowly penetrate into that marketplace and tell our own story. One of the vehicles we've used to this end is our website. It's the beginning of what lies ahead. It is our future.

Are you the only tea company in North America that owns its own tea farms?

I believe that's correct, yes, at least on the level where we're situated. There are different levels of the tea segment. There is a mass-market tea segment, which we are not planning to enter, and the specialty tea segment. I believe we are the only North American specialty tea company and maybe even in the world that owns their own farms. Most companies don't even use their own tea farms anymore. Also, interestingly, no other producer has really been able to create their brand as we have.

Regarding sustainable, organic farming and biodynamic farming, was that something that your father had learned along the way by managing other tea farms? How did you have that integral knowledge to start this?

The whole concept of 'organic' or 'biodynamic' today is the new cool thing and considered to be the latest trend. In reality it is not. It's what was done traditionally. For generations, everything was done organically and biodynamically. We're not trying to do anything new, but rather, by going back to the 50s and 60s, we're doing what was always done. That was the kind of model that was always used from time immemorial. But what happened in the late 60s and 70s was that all the chemical companies started coming in and really pushing their products. What we've done is just go back to basics. We really didn't know what biodynamics was at first, but if you look at the principles of biodynamics, it was what we were always doing: using compost, engaging in biodynamic-type preparation of the soil, using the energies around us. These were things that were very ingrained in our culture. If you go back and read about Rudolf Steiner, a lot of what he did in terms of setting up the whole biodynamic system was implemented on the basis of the traditional Indian agricultural system. What we were doing, although not formally, was what is now called 'organic' and 'biodynamic'.

We were reintroduced to the recognized methods of organics and biodynamics through our travels in Europe in the 80s, and that is when we formalized the process.

Do you think that your business model has encouraged your competitors to meet or match your high standards and values? Your website states that you offer wages and bonuses that are higher than normal in the industry, specialized medical facilities, schooling and housing, livestock, and other benefits that pertain to sustainability on many different levels. So what are your competitors saying? Are they trying to match your models?

When we started off, and this may be true even today, our family was regarded with great dislike in the tea-growing community for several reasons. For one thing, we did not make our way up by way of the traditional business model or from a business family. Secondly, we have raised the standards to such a high level within the community that it has forced everybody else to elevate their own standards so as to keep pace with us. All of the other owners, whether they like it or not, have had to come to embrace our principles. We are proud to say that today, within our region of Darjeeling, about fifty percent of the farms have tried to follow our model and are now organic. So we have been a very strong leader and proponent of what we do, and by taking this to other communities we have found, whether it is out of genuine willingness or just as a result of the pressure of circumstances, that other companies in the region have had to improve their product and working standards.

Biodynamic, organic, fair trade... how do you feel about the certification system? I have heard it can be very challenging and expensive for companies to obtain all of these certifications.

You're absolutely correct. It's very much a two-edged sword. The certifications have their place, but also, over time, they have become big business. If you go back in time to a traditional era, when a farmer came to you and said, 'Here are my crops, I have grown them organically,' you would believe him. What has happened over the years is that there are so many companies trying to play a role in this marketplace that you have to find some system to regulate what is going on. Not everyone is doing this out of conviction, from the bottom of their heart.

That being said, in one way, certification is good, given the world that we live in. Still, I wish there was more harmonization of standards amongst the various countries or regions of the world. We have literally about a dozen certifications and, apart from the demands on time and the complexities of the various processes, it is an extremely expensive proposition. We operate all over the world. Hence there is, for example, a Japanese protocol of certification, and there is one for the EU, but the Swiss don't follow EU, so that there is a separate Swiss criterion. The UK has its own standards, while Canada and the U.S. have their own certification systems as well.

So because we're selling in all these markets, we have to comply with all of these standards. The process becomes extremely time-consuming, tedious, and expensive, and it tends to lose its meaning. But all the same, there is a need for certification.

Also, you will see that all the farms that we own are fair trade certified and that they are all models of the fair trade concept. In fact, they were among the first fair trade farms in the world. Nevertheless, Ineeka does not use the fair trade logo. Why? Because use of the logo has become incredibly cost-prohibitive. I believe in the concept, but there is a double-edged sword there.

I co-authored a book called "Heart Centered Leadership", and the title speaks for itself. It's all about leading from the heart, putting your people first. It's basically what you're doing within your business model. I think of Ineeka as a shining example of a heart-centered business model. Would you agree with that? Skeptics might say it can be difficult to sustain a healthy bottom line when social responsibility is a company priority. What are your thoughts on this?

To be honest, there are times we feel that we're leading more from the heart than from a business standpoint. Literally, for my family, it is all about doing the right thing for the people. It all starts from there. At the same time, we are very conscious about economic sustainability. Without that, your whole model is going to collapse. We are a living example of how a company can create a very successful business model by leading from the heart. We don't have shareholders to answer to. Our shareholders are the 25,000 people who live and work on the farms. That's really the ultimate criterion of success. What more do businesses need to do? Pay their CEOs multi-million dollar salaries?

What advice would you offer companies or entrepreneurs who want to integrate a higher standard of corporate and social responsibility into their businesses?

I think the key thing is to be true to what you are doing and to be true to who you are and to follow that spirit. To give you an example, Ineeka and all the copy that you see and all the designs that you see, everything that we've done we've done ourselves and told our story. We have not used any branding firm, any design company, any copy-righting. This is our story. What's more, there is actually a physical place in the world where you can go to see firsthand what we're talking about. Not all companies have that physical place, but still, you need to be completely true to what you're doing. All through this, as discussed before, the people – your employees, your customers – have to come first. That's what's going to help expand and energize this movement and so make this world a better place.

Do you have or have you ever had a mentor?

My father has been the best mentor I've ever had. He has taught me to be true to who we are and to put the people first and to just do the right thing. He's been a great influence in my life. Also, over the years I've met fabulous people who have led me through this daunting maze of international business. It's interesting. We have literally had people who have come to us without any expectations and said, 'I want to do this with you and I am going to help you navigate through this.' Just to give you some names: Mark Retzloff, founder of Wild Oats, Eden Foods and Horizon Dairies. We don't do business together, but Mark and his wife travel every year to our farms to connect with the people. He truly believes in what we're doing. There's also Drake Sadler, who is the owner of Traditional Medicinals, Horst Rechelbacher of Aveda, and Dipak Jain, who is the Dean of the Kellogg School of Management. None of these people has anything to gain financially from what we're doing, but they have all come together to help me navigate through all this from an international standpoint. But the roots, the standards, the heart of our business, have come from my father.

In closing, I'd just like to ask you, what does the word "community" mean to you?

Community is not just us, as in the 25,000 people working and living on our farms. You're part of our community as well. Community is these tentacles outstretched into the world and these relationships that we have created with people all over this beautiful planet.

By the very fact that you're talking to me, you're somewhat related to the person who's plucking the tea. Let me explain it differently.

Let's say I have a garden and I'm keeping it very clean. I have a very nice environment surrounding me. My neighbor begins to observe what I'm doing and so he begins to shift his perspective and make some changes. Even if he only does ten percent of what I'm doing, he's part of my community because I'm affecting him. Similarly, by your drinking a cup of tea, you've become a part of our community. That's how we're hoping to grow this community – by touching other people who may not know or realize that they're actually an integral part of what we're doing.

We cannot change the world by dictate. Who are we to tell people what to do? What we can do is make a difference within the environment and the communities that we touch, even while we cultivate the hope that other people elsewhere will do a small part of what we're doing in their own little 'Ineeka.'

The famous Vietnamese monk Thich Nhat Hanh suggests that the awakened mind begins with making happiness your morning's intention, which begins by intentionally smiling "with your whole being," leaving no place for criticism or pessimism to reside within you. Joy is always located within the present moment, because it is the only moment that exists. You can choose to awaken happiness at any time. It is always there for you to see it.

Perfection is everywhere, if we only choose to recognize it.
~ *Okakura Kakuzo*

5

CONSCIOUS OPTIMISM

The optimist sees the rose and not its thorns; the pessimist stares at the thorns, oblivious to the rose.
~ *Kahlil Gibran*

We all dream of things that would make us happy. These take many forms: a fulfilling career, robust health, a supportive circle of family and friends, a beautiful home, or a life filled with travel and wonderful experiences, as well as time to enjoy them. There is nothing wrong in fact with aspirations and ambition. A life of purpose drives individuals to pursue their most cherished dreams and make them a reality.

But ask yourself this: If all these grand, external achievements were suddenly taken away, could I still be happy? Could I still view the future with a sense of optimism? Could I look into my heart and know that the best in life is yet to come?

These questions may sound ludicrous. After all, anyone who has realized a dream and seen it snatched away by a twist of fate or by their own doing knows quite well that this can be a devastatingly difficult turn on the journey of life.

Some recover from the lows in life. Others never do. But living through anguish and defeat forces people to make choices. It isn't pretty, and it's never pleasant to endure. Yet these upheavals compel "the walking wounded" to rethink every aspect of their life as they have known it. Their goals, their beliefs and what it really means to be happy all come into question.

We are all human. We all have to find our own way to renewed optimism, when disappointments come calling.

How do we move past disappointments? How do we rebuild our lives? How do we find the road to happiness, especially when the road we thought would take us there is unexpectedly washed out from under our feet?

These questions plague millions of people around the world today, people who have lost their jobs, their homes and possibly their faith in humanity after financial or personal crises.

But like anything in life, perspective is everything.

There are some people who live in a dream world, and there are some who face reality; and then there are those who turn one into the other.
~ *Douglas H. Everett*

What does it mean to be intentionally optimistic? It can mean something as small and commonplace as a young man having big dreams of owning a house, even though he has no down payment or fulltime job. Or it can mean something as grand and out of the ordinary as building a multi-billion dollar empire by "delivering happiness". It can also mean remaining heroically steadfast and eternally optimistic while dealing with a devastating disease.

Conscious optimism began with an idea and one red paperclip for Kyle MacDonald, a Canadian entrepreneur and author who traded his way from that single twisted piece of metal right up to a house in a series of online transactions over the course of a year.

It all began with the following ad on *Craigslist*:

This might not surprise you, but this is a picture of a paperclip. It is red. This red paperclip is currently sitting on my desk next to my computer. I want to trade this paperclip with you for something bigger or better, maybe a pen, a spoon, or perhaps a boot. If you promise to make the trade, I will come and visit you, wherever you are, to trade. So, if you have something bigger or better than a red paperclip, email me. Hope to trade with you soon!

Kyle PS: I'm going to make a continuous chain of 'up trades' for bigger or better things until I get a house.

Inspired by the childhood game *Bigger, Better,* MacDonald, who was 25 at the time, made his first trade, a red paper clip for a fish-shaped pen on July 14, 2005. Twelve months later, in July of 2006, with the fourteenth transaction, he reached his goal of trading up to a house, exchanging a Corbin Benson directed movie role for a small house in Kipling, Saskatchewan. As time went on, he realized something even more significant than his original intention. McDonald was in the business of granting dreams.

As a teenager, McDonald was constantly coming up with innovative, moneymaking ideas. Friends and family have said they were not surprised when Kyle finally achieved his goal, often working 20 hour days answering enquiries, negotiating trades, and fielding calls from the media. Shrugging his shoulders, he says, "Sometimes I forget to do the simple things, like eat and sleep."

If I started small, thought big, and had fun, it could all happen.
~ *Kyle MacDonald*[16]

Who would have thought that one red paperclip could be traded for a house? MacDonald was served well, it would seem, by his unwavering sense of optimism.

Envision, create, and believe in your own universe and the universe will form around you.
~ *Tony Hsieh*[17]

Tony Hsieh has built a multi-billion dollar online empire on the basis of this injunction.

In his book *Delivering Happiness: A Path to Passion, Profits, and Purpose*, author, entrepreneur, and creator of Zappos.com, Tony Hsieh, talks about the importance of balancing work and life in a way that fully integrates one's being and increases the prospect for greater happiness.

If the research shows that vision, meaning, and a higher purpose leads to happiness, what is your company's higher purpose? What is your higher purpose?
~ *Tony Hsieh*

No stranger to high-handed deals in corporate boardrooms, Tony Hsieh's story reads like a script from a movie.

In 1999, at the tender age of 24, Tony Hsieh sold LinkExchange, the company he co-founded, to Microsoft for $265 million. Once the deal closed, he signed on as an advisor and investor and eventually became CEO, in which role he helped the company grow from almost no sales to over $1 billion, while simultaneously making *Fortune Magazine*'s annual "Best Companies to Work For" list.

In November 2009, his online retail organization, Zappos.com Inc., was acquired by Amazon.com in a deal valued at $1.2 billion on the day of closing.

Chase the vision, not the money.
~ *Tony Hsieh*

Clearly Hsieh is living with passion and purpose and getting rich doing it. He has realized such success as an entrepreneur that money no longer motivates him. He has stayed on at Zappos, earning a salary of only 36,000 dollars a year.

"Happiness is about being able to combine pleasure, passion, and purpose in one's personal life," says Hsieh.

It would seem that the key to conscious optimism has nothing to do with external factors. In fact, spending a lifetime acquiring expensive gadgets, homes, cars, and other symbols of success long prized by society will only satisfy human beings to a very limited extent. And, as Marcus Aurelius Antoninus once wrote, "Very little is needed to make a happy life; it is all within yourself, in your way of thinking."

So why does happiness seem so elusive? And why is there such a heightened awareness of "the joy factor"?

Even world leaders have come to be more concerned with defining and measuring happiness. Recently, French President Nicolas Sarkozy proposed that his nation's economic progress be monitored by various "happiness indicators", such as leisure time, access to education, health, social relationships, and hobbies. He has made it his intention to make joy and wellbeing the key indicators of growth, shifting the attitudes of his nation to measures of wellbeing and sustainability rather than remaining fixed on traditional benchmarks like gross domestic product (GDP).

And, on the other side of the world, a small country has placed happiness ahead of government politics. In the remote Himalayan kingdom of Bhutan, policies have implemented to ban advertising, wrestling channels, plastic bags, and traffic lights, as these things are deemed to interfere with "Gross National Happiness".

How do you measure GNH? "The government (of Bhutan)," *The New York Times* explains in a report, "has determined that the four pillars of a happy society involve the economy, culture, the environment and good governance. It breaks these into nine domains: psychological well-being, ecology, health, education, culture, living standards, time use, community vitality and good governance, each with its own weighted and unweighted GNH index."[18]

The very least you can do in your life is to figure out what you hope for. And the most you can do is live inside that hope. Not admire it from a distance but live right in it, under its roof.
~ Barbara Kingsolver

A couple of years ago, while filming his documentary, *Adventures of an Incurable Optimist*, Michael J. Fox visited Bhutan. He noticed that these optimistic people were fulfilled and had exceptional relationships and that, moreover, they did not need material possessions to be happy.

In a 2009 interview with *Good Morning America's* Diane Sawyer, Fox said "I sat down with a farm family, and I found... there were even these little differences in the way the farm family would talk to me... about how they all were there for each other.... So, it's a sense of unity. We can, all of us, potentially heal the world, and we all have a part to play in improving the lives of the people around us."

Actor, family man, activist, and incurable optimist, Fox heads up the Michael J. Fox Foundation for Parkinson's Research. As a sufferer of Parkinson's for the last 20 years, he has been grappling with the issues of fear, loss, identity, and acceptance. Yet, in spite of all this tragedy and strife, Fox has come through even stronger, saying that he never imagined his disease would redefine his outlook on life *for the better.*

"Your happiness grows in direct proportion to your acceptance and in inverse proportion to your expectations," Fox told Sawyer. "Acceptance doesn't really mean you're resigned to it. It just means acknowledging that that's what it is."

Conscious optimism is all about feeling contented and at peace with your situation each and every day of your life. That may sound like an impossible task, especially in this imperfect, fast-paced world of ours. But research has shown that people who can achieve that inner core of peace and happiness are more creative. They're more resilient. They're able to bounce back more easily from life's challenges. They are also able to see the possibilities for happiness even in failure.

To reach that state of conscious optimism requires commitment and practice. It requires re-training the mind, changing negative habits and belief systems, and taking responsibility for one's own life. But the rewards for such a shift in consciousness are powerful and life-altering.

If you heed life's miraculous call and put past tragedies behind you, your ability to stretch yourself out and reach for happiness again will most certainly grow and blossom. But the first step is to embrace those wounds and bless them. Once you consciously express your appreciation for the hand you have been dealt in life, you lay a new groundwork for a more fulfilling state of being.

Many other components also play a part in mastering the art of conscious optimism: kindness, compassion, love, and forgiveness. But, above all, it is a call to action, one that compels each and every one of us to connect with our spirit and the world around us and actually commands us to be happy.

As Aristotle once said, to be truly happy in life is "the be all and end all, the goal of all goals." Centuries later, this ancient Greek philosopher's take on real happiness still holds true.

Happy For No Reason: An Interview with Marci Shimoff

For those who do not know her, Marci Shimoff is the woman behind the biggest self-help book series in history, *Chicken Soup for the Soul*. Her six bestselling titles in the series, including *Chicken Soup for the Woman's Soul* and *Chicken Soup for the Mother's Soul*, have sold more than 13 million copies worldwide in 33 languages. They have also been on the *New York Times* bestseller list for a total of 108 weeks. Shimoff is a featured teacher in the international film and book phenomenon, *The Secret*.

Shimoff's recent book, *Happy For No Reason: 7 Steps to Being Happy from the Inside Out*, offers a revolutionary approach to experiencing deep and lasting happiness. Here, in this interview, Shimoff shares her lessons on defining true happiness and reaching a state of conscious optimism.

What is the difference between a happy person and a "happy for no reason" person?

Most people in our culture are trained to look for circumstantial happiness. We have this inner dialogue with ourselves that goes something like this: 'When I have a great relationship and the right job and enough money, then I will be happy.' I call this 'happy for good reason'. There's nothing wrong with having good reasons to be content with your life, except that, when they go away, there goes your happiness. What I define as 'happy for no reason' is an inner state of peace and wellbeing that doesn't depend on circumstances. People who are happy for no reason don't look to their life experiences as the source of their happiness. They bring their happiness to their life experiences.

But don't most people associate their level of happiness with the external world?

I think we have been trained to do so, yes. We also have a very big industry called advertising, whose sole purpose is to let us know that we really need such and such a product in order to be happy. These are insidious messages. They creep into our subconscious, and it is very hard to avoid them.

There is a lot of training that we have to do with our own psyche, in order to recognize that being happy is actually a matter of acquiring certain habits that will create an inner state of happiness. In fact, there are tremendous studies that have been done to show that these external factors will only satisfy us to a very limited degree. Daniel Gilbert, a professor of psychology at *Harvard University*, has done some fascinating research on this topic, and it proves that we have a very faulty ability to assess what will make us happy in the future.

First of all, our future expectations never make us as happy as we think they will. Secondly, when we do get what we thought we wanted, we very quickly become acclimated to it and return to our original happiness set point, our default setting, so to speak.

There is a common misconception that money can buy happiness, but I think you would argue that point. In your book, "Happy For No Reason", certain statistics are brought to light about people who had won the lottery. Within a year, we learn, they had gone back to their original happiness set point!

Yes. It has also been shown that, once you have your basic needs met, no amount of money makes you any happier. So the added millions don't matter!

Would you say, then, that it's a purposeful decision to become "happy for no reason"?

It's not just a decision. It's a decision to practice certain habits. Happiness is a physiological state. It can be measured. There are several physiological markers or indicators of happiness. So it's not just a matter of deciding today to be happy and then all of a sudden you are. It's a matter of deciding to take responsibility for your happiness and then practicing the habits of happy people. It's like playing tennis. You can't just decide to be a fabulous tennis player and then wake up tomorrow morning and find yourself able to play Wimbledon. You have to practice the habits of great tennis players. It's the same with happiness. You have to practice the habits of happy people.

One of the more fascinating happiness factors that your research uncovered is the beguiling nature of the happiness set point, which you just mentioned. Can you expand on this concept?

Yes. Actually, one of the main people involved in the happiness set point research was Sonia Lyubomirsky of the University of California, Irvine. What they found was that fifty percent of our happiness set point is genetic, ten percent is affected by our circumstances, and forty percent stems from habits of thoughts and behavior. That forty percent is the piece that we can really do the most about, in order to shift our happiness set point. A lot of people haven't taken responsibility for their happiness and they say with resignation, 'Oh, I was just born with unhappy genes,' or 'I just don't have the right circumstances.' It's very clear that, in both of these cases, we all have the ability to take greater responsibility for our happiness, because the root issues of the matter do not lie in just our genes or our life situation.

What would you say to someone who has the limiting belief that they can't change their habits?

The first thing I would say to them is: you can't blame it all on your genes and you can't blame it on your circumstances. The place you need to go to and examine is your own habits. When you want to change your habits, it's important that you do it in small pieces, in small ways, consistently. Most people spend more time on their hair than on improving their happiness every day. We just haven't made it a priority.

Ironically, happiness is what we all want. Aristotle said, 'It's the be all and end all of life, it's the goal of all goals'. The Dalai Lama says that it's the purpose of life. We all want to be happy. We've just been going about it the wrong way. So how do we do it?

First, we need to shift our attention from where we've been accustomed to looking for happiness. You know, we've been looking for happiness in all the wrong places. We need to shift our attention to looking for it in the right places, which is in our habits, specifically in the habits that we practice every day.

There are seven main headings that these happiness habits fall under, and we really need to attend to all seven of these areas in order to raise our happiness level. We have to take responsibility. That's the first step. We have to take care of our mind, body, heart, and soul, and then we have to live an inspired life, a life that is aligned with our specific purpose and passion, so that we have meaning. We need to surround ourselves with support and with the people who are going to boost our own happiness and help sustain it.

First and foremost comes taking responsibility for your life, taking ownership of your happiness. The second habit has to do with the mind, and it's about not believing everything that you think. Then there is the body, and it's about making the cells in your body happy, because it's not just a mental decision to be happy. You have to strengthen your decision to be happy on a physiological level. There is in fact a physiology of happiness. Then there's the heart. It's about living life with love and gratitude and forgiveness and kindness. There is also the spirit, which is about connecting and plugging into your soul, and then there is your purpose or passion, which promotes your living an inspired life. Finally, there is your support system, which is to say, surrounding yourself with happier people.

My next question has to do with the hundred people whom you interviewed. The one belief that they all held in common was the notion that this is a friendly universe. I find that fascinating.

Einstein said that the most important question we can ask ourselves is, 'Is this a friendly universe?' What I found is that people who are happier believe that ultimately this is a benevolent universe and that, when things happen to us, they happen for some sort of good reason. There is a measure of blessing or gift in everything that happens to us.

I love that adage from your book, "Rejection is God's protection."

I love that phrase too. Here is another phrase that I love. I just heard it recently, and I'm not sure who to quote on it. It goes something like this: 'Life doesn't happen to you, it happens *for* you.' What it means is that you should assume, as a working hypothesis in life, that everything that is happening to you is happening for your highest good. The problem is that you may not understand it that way right now. When I am speaking to an audience, I ask them how many people have been through a challenging time or a crisis. Everybody raises their hand. Then I say, 'How many of you would say that that experience was one of the best things that has ever happened in your life?' Almost everybody raises their hand. In retrospect, we are able to see why the challenge or crisis was a blessing. Happier people are actually able to have faith or trust that challenging times are a blessing even while they're going through them.

That sounds a little daunting. After all, we're only human. How do we master this discipline?

It's a practice, the practice of looking for the lesson or the gift in our difficulties. One of the questions that I suggest people ask themselves goes like this: 'If this were happening for a higher purpose, what would that be?' These are muscles of perspective that we have to build.

But it's not just the brain you're changing. You're also changing other bodily functions related to the brain, such as your heart rhythm coherence.

There was a quote from the book that referred to the fact that you used to have pain in your heart, but the pain could not be attributed to any physiological cause. Now you no longer experience this "phantom pain". It makes sense that a person can, on occasion, experience physical problems brought on by mental, emotional, and spiritual challenges. The brain seems to be a significant piece of the puzzle.

Yes, but it's more. Beyond the brain, it's the heart as well. There is research from the Institute of HeartMath which shows us that, when we feel greater love, compassion, and appreciation, we go into heart rhythm coherence, which means that our heart rhythms are calmer and more consistent. In order to achieve this, I think it's a matter of changing those habits of ours that do not serve us. More positive habits can change the brain's neuropathways. They change the heart rate variability, that is, our heart rhythm coherence. They also change the neurochemicals in the brain, the serotonin and the oxytocin. We are building muscles that are going to change our physiology, so that it makes it easier for us to feel increasingly happier as time goes on.

Let's talk about fear for a moment. We all get caught up in the media headlines: job losses, financial and environmental crises, war, terrorism, and so on. How do we "unplug" from the fear and embrace a "happy for no reason" state?

The first way to do it is to recognize that it's an important thing to do. What you put your attention on is what grows stronger and more dominant in your life. Many people get caught up in focusing their attention on all the negativity that is occurring in the world. They spend hours 'feeding' that in themselves. When you're watching the news, it's like you're taking in food. It's registering in your body. I am not saying to be oblivious to what's going on in the world. That's certainly not what I'm suggesting, nor am I about denial. What I'm saying is that we overexpose ourselves to the negativity. It's a bad diet. We are indulging in a bad mental diet.

I always say, "Garbage in, garbage out."

Yes. If people looked at all this as though they were taking in junk food, I think they would understand it more easily. It's junk food for your brain, for your heart. Do you know that there is research which shows that seeing a horror film will change your physiology for six weeks? Psychological residue from the horror film will last in your body for six weeks. Our senses take it all in and register it very deeply, and it's the same with everything we expose ourselves to, such, for example, as the negativity of the people around us. We have to be aware that everything around us is constantly influencing us.

Everything in the universe is energy. Everything vibrates at a certain energetic level. So ask yourself: What are you consistently exposing yourself to from the point of view of energy? There is the energy in food, there is energy in the people around you, there is the energy of the news, there is the energy of what you are reading, there is the energy of the movies you are watching, there is the energy of your environment. Are you in an environment that surrounds you with beauty? You don't have to have a ten thousand square foot house. You can create beauty in a small space where everything that your eyes fall on becomes food for you.

One of the principles in "Happy For No Reason" is, "let love lead". Tell us a little bit more about that.

I believe that love is the highest energetic vibration on the planet and that it is really our ultimate purpose for being here. Our purpose should be to expand our capacity to give and receive love, and we do that through the heart. I don't mean sentimental or romantic love. I mean appreciation for things just as they are, in a spirit of non-judgment, compassion, forgiveness, loving kindness, and unconditional love. My next book is on the subject of love. I have just interviewed over 150 people – I call them love luminaries –who are living more and more in this state. It's not just that they're happier. There's more to it. It's all about being in love with life. It's about *being love*, it's not about being *in love*.

Being love and living love – it's the key. Love luminaries are able to get a lot more done because they are in an energetic flow. They love what they are doing. They bring love to the people around them, which I believe is the basis of success. I think you can be successful by certain material standards without being loving, but it's empty and it's unfulfilling. We all know examples of very wealthy, powerful people who are hard, cynical, and unhappy.

How important is a sense of gratitude? Do you think that a sense of gratitude is lacking in many of today's leaders?

Absolutely. Gratitude is the fast track to happiness and success. What we put our attention on, we get more of. There is a saying, 'What you appreciate, appreciates.'

Would you say that contributing to something greater than yourself leads to a happier and more fulfilling life?

A lot of research has been done on altruism, giving, and generosity, and it has been shown that people who are very generous and altruistic are happier and healthier. First of all, when you are giving from fullness, then it contributes to a happier life because you are overflowing. It expands you. When you are giving from lack, which a lot of people do, it actually burns you out more. It makes you more stressed.

How do you move from giving because you feel obligated to giving out of a sense that giving actually expands you?

Two factors enter into play. Number one is: take care of yourself. Give to yourself first. That's the very first place you have to give. Secondly, find small ways in which you feel inspired, where you give with a sense that there is something at work beyond you. It could be something simple, like being nice to the person in the grocery store line behind you. Just find little ways that aren't going to drain you to the point where you find yourself over-giving. Do small acts of kindness that way. Find ways that feed you, so that you're not influenced so much by the idea that it's something you should do, but rather because such and such a course of action would feel good to you. The test is to ask yourself the question: 'Am I doing this so that I won't feel guilty or because it will feel good?'

Do "happy for no reason" people, once they start practicing these habits, become proactive and therefore more productive?

Yes. People who have an inner core of happiness, of peace, and well being are more creative, more resilient. They are able to bounce back more easily from challenges. They see more possibilities.

I am a firm believer in "optimistic consciousness". What does this phrase mean to you? How can we shift toward greater happiness in our own lives and thereby contribute positive energy to the lives of others?

Optimistic consciousness means being able to look for and see the gift or the beneficial aspect in any situation. It ties back to what we talked about earlier, a friendly universe. Optimistic consciousness is harboring the belief that there is always a blessing in everything and that you are meant to look for what that blessing is. It's also about expecting the best and projecting the energy of positive expectation out into the universe. It's about looking for the good in others. Everybody has good and not so good qualities in them. When we focus on people's strengths and their better qualities, we get more from them. Remember, what you appreciate, appreciates. When you are appreciative, when you are optimistic, when you are seeing the best in people and you are bringing that out in them, you redouble the dynamic and get more of the same. It's about putting more of your conscious, creative energy towards the possibilities of what could be rather than complaining about what isn't.

There is a saying that I think relates to what you've been saying: "Don't focus on what if, focus on what is." Blaming and finger pointing are futile. Inspired, openhearted energy can move mountains.

In closing, I wanted to ask you about how our happiness influences those around us. How do you explain the fact that our moods and outlook can be incredibly powerful and affecting, even in the most seemingly insignificant interactions with others?

We consistently impact the people around us with our attitudes and emotions. There is a phenomenon called "emotional contagion" which means that we 'catch' the emotions of the people around us just like we catch their colds. We know that, the happier we are and the more we are vibrating at a higher energetic level, the greater is our actual ability to influence the people around us and render them happier.

Gandhi's famous quote says it best: *'Be the change that you want to see in the world'*. I would add the following maxim: *Be the happiness you want to see around you.*

TRY THIS

Look for the Lesson and the Gift

1. Sit quietly by yourself. Close your eyes and take a few deep breaths.
2. Recall a specific situation that has caused you to feel wronged or to blame others. Picture the person or people involved, the setting, and what was said or done.
3. Imagine taking several steps back and observing the situation from a distance, as though you were watching a movie on a screen.
4. What part of what happened can you take responsibility for? Did you ignore signs that should have clued you in that there was a problem? Did you act in a way that might have provoked the situation? Did your thoughts or actions escalate the situation?
5. What's your lesson to learn from what happened? Do you need more patience or better boundaries? Do you need to listen more, say less?
6. Ask yourself: If this were happening for a higher purpose, what would that be? Can you find the gift?
7. Write down the most important thing you can do differently as a result of finding the lesson or the gift.

Incline Your Mind Toward Joy: The Daily Happiness Awards

Throughout the day, look around you with an eye to giving out awards.

1. Be creative. For example, as you look at flowers, notice the one that could get the "Most Unusual Color" award or find one that's had the hardest struggle to survive, but made it, and give it the "Best Blossom of the Day" award.

2. Look for extraordinary smiles, efficient service, or ingenious solutions to everyday challenges. There's no limit to the type or number of awards you can give in a day.

3. Invite other family members or friends to play this award game, and at the end of the day, tell each other the awards you've given out.

(Reprinted with permission: © 2008 Marci Shimoff www.HappyForNoReason.com).

Heaven and earth and I are of the same root.
The ten-thousand things and I are of one substance.
~ Zen Master Sêng-chao/Sōjō (384-414C.E.)

6

THE COLLECTIVE
GLOBAL BRAIN

Practical application of consciousness seems remote compared to technology. Would you rather be enlightened or own an iPad? In modern society, the choice is all too obvious. But it's a false choice, because people don't realize that the things they most cherish and desire are born in consciousness: love, happiness, freedom from fear, the absence of depression, and a vision of the future. We achieve all these things when consciousness is healthy, open, alert, and expansive. We lose them when consciousness is cramped, constricted, confused, and detached from its source.

~ Deepak Chopra[19]

There are many mysteries that confound science. One of the most intriguing in recent years has been the idea of a collective consciousness at work in our universe. Does it really exist? Is it more than just a fanciful notion? It may have seemed so just a few short decades ago. But that is not the case today.

We've all had experiences where we were thinking about someone and the phone rings, or we suddenly meet someone we haven't seen for years right after recalling something about them from the past. Or, in other more vivid and pressing instances, we suddenly awaken from a deep sleep, "knowing" that someone we love is in trouble or hurt.

Sometimes we come across the exact book or message we need to get us through a difficult time. Serendipity? Chance? Coincidence? Happenstance? We have many words to explain away the significance of these puzzling occurrences.

But is there another explanation? Might everything that happens to us on a day-to-day basis be more than just random occurrences with no meaning?

What about the influence of our own thoughts on our personality, our health, and even our life expectancy? Could our own thoughts be altering our reality or, on a broader scale, affecting our world?

Many scientists think so.

Take, for example, Dr. John Hagelin, the world-renowned quantum physicist, educator, public policy expert, and supporter of world peace.

For the last quarter century, Dr. Hagelin has led an international investigation into the nature and origin of consciousness, including higher states of human consciousness.

Among his many scientific contributions over the years, Dr. Hagelin has published groundbreaking research that established the existence of long-range "field effects" of consciousness generated through collective meditation. Remarkably, Dr. Hagelin's research has showed that large meditation groups can effectively defuse acute societal stress. His research has also indicated that the positive effects generated by large meditating groups can be used to prevent violence, mitigate social conflict, and provide a practical foundation for permanent world peace.

All this may sound like the stuff of science fiction. But not so, says Dr. Hagelin. In his seminal book, *Manual for a Perfect Government*, Dr. Hagelin concluded that, through educational programs and policies that effectively harness the laws of nature and the development of human consciousness, it is possible to solve and prevent critical social problems and profoundly enhance what government can achieve.

If Transcendental Meditation were taught to as many individuals as possible on this troubled planet of ours, there would be less stress in the world, says Dr. Hagelin. People would realize their full creative potential. A new groundwork would also be established for society's greater receptivity to fresh and innovative ideas, allowing them to be implemented more effectively at all levels of society.

More remarkable still is Dr. Hagelin's conclusion that, by harnessing the power of Transcendental Meditation, we frail, imperfect humans could learn how to become peacemakers from within our own selves. That single achievement alone has the potential to become the great equalizer for all mankind, as well as a great neutralizer of crime, religious tensions, and terrorist threats to national security.

The bottom line is simple. When the "collective intention" of meditation is properly understood and practiced, the resulting state of "pure consciousness" that is manifested is good for our own betterment and that of our 21st century world. The science shows that such a global outcome is possible if like-minded individuals and organizations around the world commit themselves to educating the public about meditation techniques. But, as Dr. Hagelin says, "The time to act is now."

The Phantom DNA Effect

Other researchers have also made great strides in recent years in understanding how communication with the deepest levels of consciousness can have a profound impact on our well-being.

Fascinating discoveries by Russian molecular biologists have revealed that DNA has a mysterious resonance that has been termed "the Phantom DNA Effect".[20] It is known that DNA reacts to voice-activated laser light, when the latter is set at the specific frequency of the DNA itself. Therefore, it seems it is possible to change not only the information patterns in DNA, but more significantly, the mode of communication with the DNA itself.

This new phenomenon was first observed in Moscow at the Russian Academy of Sciences as a surprise effect during experiments measuring the vibrational modes of DNA in a solution using a sophisticated "laser photon correlation spectrometer". These effects were analyzed and interpreted by Dr. Vladimir Poponin. Dr. Poponin is a quantum physicist who is recognized worldwide as a leading expert in quantum biology, including the "nonlinear dynamics of DNA and the interactions of weak electromagnetic fields with biological systems". He is the Senior Research Scientist at the Institute of Biochemical Physics of the Russian Academy of Sciences and has also worked with the Institute of HeartMath in collaborative research projects.

The experiment went something like this: First, a container was emptied to create a vacuum, so that all that was left were photons or particles of light. The scientists measured the distribution (i.e. location) of the photons and found they were completely random inside the container – which was the expected result.

DNA was placed inside the container, and the distribution of the photons was re-measured. This time, the photons were lined up in an ordered way and aligned with the DNA. In other words, the physical DNA had an effect on the non-physical photons.

After that, the DNA was removed from the container, and the distribution of the photons was measured again. The photons remained ordered and lined up where the DNA had been. What were the photons connected to? Why did they align with the DNA? It was discovered in later experiments that the "phantom DNA" remained in the vacuum for as long as a month in later experiments!

The scientists were led to the following conclusion: "We believe this discovery has tremendous significance for the explanation and deeper understandings of the mechanisms underlying subtle energy phenomena, including many of the observed alternative healing phenomena. This data also supports the heart intelligence concept and model".

Scientist, visionary, and scholar, Gregg Braden, says that, as a result of these experiments, "We are forced to accept the possibility that some new field of energy, a web of energy, is there, and that the DNA is communicating with the photons through this energy".[21]

At the Institute of HeartMath, researchers conducted a study called "Local and Nonlocal Effects of Coherent Heart frequencies on Conformational Changes of DNA". In this experiment, scientists placed placental DNA, considered to be the most pristine form of DNA, into 28 vials. Twenty-eight researchers chosen for their emotional intelligence, i.e. their ability to feel strong emotions, each received a vial of DNA. The researchers were instructed on how to generate and experience these emotions in order to facilitate the study of the effect of these strong feelings on the encapsulated DNA.

The scientists discovered that, when the researchers focused and felt intensely the emotions of love, gratitude, and appreciation, the DNA responded by relaxing and unwinding. In effect, the DNA strands were actually lengthened.

Conversely, when the researchers felt anger, fear, frustration, and stress, the DNA responded by tightening up. It became shorter and switched off many of its codes.

Scientists now know that the heart sends the brain twice as many signals as the brain sends the heart — which gives, it must be said, a whole new perspective on the term "emotional intelligence".

The Institute of HeartMath has known about this phenomenon for quite some time. Their "emWave technology" for stress reduction provides scientific evidence for the ever-present relationship between the heart and the emotions on the one hand and physical and mental well-being on the other.

If you need further scientific proof that our thoughts and emotions have a profound affect on our health and our environment, look no further than the work of Dr. Masaru Emoto.

Dr. Emoto was born in Japan and practices as a Doctor of Alternative Medicine. His photographs of the physical effects of emotions as manifested in the physical form of water were first featured in his self-published works, *Messages from Water* (Vols. 1 and 2) and *The Hidden Messages in Water*, the latter selling over 400,000 copies internationally.

Emoto studied the effects that various focused intentions, expressed through written and spoken words as well as music, had on water samples. These directed manifestations of intention appeared to actually change the expression of the water. Using a powerful microscope in a very cold room, along with high-speed photography, he developed a technique to photograph newly-formed crystals on frozen water samples.

What he discovered was that the crystals formed in frozen water revealed changes that were in direct correlation with the specific, concentrated thoughts that were directed toward them. Water from pure sources such as spring water and water that had been exposed to "loving words" showed brilliant, intricate, and colorful snowflake patterns. Polluted water, or water exposed to negative thoughts, on the other hand, formed incomplete, asymmetrical patterns with dull colors.

In the end, he concluded that the implications of this research create a new awareness of how we can positively impact the earth and our personal well-being. Thoughts create experience and can alter physical reality. It should be noted as well that a significant fraction of the human body and of the earth is comprised of water.

So what does it all mean? Like Dr. Emoto, I have always been a firm believer that our thoughts are "things". Thoughts have their own energy frequency. Whether you believe in the power of positive thinking or believe that how you think translates into how you feel and therefore how you act, it appears from this research that our thoughts seem to quite literally give a shape and a pattern to the events of our lives as they unfold.

Collective Consciousness and Science

Robert Kenney PhD has been studying the notion of collective consciousness for years. His research in the area of collective intention or global consciousness is far-reaching and profound. In an article entitled *The Science of Collective Consciousness*, Kenney discusses some of the studies that have been done to determine the existence of collective intention. "With more and more people talking about collective consciousness, it seems natural to wonder, 'Is there any scientific research to back it up?' The answer, increasingly, appears to be 'yes.' In fact, a growing body of recent research suggests not only that a field of awareness and intelligence exists between human beings, but also that through it we influence each other in powerful ways".

Kenney goes on to discuss a particularly compelling "distance healing" experiment: "Just as we can create order in physical systems through focused attention or intention, a number of experiments have suggested that two or more people can create synchronization or coherence between their nervous systems. For example, in research funded by the Institute of Noetic Sciences and others, Marilyn Schlitz and William Braud have shown that individuals who are calm and relaxed can intentionally reduce the anxiety of others in distant places, and that people consciously focusing their attention can help others in remote locations to concentrate their wandering minds. In another area of inquiry – that of distance healing – 67 percent of 150 controlled studies have shown that individuals and groups can use intention, relaxation, enhanced concentration, visualization, and what is described as 'a request to a healing force greater than themselves,' to heal others to a statistically significant degree. Healing effects and tele-prehension have increased, when participants felt empathy and rapport, or when they meditated together".[22]

The Road to Collective Consciousness: An Interview with Dr. John Hagelin

There are a few scientists in this world who have fulfilled Einstein's dream of arriving at a "theory of everything." Dr. John Hagelin is to be found among this rare elite. Acclaimed for his groundbreaking research in the fields of electroweak unifications, grand unification, super-symmetry, and cosmology, Dr. Hagelin is currently the Director of the Institute of Science, Technology and Public Policy, a leading science and technology think tank. He is also the International Director of the Global Union of Scientists for Peace, an organization comprised of leading scientists throughout the world who are dedicated to ending nuclear proliferation and establishing lasting world peace. We talked to Dr. Hagelin about the science of human consciousness and how it just may be the vehicle for the most advanced scientific breakthroughs of our time.

What is your definition of "consciousness"?

Consciousness is the pure inner wakefulness that underlies our ability to experience. It is the most fundamental level of our being, pure subjectivity, our core reality. It is the source of our thoughts, but it is beyond thought, unbounded, beyond limitations of time and space. It is identical to the Unified Field discovered by modern quantum physics, the non-material foundation of the entire manifest universe.

Many scientists assume that consciousness is an epiphenomenon, a byproduct of the functioning of the material brain. And certainly the active modes of consciousness – that is to say, perception, memory, cognitive processing – are wholly dependent upon our brain's neurological processes. But meditation, properly understood and properly practiced, allows our mind to settle to quieter and quieter levels of functioning, until mental activity ceases altogether and pure inner wakefulness alone remains. The resulting state of 'pure consciousness' constitutes a fourth state of human consciousness, physiologically and subjectively distinct from waking, dreaming, and deep sleep. It is the direct subjective experience of the Unified Field. This experience, in turn, produces dramatic and scientifically demonstrable benefits to mind and body. And it supports an entirely new scientific paradigm, in which consciousness, that is to say, the Unified Field, is primary and matter is secondary.

It is well known that your mission and the mission of the long list of organizations you are affiliated with is that of world peace. Focusing on quelling violence is the first step towards this end. How are these remarkable findings about the ripple effect of meditation being put to good use?

More than 50 replications and 23 studies published in leading peer-reviewed journals have confirmed that large groups of peace-creating experts practicing specific, advanced meditation techniques can neutralize acute ethnic, political, and religious tensions that fuel violence, terrorism, and social conflict. These groups cause marked reductions in crime, terrorism, and even open warfare in war-torn areas, with simultaneous improvements in social trends and international relations. Such studies demonstrate that the scientific knowledge and technologies are now available to end terrorism and conflict, to achieve sound and deep-rooted national strength and security, and to create permanent world peace. Consequently, I am working every day with like-minded individuals and organizations to establish peace-creating groups in every nation, as well as one large group of 8,000 experts to create an immediate global impact. By establishing these groups and implementing these technologies, every country can ensure national security and the peace and safety of its citizens. But the time to act is now.

What is the relationship between the power of intent and collective meditation? For instance, when meditating, does one focus on a specific outcome or cause to increase its probability of happening?

The power of one's intention to create a particular effect depends on the depth and power of consciousness which entertains the intention. Much has been written in recent years about manifesting desires, that is, our mind's ability to manifest outcomes in the material world through mere intention. But unless we can operate from the deepest levels of the mind, our capacity for manifestation will always fall short.

Over the last fifty years, physics has explored progressively deeper levels of nature – ranging through the molecular, atomic, nuclear, and subnuclear – culminating in the recent discovery of the Unified Field, a single, universal, unified field of intelligence at the basis of all forms and phenomena in the universe. Each level of nature's functioning – from the superficial to the profound – has its own unique reality and structure, and each deeper level has exponentially greater power than more superficial levels, with the Unified Field representing the most powerful level of all.

Our own minds mirror this hierarchy of nature. We can entertain desires at the surface level of mind, where they won't have much potency, or we can dive within to deeper and deeper levels of mind, accessing much more powerful, quantum levels of thought and ultimately the Unified Field itself, the most powerful, limitless, universal level of our own pure consciousness. An impulse on that level will draw its support from the totality of natural law that governs the universe – which means that from there we can truly move mountains.

Collective meditation always enhances the power of intention. But interestingly and ironically, intention itself represents mental activity, which may interfere with the meditative process that allows the mind to settle down to its deepest, most silent levels. In my view, the greatest power of collective meditation is generated when participants dive deep within themselves to the level of life beyond thought and intention – that is to say, their own pure consciousness, the Unified Field. The resulting enlivenment of the Unified Field brings holistic, life-nourishing benefits to bear on both the participants and the larger society.

The personal benefits of meditation have long been recognized and are (thankfully) being brought to light in mainstream society. We know that meditation can improve our physical, emotional, and spiritual well-being. Is it fair to say that someone who practices meditation and truly reaches the deep field of consciousness is in fact contributing to the well being of the entire planet?

This statement is not just fair. It is a scientifically confirmed reality today. As noted in the answer to the question posed above, more than 50 replications and 23 studies published in leading peer-reviewed scientific journals show that large groups of meditating experts can neutralize acute ethnic, political, and religious tensions that fuel violence, terrorism, and social conflict. The result is a marked decrease in crime, terrorism, and open warfare, along with improved social trends and international relations. This far-reaching, peace-creating effect in society is the natural byproduct of many individuals diving deep within themselves and experiencing and enlivening the Unified Field, the most fundamental level of nature's intelligence, which is our own consciousness in its pure state. Direct experience of the Unified Field therefore cultivates not only individual enlightenment, but also a tangible, measurable effect of peace in the world. (For more on this topic, see www.PermanentPeace.org and www.InvincibleDefense.org.)

I believe that true leadership begins within and that one must first pursue that age-old piece of wisdom that tells us how important it is to "know thyself". Do you feel this statement is true?

Yes, absolutely, but we need to clarify the deeper meaning of this statement. The maxim, 'know thyself', should mean more than inner clarity about our own goals, desires, strengths, beliefs, etc. To truly know ourselves, we need to dive deep within and experience the limitless, infinite reality of our own pure consciousness, the core unity at the basis of both our individual life and all the apparent diversity of the universe. On this most profound level of existence, we can truly 'know the Self", that universal ocean of pure life where we are all one. The experience of this reality on a permanent basis is called Enlightenment, and when we know ourselves fully in this way – from the surface level of our life to our inner, unbounded core reality – then we are truly in a position to lead others.

The field of unity and the power of collective consciousness have become scientific certainties, based on your research and that of others. Do you feel the movement to bring this information to the world (i.e. to schools, workplaces, political organizations, etc.) is your greatest challenge?

The receptivity of social organizations to the scientific knowledge of unity depends directly on the quality of the collective consciousness of society itself. A rising and coherent collective consciousness will allow and support quicker acceptance and implementation of new, life-nourishing ideas and programs; in contrast, stress-ridden, incoherent, violence-prone collective consciousness will not be open to positive change. For this reason, I feel that the most crucial needs today are:

I.   That as many individuals as possible learn to transcend effort-
      lessly through the Transcendental Meditation program, thereby

dissolving stress, unfolding their full creative potential, and becoming peacemakers from within themselves.

2. That establishment of large groups of peace-creating experts in every nation, whose collective practice of the Transcendental Meditation program and its advanced techniques can defuse social tensions and violence in society and thereby create the basic grounds for more receptivity and more rapid implementation of these new ideas.

For these reasons, in July 2006, I founded the Invincible America Assembly, a group of 2,000 peace-creating experts in the heartland of the U.S. The purpose of this group was to raise the collective consciousness of the U.S. The impact on U.S. social trends, crime rates, etc., was immediate, and research continues to verify the group's positive influence. Now, in my work with organizations teaching and implementing the Transcendental Meditation program, I have found a growing openness and receptivity that was largely missing even five years ago. Schools, businesses, homeless and rehabilitation programs, and other national and international organizations are now embracing the Transcendental Meditation program and the great benefits that it confers, as demonstrated by over 600 scientific studies confirming those benefits (see www.tm.org). And with the implementation of each new program, collective consciousness is being positively enhanced as well. Therefore, I look forward in the years ahead to rapidly accelerating public acceptance of this profound knowledge of unity and these life-transforming programs.

Just as a gorgeous blossom
brilliant but unscented,
so fruitless the well-spoken words
of one who does not act.
~*The Dhammapada*[23]

7

BENEVOLENT REVOLUTION

It is one of the most beautiful compensations of this life that no man can sincerely try to help another without helping himself... Serve and thou shall be served.

~ Ralph Waldo Emerson

Is it possible for a single human being to change the world? Or even a small group of people? Are individuals from every walk of life and companies of all sizes becoming more aware of their responsibility to give back to those who have far too little in life? It seems so. Whether it's Warren Buffett's astonishing 31 billion dollar pledge to the *Gates Foundation* or a more commonplace ten-dollar donation, people are coming to learn that it's precisely what we give that makes us rich.

As the whimsical children's author, Dr. Seuss, once wrote in his famous tale, *The Lorax:* "Unless someone like you cares a whole awful lot, nothing is going to get better. It's not." A heartfelt commitment to this profound insight now drives some of the world's most innovative companies. And, across the board, they are discovering countless new ways by which to inspire individual employees to tap into their philanthropic spirit, even as they meet that critical bottom line.

Many captains of industry and corporate leaders are beginning to realize that we are responsible for the world in which we live. With this in mind, they have reached out in support of charitable organizations that can wisely distribute their abundant wealth. Richard Branson has been quoted as saying: "Ridiculous yachts and private planes and big limousines won't make people enjoy life more, and it sends out terrible messages to the people who work for them. It would be so much better if that money was spent in Africa – and it's about getting a balance."

Literally translated, the word philanthropy means, "love of humanity". By very definition, philanthropy is only philanthropy when it stems from giving without personal gain. Which is to say that it begins and ends with an unselfish motive, that of helping one's fellow man without seeking recognition or reward.

Most of us know that charity is its own reward. The true wealth of charity is measured by good deeds, not ego and material gain. That's why many affirm that they get back far more than they give. In other words, what they receive is the joy of love in action, the manifestation of their gift of time or money in such a way as to make a visible difference.

Interestingly, good people doing good work experience benefits that go beyond just their contentment in the knowledge that they are advancing the well-being of humanity. A study conducted in 2006 examined the brain activity of 19 men and women, each of whom was given money ($128) and asked to make choices about whether to keep the money for themselves or to give some or all of it to charity anonymously. The outcome was fascinating. The participants who gave the money to charity experienced an extremely high level of pleasure. The researchers concluded that, "The warm glow that many donors get from giving to charity involves the same brain mechanisms that evoke pleasurable sensations after sex, eating good food, and using heroin or other drugs."[24]

A revolution starts with one idea, followed by action.
~ *Jim Knight, Senior Director of Training, Hard Rock International*

One of the most outstanding beacons of meaningful, modern-day philanthropy in our day is Hard Rock International.

Surprised? So was I. Since the company's first rock 'n' roll cafe opened to the public in London, England on June 14, 1971, founders Isaac Tigrett and Peter Morton have made it their business and their abiding passion to use Hard Rock International's extensive network of cafes, hotels, and casinos around the globe to benefit the planet.

As Tigrett and Morton once said, "Charitable work will always be integral to what Hard Rock is."

Since 1971, Hard Rock has been committed to a wide range of philanthropic causes and activities. Their passionate and dedicated team members in their local Ambassador programs help a myriad of communities around the world on a daily basis. In every way imaginable, Hard Rock puts its philosophy of "Love All, Serve All" to work so as to benefit young and old, the sick and the poor.

You see that spirit in the company's involvement with charities like the Columbian-based children's initiative Pies Descalzos Foundations (The Bare Feet Foundation), the Children's Miracle Network, and other youth organizations. Hard Rock International's concern for the planet drives its collaboration with the Arbor Day Foundation, which inspires people to plant, nurture and celebrate trees. The list of charities that Hard Rock helps is extensive and wide-ranging.

All manner of men, women and children have found it within themselves to engage the spirit of giving for the betterment of others. From contributing to Farm Aid to helping to educate African farmers through the Wildlife Conservation Society and more, Hard Rock, like other top philanthropic-service corporate models today, knows how to tap into the compelling passion that people have to do something meaningful with their lives. This new face of philanthropy highlights, moreover, three key ingredients of the process: belief, passion and purpose.

Our differentiator may be rock, but philanthropy is our soul.
~ *Annie Balliro, Senior Director of Philanthropy, Hard Rock International*

The spirit of Love All, Serve All thrives on believing and achieving. It has heart and the wisdom to use it well. And it is also about giving people purpose through their passion. If we couple this with our own innate faith in mankind, we can change the world for the better, even if that world is just our own neighborhood.

Take Time to be Kind: An Interview with Annie Balliro and Jim Knight

Today's brightest corporations have a new and dramatically changing face, one that speaks to the need for heart-centered leadership in all manner of ways, both on and off the job. As we have seen, one of the best examples of this new corporate model at work can be found in Hard Rock International.

In the following interview, we talk to Jim Knight, the Senior Director of Training for Hard Rock International, and Annie Balliro, the company's Senior Director of Philanthropy, to learn how big business and the need to better mankind are finding powerful new ways to coexist and change the world.

I co-wrote a book entitled "Heart Centered Leadership". What does this term mean to you both in the context of Hard Rock Cafe's basic tenet of Love All, Serve All?

Jim:
The phrase 'Heart Centered Leadership' represents a way to courageously lead others by using time-tested principles that revolve

around living a positive way of life. This has implications for both the leader and the people they lead. Certainly, results-oriented objectives are imperative to the success of any business, but how you get there – by treating people a certain way and behaving a certain way – makes the difference in both business sustainability and in living a positive and productive life.

Annie:

I had not heard of the specific term, 'Heart Centered Leadership', but after a little research I actually laughed out loud, since utilizing the truth as a key principle for behavior (both in and outside the workplace) has always been a valuable guideline in my personal toolbox. The truth, although not always the most popular path, will always lead you in the right direction.

Your company tenets are: "Love All, Serve All", "All is One", and "Take Time to Be Kind". They pervade the atmosphere of Hard Rock. How did you set out to incorporate these admirable guidelines throughout the various levels of your company?

Jim:

That was initially pretty easy, as these were guiding principles brought to the organization by the company founders soon after the company's inception in 1971. When you have a group of like-minded people on a single mission to literally revolutionize 'the system', powerful things happen. This was the case when the founders, Isaac Tigrett and Peter Morton, decided that business and spirituality could co-exist. These company mottos, along with 'Save the Planet', have been an integral part of the way our employees think and act. Today, they are a clear and present influence in every imaginable way for both guests and employees. They make their way into all of our brand and training collateral, they are emblazoned on the walls of every property and they are manifested in our local Ambassador programs, which is our internal name for the volunteer group of employees who dedicate their time and talent to giving back to the community.

Annie:

Hard Rock International's mottos, LOVE ALL, SERVE ALL, TAKE TIME TO BE KIND, SAVE THE PLANET and ALL IS ONE, are more than just words on our walls. They are the guiding principles by which we behave as 'Hard Rockers' (i.e. Hard Rock employees) and have been since day one.

Hard Rock has accomplished so much through your philanthropic programs and events and the deep expression of commitment to your global partners, employees and suppliers. Was there a defining moment when Hard Rock made the decision to create a business model that stood for altruistic values, while still remaining profitable? What was the company's most difficult setback when initiating this?

Jim:

Since the company's value system organically included philanthropy, I do not think Hard Rockers saw this happen as a single defining moment, but rather, simply as a way the company exists. Remember, this has always been a part of the organizational DNA. There was certainly a time when things got a little more challenging for us in terms of integrating these programs, when company results were going in the wrong direction for a variety of reasons. Sadly, this placed philanthropy on the back burner for some time. However, some strong company leadership changed all that. In 2004, Hard Rock hired new President and CEO, Hamish Dodds, who in turn hired and promoted some key executives and made philanthropy a prevalent part of the business again. In fact, Hamish even created a Senior Director of Philanthropy, a senior-level position solely focused on this area of the business. The idea of philanthropy for the company was the same as it was over three decades before that, which was the notion of bringing together an organized group of like-minded people who are attracted to the company mores in the first place when they apply for the job and who will galvanize around a heart-centered mission and a purpose bigger than themselves. People inherently want to do meaningful work. This includes doing something rewarding for the community, the Earth, or others less fortunate.

By the company's continuing support of a philanthropic mindset in everything it does, corporate profitability has flourished in many ways. Employees tend to stay on with the company longer, social-minded guests resonate with the philanthropic mission, strategic partners and vendors tend to be more open to donating product or services in support of an altruistic initiative, and celebrities and artists are more likely to want to take part in these charitable events.

Additionally, we have found that some of the best programs are not the global initiatives that Hard Rock spearheads, but rather the locally generated initiatives that individual corporate properties have taken on as a labor of love to make a difference in their own community. This is as much a part of employer loyalty as anything else. The only real setbacks in doing this type of work are the occasional roadblocks of time and money, which ultimately just become excuses. For example, sometimes it costs a property more money and extra effort to do the right thing, such as implementing a recycling program and using recyclable products, versus taking the cheaper and easier path of not doing so. Once the individual or collective mindset turns to a 'can do' attitude and people realize that something can always be done, that's when the setbacks simply become a thing of the past.

Annie:

Philanthropy is not an 'add on' to existing programs at Hard Rock International, but rather a founding cornerstone by which all global programs are created across all our properties. The spirit of LOVE ALL, SERVE ALL has been an integral part of our DNA since day one.

Money, celebrity and power aside, how, in your opinion, can one person begin to make a difference in terms of the social injustices and the ecological tragedies we are facing in the world today? Also, do you think there's a wake up underway?

Jim:
I believe a single committed person can make anything happen... and that includes changing the world for the better.

There are scores of individuals who have worked hard to attain a level of position where they have a monster platform and a powerful voice which can influence and impact others to act. Those that do philanthropic work, not for themselves, but for the good of others, are inspiring and motivating people to go out and do the same in turn.

A more realistic approach is to look at it from an individualistic view. Most people in the world are not going to attain this exalted level or platform. However, every person can do something to make a difference. Whether it be making the simple decision to stop littering or the more committed act of joining some type of volunteer community service project, each act a person undertakes makes our world better. The social injustices and ecological tragedies that you mentioned may be problems that occur on a more grandiose scale, but I truly believe that the more socially-conscious individuals we have on this earth, the more they will eventually outnumber those that cause these larger issues in the first place.

A revolution starts with one idea followed by action. I think that, in today's world, it is almost considered outmoded behavior if a person is unaware of how their actions affect the planet and its population. Philanthropy cannot be a momentary movement or fad, but rather a way of life.

Annie:
Every Hard Rocker is encouraged to make a difference in some way, whether through our global philanthropic programs or as our local Ambassadors in every community we live in. Hard Rock

International is filled with great examples of one individual who made an impact in their marketplace and through a passionate commitment to a local program grew their support into worldwide brand initiatives.

This may be difficult to answer considering how many programs you are involved in, but what was the most inspiring charitable event you have initiated, and why?

Jim:

Tough question – but I think the one that made the biggest impact in my life is Give Kids the World Village, which is affiliated with the Make a Wish Foundation, where terminally-ill kids get free trips to Disney World and a free family meal and T-shirts from Hard Rock. We received many letters each year stating that the Hard Rock made their entire vacation. I had the opportunity to go out on occasion with the Ambassadors to hang out with the kids and even build one of the village buildings. I am also very excited about the work we do with World Hunger Year (WHY), which focuses on poverty and child hunger-related causes. We work with several charities in multiple countries and each year we do internal staff contests to provide opportunities to the winners to travel with the Hard Rock CEO to one of the recipient countries and actually see where the funds go. The stories that come out of those experiences are remarkable and uplifting.

Annie:

There are literally an infinite number of programs that inspire me. I am repeatedly amazed by the Hard Rock spirit, exemplified by our team's commitment to the notion of LOVE ALL, SERVE ALL, and our accomplishments as a global brand, as well as the accomplishments within our local communities that take place on a daily basis. Every Hard Rock International philanthropic program, every Hard

Rocker in every Cafe, Hotel, and Casino and on our Corporate Team is a valuable part of our efforts to raise awareness, our fundraising and the dynamics of sustainable change for deserving charity partners.

What (or who) inspires you and keeps you going? How do you inspire and instill hope in others?

Jim:

I have several personal Hard Rock heroes. The passion and energy that Annie Balliro brings to the job as our Senior Director of Philanthropy is infectious. Just when you think you can't make something happen, she's able to lift you up and inspire you to do more for the world…one act at a time.

I also get very motivated when I hear about the local stories of individual Hard Rockers, the good deeds they do in their own properties with no direction from the company. I love teaching others about philanthropy because it's my own way to use my individual talents to communicate the concept of mass messaging to those that want to hear, but I also like the personal reinforcement that comes with teaching something. Every time I teach the class or have a side-bar conversation about philanthropy, it gives me the extra jolt I need to look for opportunities to do more and share best practices. I have been with Hard Rock for 20 years now, so I do need some inspiration from time to time! When all is said and done, philanthropy is one of the key fundamentals of the Hard Rock brand that has kept me here for more than two decades.

What does Hard Rock stand for? How has philanthropy changed the idea of who you are as a company?

Jim:

Hard Rock is all about 'spreading the spirit of rock 'n roll'. However, the way in which we do this is what garners us some internal and grass roots recognition. Annie has been quoted as saying, 'Our differentiator may be rock, but philanthropy is our soul'. I think people who discover the things we do in this realm become bigger fans of the brand. It's one of the core elements that separate us from the rest of the competition. The world may not know about all the charitable acts the company accomplishes, but our internal 30,000 plus employee base certainly does. For many, this makes the job bigger than a paycheck. It's a cool thing to be able to work for a company that you respect, make a decent living serving others and then lay your head down on the pillow each night, knowing that you also did something personally for someone less fortunate. That's the beauty of philanthropy.

That's who we are. That's how we roll.

TRY THIS
Companies that embrace philanthropic efforts enjoy a number of significant advantages that contribute to the mutual benefit of both management and employees on every level:

1. Loyalty and morale rise in direct correlation to the enhanced sense of personal engagement and connectedness of the employees, since they are proud to be associated with a company that cares and does good for others.
2. Top talent is retained, and company expenses associated with employee turnover are lower, which enhances the bottom line.
3. Employees experience the increased sense of personal satisfaction and reward that goes with being part of a meaningful community effort, something bigger than themselves that makes a difference in the lives of others.
4. Team building happens at a higher level, since all employees are working side by side together towards a common goal.

Listed below are some ways in which you can instigate change within your company, and, in turn, begin to make an impact for others and this planet.

1. With your employees, explore particular causes that they may resonate with. These could be charities or organizations whose mission aligns with your company's culture or mission.

2. Select an employee or ambassador to champion your organization's philanthropic efforts.

3. Organize team philanthropic events. For example, volunteer with a local Habitat for Humanity home building project. The collective group can work together to achieve something for the community while serving as an excellent team-building event for the employees.

4. Support employees' philanthropic ventures by providing paid time off for them to participate in community charitable events.

5. Select suppliers who have a philanthropic vision for their organizations.

6. Implement recycling and environmentally friendly programs at all company locations.

Sons have I, wealth have I,
thus the fool is fretful.
He himself is not his own,
how then are sons, how wealth?
~The Dhammapada[25]

8

WHAT'S WRONG WITH THIS PICTURE?

It's a really striking paradox. The richest country in the history of the earth, and everybody is p.o.'d all the time. It doesn't really speak well for the ability of material success to bring happiness, does it?
~ *Jonathan Franzen*[26]

Look at the world around you and the message is clear. We are paying dearly for a life out of balance. And the situation is getting more than a little scary.

Trust has been eroded in our governments and our political leaders. We've lost faith in many of our religious institutions. Shopping and credit card debt continues, despite a wake up call on Wall Street. The pressures of working longer and harder have left millions of people feeling tired, overwhelmed, and not sure how to cope.

The US debt is the largest in history: over $12 trillion. And deficits are projected to average over $900 billion a year through 2020.

That's over $80,000 for every American worker.[27] And to make it all the more discouraging, our tax dollars do not make even a small dent in this massive debt.

Then there's our own personal "black hole" of debt. Over 61% of Americans live paycheck-to-paycheck, meaning a job loss, sickness, or some other financial crisis could catapult many into dangerous territory.[28]

Our system is in crisis.

75% of the 400 richest Americans believe that "the best way to build wealth is to become and stay debt-free."
~ *Forbes 400*

At first glance, these problems inherent in today's fast-paced world seem far beyond our making. We are simply moving with the flow of the times and, to distract us from our woes, we shop.

So, what are we buying?

Consumers today are spellbound by the newest toys and the best deals they can find. After working hard and chasing the dreams that advertisers have invented for us, we feel we deserve all the cars, homes, luxury goods, and techno gadgets we can buy, even if we cannot afford them. And yet there's an irony that's inescapable in this consumer mindset: The more you own, the more it owns you.

Suddenly, those purchases that we simply could not live without start to feel more like a burden and a worry. America has consumption mania. We buy and we buy more. Yet our rampant consumerism and the culture of disposable-ness that it has created have only served to make life more difficult for many.

We have become a nation of consumers. Our primary identity has become that of consumer, not mother, teacher, or farmer, but consumer. The primary way that our value is measured and demonstrated is by how much we contribute to this arrow, how much we consume.
~ Annie Leonard, *The Story of Stuff*

Then there are the issues behind the creation, distribution, and disposal of what we consume. It's no secret that manufacturers of all kinds have put the bottom line above their commitment to consumers.

Look back to 2007. In that year 472 consumer products were recalled. That record figure prompted legislators on Capital Hill to dub 2007 "The Year of the Recall". We were horrified to witness the melamine poisoned pet food debacle. This recall turned out to be the largest in pet food history, affecting 1,177 products. According to media reports, the scandal cost the primary company involved more than $55 million in expenses, plus an additional $30 million in litigation settlement costs.[29] News agencies have also reported on countless foods for human consumption that were also recalled in recent years. But the news did not stop there.

Manufacturers of everything from food products to fashion, from toys to electronics, are caught up in a never-ending race to do it faster — and always cheaper.

Why? How is it that companies feel so compelled to lower production costs to this extent? Many think it is due to idealistic expectations from shareholders and unrealistic stock market projections.

The corporate hierarchy works hard at assembling plans and budget projections a year in advance. Quite often, when these plans are completed, top management discovers that the results fall far below what Wall Street expects. CEOs and CFOs are therefore left in a sticky situation. They strive to meet Wall Street's expectations and prepare to be slapped on the wrist, or worse, if they fall short. Our most recent recession has revealed, in the most devastatingly graphic examples since the Great Depression, the dangers of conforming to market pressures for growth that are essentially unachievable.

So whom do we blame? The answer is not as cut-and-dry as it may seem.

The truth is that we as a society are to blame in our quest for more goods, more money, more houses, and more toys. This desire to amass "stuff" is unprecedented in human history, and it shows no signs of slowing down.

But it's more than that. Basically, it's that we want more – more than ever in history. Reading over Annie Leonard's *The Story of Stuff* can give us some insight. Leonard has spent years researching the phenomenon of consumerism and what amounts to our obsession with shopping. Not only does it affect us negatively, but, she maintains, it is having a devastating effect on the environment.

Case in point: the U.S. has 5% of the world's population, but consumes 30% of the world's resources and creates 30% of the world's waste. The average person in the US consumes twice as much as they did 50 years ago, and we spend 3-4 times as many hours shopping as our European counterparts.[30] Shopping has become a national pastime, even a hobby for many people.

But do we really need all those things?

And where do all those things come from? As many countries in the western world continue to rely on inexpensive products manufactured in China and other offshore markets, this reliance has fueled a feeding frenzy of consumer "price wars". In their quest to keep driving prices down further in order to conform to the unrealistic demands of their bottom line, retailers must forgo quality and, in some exceptional cases, even safety. Meanwhile, the supply chain can do nothing else but follow.

What sort of impact does the acquisition of new "toys" have on the environment? How many times have we been told in recent years that it is less expensive to replace that computer, phone, or other electronic device than it would be to repair it?

This has led to incredible waste. For a fleeting moment, we feel frustration or even a sense of mourning because we know how wasteful this is. Our instincts on this are razor sharp. It has been proven that 99 percent of the "stuff" we harvest, mine, process, and transport — 99 percent of the stuff we run through our consumer system — is trashed within six months.[31]

I was thinking about this the other day. I was walking to work and I wanted to listen to the news, so I popped into this Radio Shack to buy a radio. I found this cute little green radio for 4 dollars and 99 cents. I was standing there in line to buy this radio, and I wondering how $4.99 could possibly capture the costs of making this radio and getting it to my hands. The metal was probably mined in South Africa, the petroleum was probably drilled in Iraq, the plastics were probably produced in China, and maybe the whole thing was assembled by some 15 year old in a maquiladora in Mexico. $4.99 wouldn't even pay the rent for the shelf space it occupied until I came along, let alone part of the staff guy's salary that helped me pick it out, or the multiple ocean cruises and truck rides pieces of this radio went on. That's how I realized I didn't pay for the radio.

So, who did pay?

Well, these people paid with the loss of their natural resource base. These people paid with the loss of their clean air, with increasing asthma and cancer rates. Kids in the Congo paid with their future — 30% of the kids in parts of the Congo now have had to drop out of school to mine coltan, a metal we need for our disposable electronics. These people even paid by having to cover their own health insurance. All along this system people pitched in, so I could get this radio for $4.99. And none of these *contributions are recorded in any accounts book. That is what I mean by the company owners externalizing the true costs of production.*[32]

Have we become so enthralled by the pursuit of shiny new toys that we are unable to see what such wasteful consumerism is doing to the environment? Consider this: for every one garbage can of waste we put out on the curb, 70 garbage cans of waste were made upstream to make the products in that one can.[33] Old computers, phones, and other devices and "toys" end up in our landfills, making room for newer models consumers simply have to have. Where will it end?

Any so-called material thing that you want is merely a symbol: you want it not for itself, but because it will content your spirit for the moment.
~ *Mark Twain*

Ask yourself this: Are you happier with all this "stuff" in your life? Are you letting material things determine your personal worth in this world? We may want more and more, but are we better off for it? Not by a long shot.

We have literally shopped till we drop, as the old saying goes. So why aren't we happy?

It is estimated that in the U.S. our "national happiness" quotient peaked sometime in the 1950s.[34] Whether you attribute this to cultural, societal pressure, individual unconsciousness, or simply ego, something is very wrong with this picture.

In our heart of hearts we know that we are tired of the marketing machine, and this behavior is unsustainable.

Pay no attention to that man behind the curtain.
~ *The Wizard of Oz*

More importantly, what has our attraction to "stuff" done to us as individuals – and to our planet?

Some people, like Leo Babauta, the author of *The Power of Less* and *Zen Habits* blogger, would say the solution lies in an overhaul of our habits. Babauta never sugarcoats his message. Change is difficult. Whether it is taming consumerism or a host of other addictions, it all comes down to changing one habit at a time. Keep it simple, allow yourself to focus, and give yourself the best chance for success, Babauta urges.

We have spent decades trying to juggle our "stuff" and we have spent years forgoing balanced checkbooks for the thrill of acquisition. Has this brought us balanced lives? Has it made us feel better about ourselves, or quite the opposite?

Looking into the implications of the materialism that we, as a society, have embraced is no easy thing. Without doing so, however, we can never be free. As the saying goes, "a little shopping never hurt anyone". And of course we need and want to purchase things with the intent of creating a comfortable home and living. But when acquisition becomes the primary way people display their value to the world, it's time for a change. Thousands of years ago, Aristotle said, "Balance is everything in life". The saying still applies today. So what is this all about? Why do we buy? What do we think it will do for us? Is it true that the possessions buy us happiness or peace? How long before the luster of the new items wears off? The ego is strong, and we want to look good to ourselves and to society. We want to be accepted and to be known as being progressive. But trying to keep up with the Joneses is exhausting, and many are beginning to realize that it is a losing battle.

How do we get off the merry go round?

It takes courage to ask these questions. It takes courage to consume less and to say no to the latest acquisition. Instead, it's time for us to look at what the void is. What are we missing? What is behind that void that we hope the stuff will fill?

Simplicity is the ultimate sophistication.
~ *Leonardo DaVinci*

A Life Well Spent: An Interview with Leo Babauta

Author and blogger Leo Babauta has mastered the art of paring down life to its bare essentials. His strategies are simple and straight-shooting. But they also require commitment and the faith to believe that the only way to a better and more meaningful life is "to know thyself". Readers of Babauta's books and Zen Habits website will see that the road to a life less burdened by debt and consumerism may be easier to master than you think.

The following excerpt from a recent mnmlist blog you wrote entitled "Manufacturing Content" states:

"Many of the problems we are experiencing as a society come from manufactured desire. Obesity, debt, financial crises, an overabundance of stuff, consumerism, global warming, and so on — they happen because we are never content, we are always wanting more, and can not control our desires..."

Based on this statement, do you feel that people substitute "stuff" or objects of desire to fill a void? What has happened over time that has resulted in our current addiction to food and reverence of material possessions?

We work more than ever before, we're busier than ever before, and we have less time for our passions, our loved ones, and ourselves. This leaves a void that we try to fill with entertainment, junk food, and material goods, but they never really do the job. I believe these addictions have been created intentionally by corporations looking to profit off our desires and addictions. They have created voids and desires where none existed before through advertising, and it's surprisingly effective.

How do we free ourselves from our desire for more of everything?

We must start by realizing that more and more will not ever lead to happiness and that the desire for more is never fulfilled. Next, we must realize that our actual needs, as opposed to what we desire, are very little, and that we already have everything we need to be happy. Once we realize that we can be content with very little, we are freed from the need to fill that void. Finally, we must guard against these manufactured desires. We must stop exposing ourselves to so much advertising and remind ourselves that shopping and eating and watching will never bring happiness.

In terms of our lifestyle, do you think we have reached a tipping point and are evolving in a more positive direction?

There are lots of positive signs. Many people are realizing that our lifestyle of excess is leading to global warming and the destruction of the nature we all love, as well as an excess of debt and financial ruin. Many people are cutting back either voluntarily or because of the recession. Many people are learning to connect as people rather than as consumers and corporate employees. However, it's all very much up in the air. We can only win by waking up.

What is your advice to people who hold on to the belief that life is hard?

Life is easy. Trillions of people have done it. It's only hard if we make it hard. I'd start by letting go of the idea that things are good or bad. They just are, they just happen, and it's only in our minds that they become good or bad. So if something 'bad' happens to you, pause and realize that it's not bad. It just happened. Then move on to the next moment.

You have made significant shifts in your life over the last few years. The impetus for those changes seems to be your decision to quit smoking in 2005. Was this the catalyst that led to a dramatically simplified way of life?

I wanted a simpler life, but didn't know how to make changes. Quitting smoking taught me something about changing habits and changing my life: you do it in small bits, you focus on one thing at a time, and you do it in a way that's enjoyable. I applied these principles (and a few others) to other habit changes, and one at a time, I was successful in changing lots of little things in my life. They added up to huge changes.

Tell us about "Zen Habits" and what the message means to you.

Zen Habits, at its heart, is a rebellion against a culture of more, of busy, of excess. It's a call for simplicity, for focus, for slowness, for less, for living in the moment.

The evident honesty and sincerity in your writing is refreshing, and it's interesting that you've made a commitment to experiment with a radical transparency policy for all endeavors that involve Zen Habits. What is radical transparency and why is it important to you?

Radical transparency is simply taking what we believe about democracy and truth to its most logical extension. If we believe that government accountability is important to a democracy, then why not apply it to business, to everything? I believe that, if government were truly transparent, if we could see every email, every meeting of every government official, then there would be no corruption. The same is true of business. There would be no corrupt business practices, no sweatshops, no pollution, no toxic chemicals in our food and make-up if people could see behind the closed doors of business. Conduct everything out in the open, and there will be no shadiness. I decided to try it out myself, to lead by example, though I haven't completely figured out how to do it yet!

You have said that, in order to simplify your life, the first step is to identify what is important, then cut out all else that distracts and restrains you from doing what you love. The adage "If you love what you do, you'll never work a day in your life" comes to mind. Is it really that simple? What would you say to those who hold themselves back from seeking what they love due to responsibilities such as financial and family commitments? What about the potential risks? Realistically, is follow your bliss always possible?

It really is that simple, and yet the simple can be very hard because it means letting go of our notions of the way things need to be. We are held back by social, financial, and family commitments, but how many of those commitments are truly necessary? Can we eliminate some of them to make time for what we love? I did. I cut out dozens of commitments, cut back on my needs, said 'no' to many requests so that I could say 'yes' to what I believe is most important.

There are risks whenever you take action like this, in a bold way, but consider the risks of not changing. You lose out on what you love. You live a life you don't want. That's a tragedy.

Is follow your bliss always possible? Of course it is. It just takes a commitment to doing it and a realization that nothing else really matters except those we love and doing what we love. Is it important to have a nice car, a huge house, fancy gadgets, and a closet stuffed with designer clothes and shoes, an excess of food? Is it important to look good to your colleagues, neighbors, and society by doing whatever you think will impress them? Let go of these 'needs', and you open up the possibilities.

Is there a simple, step-by-step process that you could provide us that could break down an undesirable habit and replace it with healthier one?

Pick one habit and publicly commit to replacing it with a specific, positive replacement habit for two months. Figure out the triggers for the old habit, and commit to doing your new habit each time the trigger happens. Break the new habit into a tiny baby step to start with. If you want to exercise, commit to just getting outside for five minutes a day. Be sure to do the new habit every time the trigger happens. Each week, increase the new habit just a little – baby steps.

TRY THIS

Leo Babauta says the road to change begins with a "cheat sheet" made up of 29 ways to change your habits for the better. Using these methods he designed, Babauta says he has been able to quit smoking, stop impulse spending, get out of debt, begin running marathons, awaken earlier, eat healthier, become more frugal, simplify his life, and become more organized, focused, and productive. The following exercise, reprinted from Babauta's website, www.zenhabits.net, outlines 29 points that will help you plan, change, and prosper.

Habit is habit, and not to be flung out of the window by any man, but coaxed downstairs a step at a time.
~ *Mark Twain*

Keep it Simple

Habit change is not that complicated. While the tips below will seem overwhelming, there are really only a few things you need to know. Everything else is just helping these to become reality.

The simple steps of habit change:
1. Write down your plan.
2. Identify your triggers and replacement habits.

3. Focus on doing the replacement habits every single time the triggers happen, for about 30 days.

The Habit Change Cheat Sheet

The following is a compilation of tips to help you change a habit. Don't be overwhelmed. Always remember the simple steps above. The rest are different ways to help you become more successful in your habit change.

1. **Do just one habit at a time.** Extremely important. Habit change is difficult, even with just one habit. If you do more than one habit at a time, you're setting yourself up for failure. Keep it simple, allow yourself to focus, and give yourself the best chance for success. By the way, this is why New Year's resolutions often fail. People try to tackle more than one change at a time.

2. **Start small.** The smaller the better, because habit change is difficult, and trying to take on too much is a recipe for disaster. Want to exercise? Start with just 5-10 minutes. Want to wake up earlier? Try just 10 minutes earlier for now.

3. **Do a 30-day Challenge.** In my experience, it takes about 30 days to change a habit, if you're focused and consistent. This is a round number and will vary from person to person and habit to habit. Often you'll read a magical "21 days" to change a habit, but this is a myth with no evidence. Seriously – try to find the evidence from a scientific study for this. A more recent study shows that 66 days is a better number. But 30 days is a good number to get you started. Your challenge: stick with a habit every day for 30 days, and post your daily progress updates to a forum.

4. **Write it down.** Just saying you're going to change the habit is not enough of a commitment. You need to actually write it down, on paper. Write what habit you're going to change.

5. **Make a plan.** While you're writing, also write down a plan. This will ensure you're really prepared. The plan should include your reasons (motivations) for changing, obstacles, triggers, support buddies, and other ways you're going to make this a success. More on each of these below.

6. **Know your motivations and be sure they're strong.** Write them down in your plan. You have to be very clear why you're doing this, and the benefits of doing it need to be clear in your head. If you're just doing it for vanity, it's not usually enough, although it can be a good motivator. We need something stronger. For me, I quit smoking for my wife and kids. I made a promise to them. I knew that if I didn't quit smoking, not only would they be without a husband and father, but they'd also be more likely to smoke themselves (my wife was a smoker and quit with me).

7. **Don't start right away.** In your plan, write down a start date. Maybe a week or two from the date you start writing out the plan. When you start right away (like today), you are not giving the plan the seriousness it deserves. When you have a "Quit Date" or "Start Date", it gives that date an air of significance. Tell everyone about your quit date (or start date). Put it up on your wall or computer desktop. Make this a Big Day. It builds up anticipation and excitement and helps you to prepare.

8. **Write down all your obstacles.** If you've tried this habit change before (odds are you have), you've likely failed. Reflect on those failures and figure out what stopped you from succeeding. Write down every obstacle that's happened to you and others, things that are likely to happen. Then write down how you plan to overcome them. That's the key: write down your solution *before* the obstacles arrive, so you're prepared.

9. **Identify your triggers.** What situations trigger your current habit? For the smoking habit, for example, triggers might

include waking in the morning, having coffee, drinking alcohol, stressful meetings, going out with friends, driving, etc. Most habits have multiple triggers. Identify all of them and write them in your plan.

10. **For every single trigger, identify a positive habit you're going to do instead.** When you first wake in the morning, instead of smoking, what will you do? What about when you get stressed? When you go out with friends? Some positive habits could include exercise, meditation, deep breathing, organizing, decluttering, and more.

11. **Plan a support system.** Who will you turn to when you have a strong urge? Write these people into your plan. Support forums online are a great tool as well. I used a smoking cessation forum on about.com when I quit smoking, and it really helped. Don't underestimate the power of support. It's really important.

12. **Ask for help.** Get your family and friends and co-workers to support you. Ask them for their help, and let them know how important this is. Find an AA group in your area. Join online forums where people are trying to quit. When you have really strong urges or a really difficult time, call on your support network for help. Don't smoke a cigarette, for example, without posting to your online quit forum. Don't have a drop of alcohol before calling your AA buddy.

13. **Become aware of self-talk.** You talk to yourself in your head all the time — but often we're not aware of these thoughts. Start listening. These thoughts can derail any habit change, any goal. Often they're negative: "I can't do this. This is too difficult. Why am I putting myself through this? How bad is this for me anyway? I'm not strong enough. I don't have enough discipline. I suck." It's important to know you're doing this.

14. **Stay positive.** You will have negative thoughts – the important thing is to realize when you're having them and push them out of your head. Squash them! Then replace them with a positive thought. "I can do this! If Leo can do it, so can I!"

15. **Have strategies to defeat the urge.** Urges are going to come – they're inevitable and they're strong. But they're also temporary, and beatable. Urges usually last about a minute or two, and they come in waves of varying strength. You just need to ride out the wave, and the urge will go away. Some strategies for making it through the urge: deep breathing, self-massage, eating some frozen grapes, taking a walk, exercising, drinking a glass of water, calling a support buddy, posting on a support forum.

16. **Prepare for the sabotagers.** There will always be people who are negative, who try to get you to do your old habit. Be ready for them. Confront them and be direct. You don't need them to try to sabotage you. You need their support, and if they can't support you, then you don't want to be around them.

17. **Talk to yourself.** Be your own cheerleader, give yourself pep talks, repeat your mantra (below), and don't be afraid to seem crazy to others. We'll see who's crazy when you've changed your habit and they haven't changed theirs!

18. **Have a mantra.** For quitting smoking, mine was "Not One Puff Ever" (I didn't make this up, but it worked – more on this below). When I wanted to quit my day job, it was "Liberate Yourself". This is just a way to remind yourself of what you're trying to do.

19. **Use visualization.** This is powerful. Vividly picture, in your head, successfully changing your habit. Visualize doing your new habit after each trigger, overcoming urges, and what it will look like when you're done.

20. **Have rewards.** Regular ones. You might see these as bribes, but actually they're just positive feedback. Put these into your plan, along with the milestones at which you'll receive them.

21. **Take it one urge at a time.** Often we're told to take it one day at a time – which is good advice – but really it's one urge at a time. Just make it through this urge.

22. **Not One Puff Ever** (in other words, no exceptions). This seems harsh, but it's a necessity. When you're trying to break the bonds between an old habit and a trigger and are forming a new bond between the trigger and a new habit, you need to be really consistent. You can't do it sometimes, or there will be no new bond, or at least it will take a really long time to form. So, at least for the first 30 days (and preferably 60), you need to have no exceptions. Each time a trigger happens, you need to do the new habit and not the old one. No exceptions, or you'll have a backslide. If you do mess up, regroup, learn from your mistake, plan for your success, and try again (see the last item on this list).

23. **Get rest.** Being tired leaves us vulnerable to relapse. Get a lot of rest so you can have the energy to overcome urges.

24. **Drink lots of water.** Similar to the item above, being dehydrated leaves us open to failure. Stay hydrated!

25. **Renew your commitment often.** Remind yourself of your commitment hourly and at the beginning and end of each day. Read your plan. Celebrate your success. Prepare yourself for obstacles and urges.

26. **Set up public accountability.** Blog about it, post on a forum, email your commitment and daily progress to friends and family, post a chart up at your office, write a column for your local newspaper (I did this when I ran my first marathon). When we make it public – not just the commitment but the progress updates – we don't want to fail.

27. **Engineer it so it's hard to fail.** Create a groove that's harder to get out of than to stay in. Increase positive feedback for sticking with the habit, and increase negative feedback for not doing the habit.

28. **Avoid some situations where you normally do your old habit**, at least for awhile, to make it a bit easier on yourself. If you normally drink when you go out with friends, consider not going out for a little while. If you normally go outside your office with co-workers to smoke, avoid going out with them. This applies to any bad habit. Whether it be eating junk food or doing drugs, there are some situations you can avoid that are especially difficult for someone trying to change a bad habit. Realize, though, that when you go back to those situations, you will still get the old urges, and when that happens, you should be prepared.

29. **If you fail, figure out what went wrong, plan for it, and try again.** Don't let failure and guilt stop you. They're just obstacles, but they can be overcome. In fact, if you learn from each failure, they become stepping-stones to your success. Regroup. Let go of guilt. Learn. Plan. And get back on that horse.

Be content with what you have, rejoice in the way things are. When you realize there is nothing lacking, the whole world belongs to you.
~ Lao Tzu

Appreciative Inquiry

Need to get a handle on why you are dissatisfied with your life – or trying to figure out why certain aspects of your life aren't working? Try a process called "Appreciative Inquiry". A.I. is the practice of asking unconditional, positive questions. The intent is to seek the positive or to focus on what is working versus what is not working. There is a "4 D" cycle of inquiry:

Discovery: Appreciate what is and acknowledge the best of what is now.

Dream: Imagine what might be so that you can develop a clear vision.

Design: Determine what should be with implementation and action plans.

Destiny or Delivery: Results that would come through implementation.

The idea is that a series of questions would be designed under each of the 4 Ds. This is a method most often used in organizational change, but it's also useful for strategic planning, diversity management, and customer service.

This process can also be applied to discovering what is working in our personal lives and where we need to make modifications.

Here is how this might work in business:

Examples under Discovery: "If you could keep three things in this organization that give life to it, even though there is change taking place in it, what are those three strengths?" "Share the best example of something you did in your organization that was a source of innovation and success." Yet other examples could be: "What do our clients want us to become?" "What would give us the biggest bang for the buck?"

We can borrow from this process and use it in our personal life to gain clarity, purpose, and happiness.

The Practical Application of Appreciative Inquiry in our Personal Lives

Pick a particular aspect of your life that you want to focus on, happiness, for example. Some possible questions are:

1. Under what conditions do I excel? When I am operating at my best, what am I doing?
2. When I have felt genuine happiness, what was I doing or what was happening in my life?
3. Who of my friends and family put a smile on my face and why?
4. What are my talents and what are the benefits I realize when I have the opportunity to express them?
5. How do I put those talents into place in my daily life?
6. What is one thing that I can do tomorrow (today, this week, this month...) that moves me a step closer to creating the life that I want?
7. What resources are available to me to help me take this step forward?

The awakened mind is often represented in eastern philosophy by the flowering of a lotus blossom. Zen (Chan) patriarch Hakuin, remarked that the "eighty-four thousand troops" hiding inside the threads of a lotus flower symbolized the realization of the awakened mind. The true power of Kensho (awakening) lies inward, not outward.

When the titans fought with the king of gods...he led eighty-four thousand troops into the holes of lotus threads, where they hid. Unable to attack them, the king of gods retreated
~ The Record of Lin-Chi

9

MAKING THE CONNECTION

Darkness cannot drive out darkness; only light can do that...
~ Martin Luther King Jr.

There are many paths that I have followed to discover my true self, and these experiences have taught me many things. Most of all they have revealed that I am not alone on this journey towards a greater connectedness to the "world within".

My always-present inner self is confronted at every turn by the endless challenge of discovering ways to manage the many emotions that I feel in a day and learning how to flip the switch so as to discard those that are not serving me well.

There are many ways to calm the savage beast: exercise, breathing techniques, NLP (Neuro-Linguistic Programming), and so on – the list is almost infinite. But many experts believe that it is the practice of meditation that is the most transformative of all.

Vast numbers of people are discovering meditation's myriad benefits. In fact, a government survey in 2007 found that about 1 out of 11 Americans, more than 20 million, had meditated in the year prior to the study. And a growing number of medical centers are teaching meditation to patients for relief of pain and stress.[35]

Meditation allows us to stay in the present moment and makes us alert to our thoughts and actions. It creates a stillness of the mind, wherein we assume the role of "witness" in all of the activities of life, from waking to sleeping. Meditation can soothe our bodies and calm our minds. This can be very beneficial in our personal lives, as well as in the workplace.

In a *New York Times* online article, internationally renowned psychologist Daniel Goleman cited a research study on the benefits of meditation in the workplace. Richard Davidson, head of the Laboratory for Affective Neuroscience at the University of Wisconsin, conducted the study with Jon Kabat-Zinn, a teacher of mindfulness meditation from the University of Massachusetts Medical Center, in order to see how a group of people at a high-stress biotech company could be helped by mindful meditation. He writes that the right prefrontal area of the brain and the amygdala show high activation levels when we are upset or feeling the effects of stress. But when we are "positively engaged, goal-directed, enthusiastic and energetic", the right side settles, and the left prefrontal area becomes activated.

Kabat-Zinn, who has pioneered this contemplative method with medical patients to ease their symptoms, taught mindfulness at a high-stress biotech company. These beginners meditated for 30 minutes a day for eight weeks. Davidson's measures showed that, after the eight weeks, they had begun to activate that left prefrontal zone more strongly and were saying that, instead of feeling overwhelmed and hassled, they were enjoying their work. So, while the Calvinist strain in American culture may look askance at someone sitting quietly in meditation, this kind of "doing nothing" seems to do something remarkable after all.[36]

According to *Canadian Business Magazine*'s 2010 article "Why Meditation Has a Place in Business," studies now suggest that the average worker is interrupted once every 11 minutes and that it takes that employee approximately 25 minutes to get back on track with their office tasks. This is just one of the everyday pressures on the modern worker. The article explains why some companies are now incorporating meditation practices into the workplace as a way to reduce stress, boost mental health, and sustain an employee's productivity.

Google, as this article points out, "continues to remain the highest-profile example of a company investing in workplace mindfulness." In fact, one of the company's original employees, a software engineer by the name of Chade-Meng Tan, has taken that need for greater employee mindfulness through meditation right to the top of Google's corporate hierarchy.

Curious about the benefits of meditation, Tan invested a portion of his Google IPO loot in research on the emerging data on this practice. Tan's journey led to the creation of the Search Inside Yourself program under the sponsorship of Google University, the company's internal educational outlet for its employees.

To date, this program has serviced an estimated 500 Google employees, teaching them mindful breathing and listening techniques, as well as the importance of developing both their emotional intelligence and business acumen with equal attentiveness. The ultimate goal, says Tan, is to make employees and businesses more effective and, hopefully, more profitable.

And yet, when used correctly, the merits of greater mindfulness can spill over into every aspect of the human experience, both on and off the job.

The practice of mindfulness is certainly nothing new. It comes out of the Buddhist tradition of meditation and has long been practiced in monasteries and ashrams for centuries, as many celebrities, athletes, and a vast number of meditators around the world now know.

So why is there all this modern interest in an age-old technique?

With a spirit of deference to the many things in life that have stood the test of time, modern-day science can now reevaluate these age-old practices with a new openness and intensity. Thanks to groundbreaking technologies, western science is now free to reexamine these ancient techniques of spiritual self-awareness to a new end and with a fresh perspective, asking the following key question: can meditation help unlock the power of the brain?

Scientists now know that people who consistently meditate have a singular ability to cultivate positive emotions and control those feelings. They have better focus and reduced levels of stress, as well as bolstered immune systems.

In fact, engaging in regular meditation is the way to actually enlarge certain areas of the brain according to writer, Mark Wheeler. In his 2009 article "How to Build a Bigger Brain," Wheeler pointed to new findings from researchers at UCLA who used high-resolution magnetic resonance imaging (MRI) to scan the brains of people who meditate.[37] The results of the study, which were published in the journal *NeuroImage*, indicate that certain regions in the brains of long-term meditators were larger than in a similar control group.

More specifically, long-term meditators showed "significantly larger volumes of the hippocampus and areas within the orbito-frontal cortex, the thalamus and the inferior temporal gyrus – all regions known for regulating emotions."

Science's new interest in the connection between brain structure and the meditation practices employed by Buddhist monks inspired veteran TV reporter Dan Rather to travel in 2008 to research laboratories in the United States and to Dharamsala, India, home to His Holiness the Fourteenth Dalai Lama, in search of answers.[38]

As Rather put it, this 21st century quest to understand the phenomenon of how meditation can change the brain has "turned brain science on its head."

For example, at the University of Wisconsin's Waisman Laboratory for Brain Imaging and Behavior, Rather found a team of researchers who had spent five years trying to understand how a Buddhist monk's meditational training could alter the brain. Neuroscientist Antoine Lutz and his colleagues believed that if someone is trained to practice compassion on a long-term basis, as monks are, that practice will somehow change their brains. This belief compelled these researchers to search for an answer to one big question: just how far can a person transform their mind and brain through meditation, particularly in that region of this mysterious, complex organ that manages emotions?

Buddhist monks like Mingyur Rinpoche volunteered their brains for this scientific study, racking up thousands of hours of meditation in the process. When asked to meditate on compassion, the researchers noted a very strong increase in the speed of oscillations once the meditative process began. What the brains of Rinpoche and the other monks were doing is called gamma activity, something that all brains do, but rarely with such intensity. But scientists were stunned to see that this activity continued after the monks stopped meditation. As Rinpoche told Rather, "If you apply meditation every day a little bit, then you change the habit of the brain function."

That is big news to brain scientists who once were convinced that the brain stopped developing in early childhood – a hypothesis that renders aging a hopeless downward spiral for the human mind. However, the more researchers studied the meditative process, the more a new picture emerged from within the dark, secretive depths of the human brain.

"The brain is a learning machine. It wants new learning. And it's actually begging for it," Michael Merzenich told Rather. Merzenich is a pioneer in brain plasticity research and a professor of neuroscience at the University of California in San Francisco.

According to Merzenich, meditation research studies do indeed show that the brain can change and modify itself long past childhood. That's wonderful news for Baby Boomers, who will dominate

North America's population for the next few decades and who will want to live, work and play with optimal brain health.

But how do we prepare and particularly educate the younger generations to tap into this unlimited source of potential enlightenment? The only way is through education, and in this respect, believe it or not, meditation is finding its way into the curriculums of forward-thinking schools around the world.

Consider, for example, the students who pursue consciousness-based education at the Maharishi University of Management in Fairfield, Iowa. University founder Maharishi Mahesh Yogi developed consciousness-based education so that people could discover "the pure consciousness within themselves as the source of all knowledge". Maharishi University believes in developing the full potential of consciousness, combining traditional academic study with a foundation of the core values of sustainability, peace, and the admonition to "be of service to (their) fellow human beings".

In keeping with the atmosphere of harmony and pure potential, the school employs a block system of education, whereby students are fully immersed in one course a month to maximize their focus and minimize the stress loads that usually accompany the juggling of several university courses at once. The cornerstone of this teaching model is Transcendental Meditation which students practice daily. It is the key, says Maharishi Mahesh Yogi, to achieving greater self-knowledge and training the mind so that one may attain higher levels of calm, connectedness, and inner awareness in all aspects of life, whether it be on campus or out in today's challenging corporate landscape.

Is the ceiling of the Sistine Chapel a 500 year-old puzzle that is only now beginning to be solved?

The last panel Michelangelo painted (The Separation of Light from Darkness) depicts God separating light from darkness. This is where the researchers report that Michelangelo hid the human brain stem, eyes, and optic nerve of man inside the figure of God directly above the altar.[39]

Thanks, indeed, to modern science and its interest in the ancient practice of meditation, the "darkness" of the mind is coming to be seen as being not so dark at all. It is emerging as a rare new universe that humans will be able to access and inhabit in greater, more powerful ways over the next few decades.

Where this journey from dark to light will take us in centuries to come, no one knows. But one thing is clear: the answers lie within. As we human beings learn to travel the brain's enigmatic realms and harness its power, we will move our ever-evolving society from dark confusion and the wasteful expenditure of mental energy to creative, enlightened clarity.

Meditation and the Brain Connection: An Interview with Dr. Fred Travis

For those who do not know it, filmmaker David Lynch has long supported the power of meditation. In 2005, the director of *Blue Velvet* created the David Lynch Foundation For Consciousness-Based Education and World Peace. The foundation funds scholarship programs to schools where students can learn Transcendental Meditation and apply this powerful tool to all aspects of their lives. As the foundation says on the home page of its website, "Change begins within." We talked to Dr. Fred Travis about his connection to this cutting-edge foundation and his take on the power of meditation to transform our brains, bodies, and lives. Dr. Travis is a highly regarded researcher and lecturer on the brain, brain development, creativity, and meditation practice.

You refer to a specific region in the brain as the "CEO of the brain". Where is the CEO located and what is its function? How does regular meditation strengthen and maintain healthy CEO brain functioning?

'CEO' means Chief Executive Officer. It is not a scientific term, but it aptly describes the prefrontal cortex. As the boss of a company integrates inputs from all departments in the company with the goals and missions of the company and business climate, so the prefrontal cortex receives inputs from all other areas of the brain and determines the next step for the person. The prefrontal cortex is the 'front of the front'. It is behind the forehead and is involved in judgment, moral reasoning, sense of self, decision making, planning, and short-term memory. Transcendental meditation practice leads to higher activity in the prefrontal cortex and the parietal cortex, both part of the attentional system. By using these circuits, the connections become richer, denser, and then more available for future activity.

It is widely known that factors like stress and fatigue can disrupt proper neurological performance. What happens to the brain after a prolonged period of stress?

Stress and fatigue move the prefrontal cortex offline. The attention downshifts to the immediate sensory present. In other words, you have tunnel vision. Your abstract thinking – supported by prefrontal activity – has downshifted to only seeing the obvious sensory nature of the experience. The fight-or-flight system is fully on. You react stereotypically and emotionally to every response, not thoughtfully. With prolonged stress, the size of the prefrontal cortex becomes smaller. Plus, stress hormones reduce the size of the memory areas of the brain in the hippocampus. Under high stress, the hippocampus becomes smaller, and memory functions are reduced.

Would you provide us with a simple explanation of the term "neuroplasticity"?

We can also refer to this phenomenon as brain malleability. When two neurons fire, their connections are strengthened. Thus, experienced taxi cab drivers have higher volume in the part of the brain dealing with spatial maps, as well as the hippocampus. The left hand of violin players that creates the chords is larger and more differentiated than the right hand that holds the bow. Rats that are given a richer environment have heavier brains. These examples explain how neuroplasticity can mold and transform the brain through habitual and/or practiced mental or physical exercises.

What role does meditation play in the development of our brain, how it functions, and the conscious states we experience?

It boils down to the concept that 'experience changes the brain.' Whatever experience you have enriches those connections. This is important. Meditations have different procedures, and so how they affect the brain is different. For instance, meditations around the themes of loving kindness and compassion increase the size of the emotional areas of the brain. Vipassana (mindfulness) increases the size of the insula, which links body states and emotions, and the cingulate, which pertains to attention switching. TM practice that leads to the experience of the 'ground state' of the mind leads to increased global functioning during tasks, which is to say that the part is processed relative to the whole.

You have researched and compared the brain patterns of meditators who practiced various meditation styles and techniques. Did you find that all meditation techniques produced similar results?

Generally, we can identify three categories of meditation with different cognitive processes:

1. Focused Attention: sustained attention on a specific object of attention;
2. Open Monitoring: dispassionate observation of changing experience;
3. Automatic Self-transcending: any technique that transcends its own steps of activity

These are distinctly different cognitive processes, and they have three respectively different EEG patterns:

1. Gamma (20-50 Hz) for Focused Attention
2. Frontal theta (4-8 Hz) for Open Monitoring, and
3. Frontal alpha-I (8-10 Hz), providing coherence for Automatic Self-transcending.

These findings illustrate that various forms of meditation can definitely affect different areas of the brain.

Research shows that people who meditate regularly achieve optimum brain integration. What, exactly, is brain integration?

Brain integration is increased alpha coherence across widely spaced brain sensors. Alpha reflects the foundational level of brain functioning that integrates localized processing. Higher alpha coherence suggests that the matrix by which we create meaning is more integrated and is working more cohesively and effectively.

What is consciousness-based education?

Consciousness-based education realizes that knowledge is the coming together of the knower and the known through the process of knowing. As such, the knower needs to be systematically cultivated along with the given information. By analogy, consciousness-based education expands the 'container' of knowledge as new knowledge is gained.

The Maharishi University of Management (M.U.M.) is very unique compared to the vast majority of American universities, particularly because of its positive, supportive population, which encourages healthy lifestyles and a commitment to sustainability both within the student body and, on a grander scale, within the world community. Why, in your opinion, aren't more schools introducing consciousness-based curriculums?

In my opinion, it's only a matter of time. More and more schools are introducing TM practice into their curriculum. In the foreseeable future, there will be entire departments devoted to the Science of Consciousness, exploring theoretically the experiences of the unfolding of one's consciousness.

Sometimes the most important thing in a whole day is the rest we take between two deep breaths.
~ Etty Hillesum

TRY THIS
The search for inner peace does not require a pilgrimage to a Tibetan monastery or an extensive stay in silence at a remote ashram. Every day we have the opportunity to connect with our inner selves, even on the job. All it requires is planning, commitment, and consistent practice.

Meditate at Work
Get into the habit of putting 15 minutes aside each day to meditate at your place of work. Use an empty conference room, a quiet stairwell, or do a walking meditation outside during a break or at

lunch. Make that appointment with yourself and don't miss it. Before you know it, you'll start to see the payoffs in terms of greater mental clarity, reduced stress, and an enhanced feeling of centeredness that can carry you through a hectic work day.

Elevator Breathing

If you find yourself rushing to an appointment, use your time in transit to calm and center yourself. Do some deep breathing during the elevator ride up to calm your mind, center your thoughts, and focus on what you need to accomplish in that meeting. It's easy to do and it works.

Be Mindful

After you've finished your daily 15-minutes of meditation at the office, stay mindful. Smell the coffee brewing. Note the color of the light filling the building, the sounds of birds singing outside the windows, or the laughter down the hall. Attune your mind to what is going on around you at all times. Tapping in enhances that mindfulness quotient. It also enhances your appreciation for everything around you and in you.

Our conditioned perception in the business world is that short-term profits are more desirable than those earned over the long term. The enlightened leader eschews the delusions of short-sided greed in favor of responsible long-term stewardship of people, profits, and valuable resources. The same is true with the wise individual regarding the stewardship and quality of the mind.

The path that leads to worldly gain is one, and the path that leads to awakening is another.
~ *The Dhammapada*[40]

10

EURO-SENSE

The European Dream is focused not on amassing wealth, but rather on elevating the human spirit. It seeks to expand human empathy — not territory.

~ *Jeremy Rifken*[41]

Despite our best intentions, we here in the United States are a long way from understanding what it really takes to make a difference in our carbon footprint. Carbon footprint is defined as the total amount of greenhouse gas emissions produced both directly and indirectly in support of human activities, a sum usually expressed in equivalent tons of carbon dioxide (CO_2).

Using 2006 data, the Union of Concerned Scientists states that per capita CO_2 emissions in the US that year were 19.78 tons, compared to 9.6 tons in the UK, 8.05 tons in Italy, and 6.6 tons in France.[42]

Looking at lifestyle may shed a little light on this. I am fascinated by the difference between us Americans and our European brethren in terms of the way we choose to live our lives.

In many European countries, you will see citizens using bicycles, public transit, and walking as their mode of transportation. In crowded cosmopolitan cities from Florence to Stockholm, you will see the vast majority of city dwellers walking the cobblestone streets, leisurely cycling to work in their business suits and silk dresses, and patiently lining up to take public transit. It is almost unheard of to take taxis in some of the "greener" cities in Europe. Many European cities have better rail networks than we do in the US. It seems to be a matter of preference, or is it perhaps a necessity? It is certainly also a matter of lifestyle.

It's definitely less stressful to hop on public transit, cycle to work, or stroll to your next destination than it is to negotiate traffic, find parking, and pay exorbitant gas prices.

Many Europeans also drive economical cars that are far and away more modest than what many North Americans deem acceptable. It is rare to see an SUV or even a mid-sized car in most European cities, but tiny Fiats, Audis, and the Smart car are to be found everywhere, humming along the streets, generously affording their owners the gift that keeps on giving of up to 50 miles of driving to the gallon.

Take for example a housing development in Freiburg, Germany. Five thousand homes were built surrounding the medieval town center and use solar power or heat produced by an efficient central heating plant. 150 homes out of 1000 have a car (compared to 640 cars per 1000 households, on average, in the US), and two-thirds of all trips in Freiburg are made on bikes or on foot.

Then of course, there is the European way of eating – the legendary sauces, the fabulous restaurants, the consumption of wine at every meal with the exception of breakfast. You might think this would create an epidemic of obesity and ill health. Just the opposite is true, and this is primarily due to a virtue we would do well to learn more about: moderation.

"More than one third of U.S. adults – that is to say, more than 72 million people – and 17% of U.S. children are obese. From 1980 to 2008 obesity rates for adults doubled and rates for children tripled. During the past several decades, obesity rates for all groups in society regardless of age, sex, race, ethnicity, socioeconomic status, education level, or geographic region have increased markedly."[43]

If you go out for dinner in many European cities, you will find the food is, almost without fail, uncommonly delicious and portion controlled. A long walk back home or to another destination for a coffee or a social visit usually follows these lovely meals. There are no king-sized portions or gallon-sized sodas and no drives home in a gas-guzzler. Now, I'm not saying every person living in Europe lives this way, but the vast majority do.

Try asking for take-out food in many European cities. They'll scoff and ask why you don't just sit and relax and take the time to enjoy your meal or coffee. Many places don't even offer take-out containers because of environmental concerns.

A six-year Greek study found that those who took a 30-minute siesta at least three times a week had a 37% lower risk of heart-related death. The researchers took into account ill health, age, and whether people were physically active. Experts said napping might help people to relax, reducing their stress levels. Among working men who took midday naps, there was a 64% reduced risk of death, compared with a 36% reduced risk among non-working men.[44]

The other impressive ritual in many cities is the afternoon lunch break. Many Europeans break for two hours or more to have a substantial lunch, which is considered to be the most important meal of the day, and, if they're lucky enough to live within close proximity to their place of business, they also enjoy a stress-busting siesta before returning to work. The evening meal is regarded as a much smaller, less significant repast, sometimes consisting of only soup and salad or leftovers from lunch. This is a much healthier way to eat than making the evening meal the most substantial of the day.

Taken individually, these lifestyle differences seem like nothing more than interesting trivia. Don't be fooled.

Europe is often held up as a cautionary tale, a demonstration that if you try to make the economy less brutal, to take better care of your fellow citizens when they're down on their luck, you end up killing economic progress. But what European experience actually demonstrates is the opposite: social justice and progress can go hand in hand.
~ *Paul Krugman[45]*

Such differences of approach tell an enormous amount about the respective cultures of the "average" American and European, their corporate work models, their level of environmental activism, and the expectations they harbor with respect to their jobs, their employers, and their own happiness.

We've all heard the saying, "North Americans live to work. Europeans work to live."

But in today's tough economy where the needs of workers and the planet often clash with corporate bottom lines, employees on both sides of the Atlantic are struggling to find their way – and their happiness quotient – in the job market.

The world has moved light years away from the 1960s, when male breadwinners went to work, women stayed home to raise their children, and middle-class incomes could sustain this accepted model.

Just look at the new face of today's "average" employee.

Many are either single-parent workers or two-income couples, often caught between raising children and caring for elderly parents. Young and old, highly-educated or not, these "average" employees now juggle a multitude of pressing demands, along with the need for job satisfaction and fair pay. And everyone across the board is painfully aware of how their day-to-day actions on this troubled, ecologically-stressed planet will impact the future of our children, the next generation.

It's a stressful balance to achieve and maintain. Yet, this pressure to balance life and work is the new reality for millions of people around the world.

How corporations respond to this conflicting reality in years to come heralds a major evolutionary shift in business attitudes and practices. Some argue that the United States could learn a lot from European corporate models. Others disagree. But consider just this one factor: Many Europeans now have access to high-quality childcare at subsidized rates, something that takes considerable pressure off the shoulders of a worker. By contrast, millions of American workers struggle to find high-quality childcare and pay dearly for it.

We all dream of recharging our batteries with a wonderful vacation. European countries legally support an employee's right to take time off, no matter what the job. But how many overworked North Americans have felt both relief and a pang of guilt for taking a holiday? Do we really miss our work so much that we foster such conflicting emotions? Or is it that we worry about being replaced by another employee in these competitive times? Maybe both sets of reasons enter into play to some extent. I also suspect that many of us have gotten into the habit of not only putting in a full day of work in the traditional 8am to 5pm time slot, but of continuing to work well beyond these regular workday hours, precisely because of the technology that has become available to us. Many companies feel that simply because it's possible for you to be reached at all hours of the day and night, you should be reached and you should respond. In addition, many of us don't take the vacation time that we have rightfully earned.

If all of this is true, American employees and businesses need to ponder the following: In a recent *New York Times* article, entitled "Hey, America Take the Day Off," the United States was ranked on par with Vietnam and Indonesia for the total amount of days off allotted to employees by corporations.[46]

The average length of an American worker's holiday is roughly 14 days. Member countries of the European Union, on the other hand, must by law provide full-time workers with a minimum of 20 paid vacation days, plus public holidays.

Naturally, some American business leaders may argue in reply that vacation practices like these lead to less productivity, something no company can afford in such a fragile global economy. But such an argument is not necessarily true.

In Luxembourg, for example, every worker is required by law to 32 days paid vacation time. As a result, one study recently reported that workers in that country are 27 per cent more efficient than North American workers are.[47]

Of course, CEOs who are still sold on a business model that has worked well up until now may balk at such a statistic. But the message is clear. Times are changing. Recognizing this and the reality that a happy, healthier employee is a more productive employee is part of that shift.

For example, in a 2010 *BBC News* article entitled "Flexible working 'good for heart'", researchers at the Cochrane Library in Oxford, England found that employees who had control of their work hours may well have better blood pressure and heart rates.[48]

Improvements like this could be just the beginning, as the decade ahead unfolds. With time, such a process of change could also help a more harmonious balance to be struck between corporate wants and 21st century employee needs.

Ethical Shifts for a New Millennium: An Interview with David Conner

Imagine a world where forward-thinking workplace initiatives and corporate social responsibility had evolved into a credible mainstream business concept and that its basic principles applied to any business of any size.

Imagine if corporations that champion the cause of Corporate Social Responsibility (CSR) could align with stakeholders to headline global environmental and social issues, new technologies, and consumer awareness.

Coethica founder David Conner, a man who has been heavily involved in the CSR movement in recent years, says it may be possible, though complex to implement.

As Coethica and Conner define it, corporate social responsibility is all about business responsibility. By focusing on an organization's ethos and its ability to balance its economic, social, and environmental impact, we can identify what will work and what will not in tomorrow's new business landscape. We asked Conner to share his views on corporate social responsibility and what we might expect for the European Union (EU) in the years to come.

Studies show that Americans work longer hours and take far less vacation time than Europeans. Do EU companies consciously value the principles of work-life balance, or are these value systems in place primarily due to societal demands?

It's probably primarily a matter of societal pressure, but in combination with innovative, progressive companies. Across Europe, there have been numerous historical examples of businesses understanding the need to ensure employees are productive through provision of housing, education, and community activity, especially during the industrial revolution (John Cadbury, Robert Owen, William Lever, and others, for example).

Today in our globalized economy, I believe the manifestations of work-life balance are becoming homogenized. Information technology has both educated us and at the same time provided new opportunities for improving how we all work and live. I'm certain there will always be cultural differences, but increased communication is already blurring time zones and opening the possibilities of work away from a traditional office environment.

The EU is one of the most densely populated regions of the world, with the majority of the population living in urban areas. A 2008 study revealed that Europeans walk three times as far and cycle five times as far as Americans. Would you agree that the European social landscape, with its deeply rooted cultural values, is more eco-friendly in nature as compared to the American lifestyle?[49]

Europeans may have a greater opportunity for walking and also cycling opportunities due to our geography and perspectives on civil planning, but I think it is vital as well to highlight the effective rail networks across Europe, the imitation of which would vastly improve the mass transit figures for the U.S. that are mentioned in the study.

What is your definition of Corporate Social Responsibility?

The European Commission's definition of CSR is: "A concept whereby companies integrate social and environmental concerns in their business operations and in their interaction with their stakeholders on a voluntary basis."

For myself, I tend to take the word 'corporate' out of the equation, as it appears to exclude businesses until they grow to a certain size. The concept of Corporate Social Responsibility (CSR) should be about companies of every size striving to achieve a sustainable balance between financial, environmental, and social pressures while maximizing profits.

In your opinion, how do the United Kingdom's CSR standards measure up compared to the rest of the world?

It's hard to define and compare an entire nation's CSR standards, when in point of fact it's difficult enough just to compare performance across different business sectors accurately.

Accountability's Responsible Competitiveness Index (2007) offers some insight, with Nordic countries, i.e. Sweden, Denmark, Finland, Iceland, and Norway, dominating the top six places. Including the UK, these are all there on the list primarily because of an approach that is historically embedded in their cultures. Every region will always have cultural differences that will impact on CSR engagement and delivery. A good example of this is the stronger philanthropic approach to corporate citizenship that has been adopted by many US companies.

My personal opinion is that UK companies are good at engaging in a traditional and holistic approach to CSR, but have room for improvement in innovation and communication.

Will mandatory CSR reporting be something we can expect in the near future?

I'm not expecting widespread specific CSR reporting to be mandatory any time soon. I'm no fan of increasing regulation, but I am a fan of better regulation. I've never been convinced by CSR as a purely voluntary option on the part of business. Unfortunately, businesses are run by real people, not automatons that fit uniformly into strategic thinking. If a few thousand years of experience are anything to go by, we are all fallible and some people are just inherently greedy.

With ISO 26000 on the horizon and the improving relationship between the Global Reporting Initiative (GRI) and the UN Global Compact, we are seeing increasing global momentum towards improved understanding, standards, and reporting. Some governments have already pushed CSR into reporting and governance requirements. These include Denmark, France, and indeed the UK, not to mention developing countries such as India and Nigeria according to recent reports, but all at varying levels of accountability. I believe this trend towards improved regulation will continue, but only incrementally, as the agenda matures and gains further recognition by the investment community in particular.

We are also witnessing the evolution of CSR reporting of the non-financial variety from the relatively superficial paper-based documents sent to a handful of people who never really read them, full of pictures of smiling employees, children, and wind turbines. The movement now is towards far more open and integrated, credibly responsive online information and reporting with improved assurance that promotes better acceptance and value.

How does CSR play a leading role in a company's reputation?

For me, CSR is a company's reputation. If you try to separate the two, then you're missing the point. CSR should be an unseen ethos that permeates an organization and influences every decision made. Every strategic approach to CSR (or all other strategies for that matter) has to begin with clarity of purpose and vision, which lies at the heart of a company's reputation. All the actions of an organization should be of a result of that clear understanding of its relationship with all stakeholders, and CSR offers in fact the tools to facilitate wider understanding through enhanced communication. It could be best viewed as a critical friend perched over the shoulder of all decision makers.

What are some of the most prevalent CSR related issues that require attention in the EU?

You have to believe it is difficult to regulate and encourage social responsibility for such a culturally diverse group of countries. It would be near impossible to give an accurate answer to the question about prevalence of issues, as many people would offer many differing perspectives.

The generic focus across Europe is sustainable development and governance, but further segmentation of Europe into western (UK & Ireland), central & eastern (Germany, Russia), northern (Denmark, Finland, Sweden), and Southern zones (Spain, Turkey, Greece) would provide additional, more specific detail with regard to regional issues. The book, *Corporate Social Responsibility Across Europe* studies 23 countries and offers particular insights about them.[50]

In some countries the problem may be weak infrastructure leading to poor governance and corruption, while in others the problem may be over-consumption leading to environmental damage.

Regulation of social responsibility is difficult enough in one country (or one business for that matter) even without the additional complication that arises from the breadth of historical, political, cultural, and market forces that characterize the European landscape. Across the EU we have opposite ends of many various spectra, which include, for example, the range from huge corporations to tiny countries, from developed nations to developing nations, from traditional agriculture to cutting edge technology, and from arctic tundra to dry steppe. You only have to look at the recent climate conference in Copenhagen as a gauge for the variation in approaches to and enthusiasm for mandatory CSR regulation.

Encouragement is a different question altogether. I don't believe it should be difficult at all to encourage CSR across wide audiences. The problem is that those attempting to encourage businesses have only ever tried one tactic, namely, preaching, never selling or educated persuasion. Ignorant of the principles of communication to a mass audience, institutions have previously failed with their monotonous messages. By altering the content and tone of the messages to suit specific segments of the population, we can effectively stimulate CSR engagement.

For business, the net result tends to be increased productivity, access to new markets, the creation of new products, the enhancement of brand image, and the reduction of operational risk. All we have to do, therefore, is understand the individual motivations of the audience better and adapt our sales pitch accordingly, to gain a broad array of economic, social, and environmental benefits.

The European Commission has recently set CSR priority initiatives on biodiversity.[51] *By biodiversity I mean the promotion of a rich diversity of plant and animal life in any given region or indeed the world. Some CSR professionals believe biodiversity will become as important and high-profile an issue as climate change. Why should companies be examining how biodiversity impacts their businesses?*

From a perspective of risk mitigation, the more obvious inducements to a fuller understanding of biodiversity include the potential problems of supply chain disruption, the loss of operational license, the damage to reputation, substantial environmental fines, and reduced employee morale.

From the opposite perspective of identifying opportunities, on the other hand, you have the potential to tap into additional benefits such as access to the growing market of ethical consumers, interest from socially responsible investors, stable long term growth, and enhanced brand image.

The media has often referred to Western Europe as a lifestyle superpower, although a recent "New York Times" article notes ominously that "the deficit crisis that threatens the euro has also undermined the sustainability of the European standard of social welfare, built by left-leaning governments since the end of World War II."[52] EU countries are currently trying to pacify investors by implementing some drastic changes: cutting salaries, raising legal retirement ages, increasing working hours, and reducing health benefits and pensions. Will the recent economic crisis redefine the European lifestyle? What effect will this have on CSR practices?

Sadly, the economic crisis will affect many lifestyles, especially the many individuals directly impacted and facing periods of unemployment. Beyond the short-term scope of belt-tightening by all in order to weather the fallout of the financial tidal wave, I genuinely believe the values at the core of behavioral decision-making will not alter dramatically. In the short term, people tend to focus their actions on their immediate surroundings and situations and adapt accordingly, while over the longer term they follow a more stable pattern of behavior, one that is supported by their values.

While the initial impact in terms of CSR practices has, predictably enough, been narrowly focused on organizational transparency and governance, from which there have arisen ethical autopsies on the leading financial institutions involved in the crisis, the underlying lifestyle-directed pressures relating to CSR will continue to intensify as a consequence of the larger global challenges such as climate change, population growth, biodiversity and natural resource depletion, the awareness of all of these being fuelled by the information explosion.

Consumers are inevitably being far more prudent with their disposable income, spending more with 'bargain' retailers, which could create additional supply chain pressures. But there has been a surprisingly strong resilience in the green/ethical sectors due to an ever-increasing awareness of their business practices and the products they offer.

It may be the entrepreneur in me, but in my estimation this presents growing opportunities for the companies and countless innovative smaller businesses and emerging social enterprises with the vision and boldness to maximize the competitive advantage CSR presents.

TRY THIS

Taking care of our own corner of the planet doesn't have be a daunting task. Even small steps we take in our everyday lives will make a difference. Some of these ideas might not be new but they bear repeating. Try putting one or more of the following suggestions into practice:

1. When brushing your teeth, fill a cup with water to rinse your mouth out instead of keeping the water running.
2. Recycle all items that you can: paper, cans, plastic and glass.
3. Choose eco-friendly products to support companies that support the environment.
4. Walk or cycle more and drive less.
5. Drive hybrids or electric cars when possible.
6. Go vegetarian one day a week. Incorporate "meatless Mondays" to make it an easy habit to keep. It will make a difference to the planet (did you know that just one pound of beef requires as much as 2500 gallons of water to produce?) – not to mention the health benefits.
7. Adjust your thermostat one degree higher in the summer and one degree cooler in the winter. You'll save approximately 5% on your energy use.
8. Buy wind or solar energy sources.
9. Turn off computers at night. By turning off your computer instead of leaving it in sleep mode, you can save 40 watt-hours per day.
10. Wash clothes in cold or warm (not hot) water. If all the households in the U.S. switched from hot-hot cycle to warm-cold, we could save the energy comparable to 100,000 barrels of oil a day.

11. Don't buy bottled water; nearly 90% of plastic water bottles are not recycled, instead taking thousands of years to decompose.
12. Buy Local. Whenever possible, buy from local farmers or farmers' markets, supporting your local economy and reducing the amount of greenhouse gas created when products are flown or trucked in.

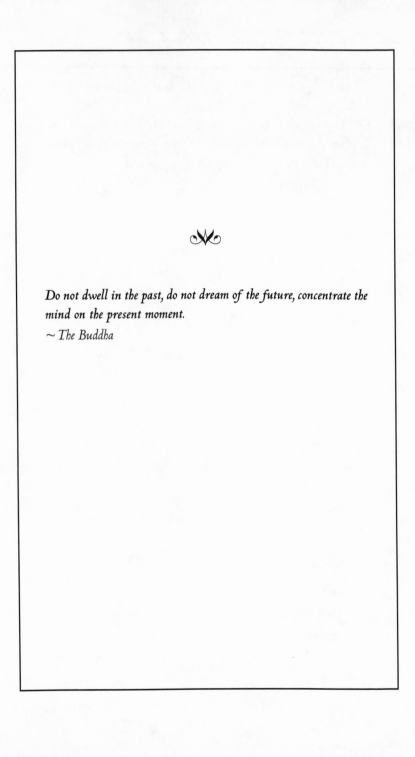

Do not dwell in the past, do not dream of the future, concentrate the mind on the present moment.
~ *The Buddha*

11

FLOWER LOGIC

Reinvent yourself before you reinvent your company.
~ *Andrea Jung, CEO of Avon Products*

I look at business in the same way that I look at nature.

In nature, the most striking manifestation of beauty I can think of is a flower. A flower begins as a seed and then grows. The stalk reaches for the sky in the bright sun, unaware of obstacles or difficulties. It just keeps growing, and its tip begins to morph into a bud. Then like quiet fireworks, this bud, so full of possibility, finally opens, revealing its full potential to the world. The flower cannot live forever so, after a time, the petals begin to fall. The stalk starts to wither, and the seeds fall from the flower onto the earth, enabling the cycle to begin anew.

In the beginning of a successful business, you begin with a seed, maybe the seed of an idea for a new business venture or a brilliant niche sector. The "seed" then goes through its initial growth stage, overcoming many obstacles, as it continues to flourish. Then the "flower" begins to grow. This expansion stage continues, until the company gets to the ultimate tipping point of victory, namely, profit!

The problem is that we never know when that tipping point is going to arrive. If we did, we could prepare for what comes next. The reality is that the "flower" does not live forever. It has to run the course of the natural evolution of business. To use the analogy of the flower, the "petals" have to drop off and die. The seeds must then become the catalyst for new ideas and new growth, in order for there to be room for the next flower, i.e. business model, to bloom.

So many companies have become caught up in an unrealistic, perpetual growth phase, and they believe it will go on forever. The harsh reality is that it almost never does. Even the most long-standing, successful companies will tell you that, as time went on, they had to rethink, reorganize, and retool their ideas and business models in order to remain relevant in the marketplace.

Toyota may be one of the best examples of this. A recent headline said, "Toyota Chairman admits to getting too big too fast".[53] This is a company that was always about quality which is an attribute they likely tried to uphold. Their crucial misstep, however, was that they changed course by embarking on a mission to be the biggest. In my mind, to think that any company can just get bigger and bigger with no regard to redesign, re-branding, or stabilization programs is to go against the laws of nature.

Do we really need a big box plaza on every corner? These behemoths are gobbling up so much land. Yet these stores seem to have found a home on every block, in every city.

How much of this do we really need?

Businesses get into a growth phase, and the expectation from shareholders and management is that they must have continual growth year after year. I find, from my own personal experience of working with upper management in some of these companies, that when this happens, the mounting pressure can become intolerable, affecting those responsible for the bottom line in ways you can't imagine. And yet most times, those in positions of leadership in these companies try to take it on and cope with it all in the name of profits, whether it makes sense or not.

We have all seen the disastrous repercussions that occur when man has tried to "push" agriculture or the environment. When we interfere with the natural order of things, we eventually pay the price. Why? It goes against nature. The flower cannot possibly bloom forever.

In business, it follows that, in order for new things to emerge, there has to be a slowing down or some form of regression phase. At the very least there must be a stabilization period. I believe that it's completely unrealistic to anticipate expansion year after year, whether it be in growth or revenue.

Think about crops. You cannot farm the same soil year after year. The soil has to "rest" and regenerate, so that it may have ample minerals and other natural growth factors to bring forth a successful crop once again.

In business as in nature, there is growth, there is maturity, there is decline, and there is re-growth. You can stay in each cycle for a certain period of time, but it certainly doesn't mean the total demise of a company once that cycle starts to wane. Even within the company there may be product lines that enjoy success for a time and then have to "die", because they are no longer what the customer desires. New, more relevant products or innovations may then be implemented that may be more in tune with consumer trends.

When I look at restaurant chains as an example and I examine the companies that were once at the top of their game, I can think of several companies that "just didn't get it". They grew, riding the wave of an innovative concept that was current at one stage. But as time wore on, the tide began to turn. Restaurant patrons are a fickle lot, and it's par for the course for them to seek out the newest kid on the block. These now defunct restaurant chains got dangerously comfortable under the guise of their past success and lost track of what was going on in the market place. Companies like this can become too self-involved and refuse to see the writing on the wall. In doing so, they become another example of a brand that needed to "die" – or at least take stock and re-brand. But they hid their heads in the sand, while their customers inevitably moved on to a fresh, new, sexier concept.

Look at our four very unique seasons. There are abundant elements at play as the world around us heeds the call for the transformation of seasons. The anticipation of spring, the reverie of summer, the falling back of autumn, and the necessary respite of nature that we call winter – all are in perfect mutual accord and are a manifestation of the natural flow of things.

If you observe the world in this way, you may see that companies that consistently propel themselves forward against these laws inherent in nature may be headed for trouble. In my observation, eventually they lose their way.

World class businesses fail because they are either unable or unwilling to discard old models of businesses when external forces have changed dramatically. We must now reinvent business to position for the age of capability.
~ *Jagdish N. Sheth.*

The Reinvention Revolution: An Interview with Mike Michalowicz

Mike Michalowicz started his first business at the age of 24, moving his young family to the only safe place he could afford, a retirement village. With limited resources and no experience, he systematically bootstrapped a multi-million dollar technology business, sleeping in conference rooms to avoid hotel costs. After selling his first company, Michalowicz launched a new business the very next day. In less than three years, he sold it to a Fortune 500 company.

With his newest multi-million dollar venture, *Obsidian Launch*, Michalowicz grows authors and experts into industry superstars.

The author of *The Toilet Paper Entrepreneur*, a book published in 2008, he is a frequent guest on CNBC's The Big Idea with Donny Deutsch, ABC News, Fox News, and other television programs.

Michalowicz also lectures for college entrepreneurial programs at Columbia University, Harvard, Penn State, Princeton, and other top schools in North America.

What is a toilet paper entrepreneur? Why do you use this term?

The toilet paper entrepreneur is really an analogy. The general concept is that I believe most people perceive entrepreneurship to be what they read in *Inc magazine* and on the cover of *Fortune Magazine*. From my experience, entrepreneurship is a lot more raw and involves a lot more of a scrappy-type lifestyle. So the concept of the toilet paper was meant to liken entrepreneurship to something that nobody talks about, which is the bathroom.

Nobody really talks about the real part of entrepreneurship. We're always pounding our chests trying to give the impression we're the all-powerful. The bathroom analogy was so appropriate, because sometimes you are stuck there with three sheets! But nobody gives up. You search around to find 'resources'. We all do it, but nobody really talks about it. It's embarrassing, it's not appropriate.

The thing is, entrepreneurship is the same way. Many times you'll feel like a complete failure and you're working so hard and nothing is coming of it. To your friends in business you'll say, 'Everything is good' or 'Everything's fine' or 'It could be a little bit better'. You don't tell the truth. That's what entrepreneurship is like. We're often caught with three sheets or, I should say, certainly without a full roll – or, in terms of the entrepreneur – without a full roll of cash and without a full rolodex of contacts. Therefore we have to be ready and willing to dig through the dumpster of life. When you think that way and you're willing to do some digging, you often find treasures and do very well for yourself.

I compare the life cycle of a business to the life cycle of a flower, which has four phases. It starts with a new beginning from "seed", followed by growth and then decline or "rebirth". The first is the start-up or development phase, the second is the growth and maturity phase, the third is the decline phase, and the fourth is either the renewal phase or the death phase. Each of these phases present different leadership challenges. How can a business identify which part of the cycle they are in, and how should they prepare to meet the challenges of each phase?

I have different names for the life cycle, but it's basically the same concept. From my experience, we first go through different emotional phases. Actually, it's kind of shocking. A lot of entrepreneurial books I read talk about the practical side, but very few talk about the emotional phases of entrepreneurship. Basically what happens in the early phase – I call it the *fear phase* – is that we start a business and we live over the edge, but many of us back away from it. Some jump into it, and there is an initial exhilaration, but then, when the phone doesn't ring and the orders don't come flying in like we thought they would, we go into the fear stage. What I think is significant about that stage is the emotional role of the entrepreneur. The reason fear is important is that it gets you running forward. Let's face it. Nothing gets you moving like the fear of something: the fear of failure, the fear of losing your savings. The fear phase gets you motivated to push forward. When the phone doesn't ring, you keep plugging along and you keep hitting the phones and making the outbound calls, until people start calling you back. It's all about survival and feeding the business. So, as the entrepreneur, you are responsible for doing everything. You wear every single hat that there is. You sell, you service, you invoice, you administer, and you do it all.

Also, what comes out during this phase is that, if you want to get to the next phase, you have to find your gift. Your gift is what you're naturally or inherently talented at. It's also a blend. It's what you can do better than everyone else but at the same time it's also what resonates with your customers. When people start buying from you repeatedly, that's the indicator that they like and want more of what you have.

Conversely, most people get this wrong and say, 'People say they love what I'm doing, they like my concept'. This may sound harsh, but we all of us lie through our teeth. We speak the truth through our wallets.

Through the early stages, you do everything under the sun to get the business up and running and continuing on. You're driven by fear, but you have to start listening to what the customer is buying repeatedly. When they start buying repeatedly, you've found your specialty, your gift.

In the next stage of growth, which is the adolescent phase, there are growth spurts, there are growing pains, but it's probably the best time in any business. It's fun, because your role as an entrepreneur now is to build a culture. This is where you start bringing people in either physically to your office as employees or maybe through partnerships and contractors. But you start scaling the business to bring other people in. Your job as the entrepreneur now changes from doing everything to being more of a systemizer. You bring people in, hiring them for their energy and their attitude, because they're a great cultural fit and you start introducing systems. You explain to them that 'this is going to be your job and just repeatedly do this and we'll grow'. Then you bring in the next employee, you look for cultural fits, and you continue to develop the systems. So phase two is all about the systems. New hires are trained to repeatedly deliver that gift, that specialty you have, consistently well. From my experience it's the most fun. The business will often start growing explosively. Clients are excited about what you have. Generally, you're new to the market. Maybe your service or product isn't new, but the way you're delivering it is unique or maybe your product or service is unique, so there's usually a lot of excitement. Customers are often more forgiving of you at this stage because you're a new business. If there's a mistake or problem, they often allow you time to fix it and get back on it. They have an appreciation and understanding because you're still a small business, and they know that everything is not going to be perfect in some cases. This is not true for all customers, but the majority are more accepting of problems in the beginning when dealing with a young, small business. A classic example of this is if you look at Google. If you rewind five or ten years ago, it wasn't perfect. The search engine was okay and sometimes it locked up and the site went down, but nobody complained. Now that Google is in its biggest stage, if it goes down for one second, we are calling them idiots. We never would have said that five years ago. That's true with all businesses, all the vendors we depend on. The customers give you more leeway initially because you're new to them.

Then you go into the stage of maturity, and from my experience it's about vision as an entrepreneur – and cheerleading. The systems you've put in place have now brought on middle-level management. It has brought on people who execute the systems, teach the systems, expand the systems and develop the systems. You, as an entrepreneur, have to take the reins at this stage. You must decide where you are focusing, where the company is going, and consistently beat the drum of 'This is our mission', cheerleading the company along at the same time. I got my own business into that stage when I sold my company and we went from rapid growth where we were bringing on ten employees a month, to bringing two thousand new people into our division because we were acquired and merged into another division. There's a lot of bureaucracy that comes into play. There are a lot of systems. So the job of the leader is to constantly say where we're headed and to turn the ship around because we're taking a new direction with very deliberate, slow-moving changes. A company of such size that has been doing so well for so long should not make changes overnight. You would lose all that loyalty you had built with your customer base.

I can only speak from what I've studied regarding the decline phase. I sold my businesses before going into that phase. I exited and sold to other leaderships, so I can't say from practical, hands-on experience. From what I've read and what I've studied and heard from other entrepreneurs who have gone through it, basically it's when a business can't get out of its own way.

It has built something that has worked for so long, and it's so ingrained into the culture that 'that's what we do'. It's like a typewriter company. Rewind to fifty years ago when the biggest typewriter companies just kept on making typewriters. They excelled at it. But then the need for typewriters declined. They had built up the perfect system to build typewriters, and that didn't translate to building computers. It was too different. It's hard to believe, but they were inside and they couldn't see the forest for the trees. All they saw was that they were consistently great at making typewriters. They were the best and decided that they would just get a bigger piece of a smaller pie. That's when they started to decline.

The entrepreneur's job here is to get outside their own industry, and that's often what doesn't happen. The typewriter guys were going to the typewriter conferences and all these events relating to typewriters. The entrepreneur in this situation should have gone to the newest conferences on computers, learning and being the lead scout on what's coming as the next 'big thing'. In other words, 'What's the biggest threat to our business?' instead of 'How do we make a better typewriter?". In this case, the entrepreneur should have asked, 'How do we embrace this new thing (which was computers), and get involved in it?'

Basically, what you have to do is start a new business within the business, a little seedling. Let it have its own little leadership team and don't have it get caught in the wheel. Open their own little facility inside your business. They may share office space, but they're off in their own corner. Let them start from the beginning and just have the backing of what your company has established financially, so that they can start getting traction. Then introduce them to your clients and try to spin it back up that way.

It sounds like the entrepreneur in this analogy was not very observant or willing to accept the inevitable. Why does this occur, do you think? Is it the fear that blinds us?

It's a great question. The emotion in the early stage is the fear, and you're off and running. Once the business gets going, I think fear turns to confidence. In the second stage of business, when you're growing and building systems, the fear phase becomes confidence and you think, 'This is working. I'm going to do more of it.' When we get to the third stage, confidence turns to aspiration, and aspiration is where we're taking the company and how we're changing the world.

As the decline starts, the problem, I think, is that fear doesn't come back. I think aspiration becomes blinding. Aspiration turns to blind faith. Blind faith is basically like saying, 'Let's go down this wrong path'. If we could invoke fear again, that would actually kickstart us to move forward.

What are a few of the most common mistakes that entrepreneurs make when starting a business?

The most common mistake I hear talked about is that people go into business under-funded. I disagree very strongly with that. I think the most common mistake on the financial side is that people aren't willing to adjust their lifestyle! When starting a business, you have to look at your existing lifestyle and recognize that, whatever income you were making prior to starting your business, it's unlikely you'll continue it when you start your new business. It's going to be one step, two steps, or ten steps back at first. I think the right approach is to say, 'How much can I adjust my lifestyle back before starting a business?' In other words, 'What adjustments to my lifestyle am I willing to make right now to start my business?' That's the best question you could ask yourself.

Why is entrepreneurship so popular with the under twenty-five set? Is it true that ten percent of college graduates are planning to start a business?

Yes, it's true, and the number is growing. Entrepreneurship is popular for two reasons. One is the perception, 'the pull' that media brings about. In particular, Facebook is a great example. Mark Zuckerberg was a billionaire at age eighteen, and there are movies about it. So the perception of the college student is, 'Instead of getting a job working for someone else, I can be a billionaire by age eighteen if I start my own business, and I'll be famous because they'll put me in movies.' So there's a lot of sex appeal to it. The unfortunate thing is that this sort of story is not common, but is perceived that way because of the media.

The second factor is 'the push'. The push is that you can't get a job. So college students are graduating and they're interviewing, but they can't get a job. So if you can't get a job, you have to do something. The result is that they're starting their own businesses. It's both a push and pull that's causing this dramatic increase in entrepreneurship.

Let's go back to the final stage, the decline or "death" of a company. How does a company get themselves out of a deep dive and into a renewal phase?

I would say that you should get as far away as possible from your industry. That would be the unique solution. Here's one example. I'm an author. I wrote a book, but the one thing I deliberately did, and it's the reason why I'm so fortunate that my book has done well, is that I didn't go to a single author convention. I didn't do anything within the industry. What I know is that it's the same five or six concepts being circulated around there. I went to different industries. I went to a convention of carpet cleaners, because it was so bizarrely different and I wanted to see what was going on. Sure enough, I came across a huge find there. One of the speakers says to the people who make the cleaning products, 'You know, there is one way to consistently increase sales by ten percent, if you put your products on the retail shelf.' My ears perked up, because books go on the retail shelf, and he said, 'If you put a I-800 number on the back of your product with a pre-recorded message at that phone number, you'll increase sales by ten percent! People go shopping, they see your product, they pick it up, and everyone has cell phones now. It's a great way of educating consumers further on your product and differentiating yourself. A lot of people will pick up their cell phone and dial the pre-recorded message to hear what else you can offer.' I put a I-800 number on the back of my book. The key was that among the authors nobody was talking about this kind of thing, I suspect because authors talk about what authors talk about. My technique was to go outside the industry. For many entrepreneurs, particularly when their business has achieved the highest level, decline is imminent. It's going to happen one day. So it's their responsibility to really break out from their industry just because it brings about innovative thoughts. It brings about different ways of tackling things. It doesn't matter where you go because business is business. Whatever you learn can ultimately be applied and spun back into your own business. Keep your mind open.

What type of leadership skills do you think are necessary to go from being an irrelevant but successful business to being a more relevant and also successful business during a decline phase?

I believe listening is huge. I'm thinking more in terms of innovation. I think the natural tendency is to suppose that we need a super-charismatic leader, that we need someone who can really rah-rah the team and get refocused. I think that's important, but I think listening is more important. If a business is in decline, they weren't listening to what was happening. They weren't listening to customers' wants. There were probably complaints coming in that they weren't listening to. I think if a business is in decline, then clearly they have a listening problem. They need a leader who listens and absorbs and infuses that listening mentality throughout the organization. We have to listen better, not talk more.

What kinds of belief systems are important in a leader during the renewal phase of a business?

An empowering belief system. Ultimately, no matter who we are, our thoughts precede how we behave. If we feel we can't do something, we'll prove ourselves right and actually not be able to do it. But if we're absolutely confident, we will do something.

I think better leaders ask better questions. A good question is 'How do I make more money?' But a better question is 'How do I bring in one million dollars more of revenue in the next month?' Asking about how to make more money is a good question, because it's forward looking and it kind of gets your mind stirring. But the answer remains true, whether you bring in one dollar or fifty dollars. If, on the other hand, you ask a better question, it changes your entire thought process and it gets you much more focused. A leader who's a good listener but also has the ability to ask really enabling, powerful questions will be the best leader.

Every answer starts off with a question. Better questions bring about better answers which mean better solutions to get your business back on track.

When you say they have to ask better questions, do you mean the questions have to be pretty specific and more timely?

And bigger. A classic case study of this was Bill Gates. His question wasn't 'How do I develop an operating system for an IBM computer?' His question was 'How do I develop an operating system that will be on every computer in the world?' It was a much bigger question which gave him a much bigger answer. Because of that, Windows was developed, and he got a much bigger and better solution.

Once a very old king went to see an old hermit who lived in the top of a tree. The king asked him, "What is the most important Buddhist teaching?"
The hermit answered, "Do no evil! Do only good! Purify your heart!"
The king protested, "But even a five-year old child can understand that!" "Yes," replied the wise sage, "but even an 80-year-old man cannot do it."

~ Buddhist parable

12

A NEW VINTAGE

I believe that children are our future
Teach them well and let them lead the way
Show them all the beauty they possess inside
Give them a sense of pride, to make it easier
Let the children's laughter remind us how we used to be.
~ *"The Greatest Love of All" by Michael Masser and Linda Creed*

Children *are* our future. This saying is as true now as it was centuries ago. Parents have always hoped and prayed that the world their offspring inherit might be better than their own. But the future facing today's younger generation is much more frightful and uncertain. Economic challenges, global warming, the threat of terrorism, war, world hunger, and genocide, not to mention the distinct possibility that the next generation might be unable to break free from a burden of debt, all add up to a tentative future.

Yet children today are being moved to change this grim forecast of the future through their own unique philanthropic initiatives, not to mention copious amounts of heart and hope.

These young dynamos are not old enough to solve global warming. They may lack the higher education and the life expertise required to engineer new, life-altering technologies, at least for now, but life in today's global village has made the world's youth wise beyond their years, as well as much more vocal about what exactly is on their minds.

Some kids, like 13-year-old Aitan Grossman, are taking a stand for a safer, cleaner, and healthier planet earth. Inspired by former American Vice President Al Gore and his environmental documentary, *An Inconvenient Truth*, Grossman launched kidEarth, a children's environmental movement.

Since its inception in 2009, Grossman's non-profit website has had some 270,000 hits from more than 110 countries. Earthday.net, the official website of the Earth Day Network (which gets 12 million viewers a year), designated kidEarth as one of the lead partners of Earth Day's 40th Anniversary. Stories about Grossman's brainchild have appeared in 50 international media outlets. Even Gore himself featured Grossman's efforts in his "Alliance for Climate Protection."

In an effort to bring attention to his cause and spread his message about environmental awareness to the world, Grossman penned a song entitled "100 Generations". Children from as far afield as Botswana, France, Taiwan, Venezuela, Ethiopia and the United States eagerly volunteered to be part of Grossman's musical project. In fact, to date, more than 100 children from five continents have recorded Grossman's song in four languages.

In a feature that appeared in March of 2010, Grossman explained it this way to the website *Amazing Kids!* "I am old enough to convince...school children from Africa, South America, Europe, Asia and North America [to] sing my '100 Generations' song with me.

That way, the world can hear that children everywhere care about the integrity of the nature that we are taking for granted, and everyone can feel our hope that the earth will stop warming soon."

Similar youthful passion and integrity are reflected in the efforts undertaken by teen activist Orren Fox to challenge the food industry and increase our awareness about the mistreatment of animals through his blog, *Happy Chickens Lay Healthy Eggs*. This 14-year-old vegetarian and gardener took a Grade 5 project and turned it into a vehicle to heighten people's knowledge about the powerful impact the food industry has on our lives – and the picture he paints is not always pretty.

Fox blogs about the dangers of junk food, making better food choices, and eating organic, as well as opting for more nutritionally sound food that is locally raised. He writes about the need to change the way egg layers and meat birds are raised and treated, so that consumers can make choices that are more ethical and kind. Fox even raises funds for this cause which is so dear to his heart, and hopes to help keep local farmers in business through his future initiatives.

Empowering orphans is what has driven Neha Gupta to pick up the gauntlet and act for change. When Gupta was nine years old, she traveled to India and saw that the orphaned children there had no hope for a better future without some type of benevolent intervention. Since then, Gupta has turned her empathy into action, raising more than $55,000 for children abandoned in the communities near her ancestral home in India.

This young philanthropist's proudest moment to date has come from watching the first class of girls at a new sewing center in one of these Indian villages establish their own business, make a living and begin to raise their lives from poverty to empowered independence. What could inspire more hope than this?

Even young people who have been brutalized by war are speaking up for change. Who would have thought that a young girl like Mariatu Kamara could walk in the light of hope after having had both her hands cut off by soldiers in Sierra Leone when she was 12 years old? Kamara was brutalized and left for dead. She was humiliated beyond imagination. And yet today this author of the book *The Bite of the Mango*, faces the future with hope and joy. Kamara works to build homes in Sierra Leone to house abused women and children through her Mariatu Foundation. She lectures about the human cost of war and hopes to raise awareness about the impact of war on children.

The world can be a perilous place, as we war-free North Americans sometimes forget. But with young people like this courageous soul intent on instigating positive change, not to mention the many others raising their voices as well in support of so many worthy causes, our children may be the ones to usher in the world's next golden age.

Miracle Miles: An Interview with Mariatu Kamara

Mariatu Kamara is a brave and gentle human being who has endured more pain and suffering in her lifetime than one could ever imagine. Her harrowing experiences as a child victim of war in Sierra Leone are the subject of her memoir, *The Bite of the Mango*. While reading her story, I wondered to myself, *How much can the human spirit endure?* But, as the saying goes, Mariatu has taken these horrific events and made lemonade out of unbearably bitter lemons.

Mariatu grew up in a peaceful village surrounded by family and friends. When rebel attacks broke out during Sierra Leone's atrocious civil war, the people of the town were forced into hiding. One day, before the fighting broke out in her village, 12 year-old Mariatu set out for a neighboring village, but she never arrived at her destination. Heavily armed soldiers kidnapped her and brutally tortured her. Finally, in a savage act of senseless violence, the soldiers cut off both her hands. Covered head-to-toe in blood and dirt, close to death and starvation, she stumbled through the countryside.

After wandering in a forest for two days, Mariatu was eventually found by a woman who took her to a clinic in the capital city of Freetown, where she spent a month recovering. Still not knowing the whereabouts of her family, she moved to a refugee camp in the west end of Freetown, where she encountered fellow amputees. Miraculously, she discovered other family members there as well.

In 2002, a compassionate couple from Canada heard her story on the news and arranged to fly her in to see them. They also attempted adoption proceedings. Although the adoption procedure failed, in that same year Mariatu was permitted to remain in Canada with a family from Sierra Leone who had opened their home in Toronto to family and friends from their country's war torn streets.

Today, in her early 20s, Mariatu is a college student studying to become a social worker and is the UNICEF Special Representative for Children in Armed Conflicts. Mariatu is a much sought-after speaker whose goals include continuing to raise funds for the Mariatu Foundation which she created to build homes in Sierra Leone to house abused women and children. She also aspires to work with the United Nations and thus raise awareness of the impact of war on children.

She is an extraordinary example of the fact that the human spirit can overcome inconceivable horrors and move on despite everything, to create a meaningful life.

I wanted to talk to this brave girl whose courage and resilience are so awe-inspiring.

What was it like returning to Sierra Leone?

At the beginning, when we were getting ready to go, I was both excited and anxious and scared at the same time. When I got there, I was so happy to see my family and friends that I eventually moved past the anxious feelings that plagued me from my past. After the first two or three days there, I was able to move beyond them and enjoy my visit.

Do you believe that the tragic events of your childhood had a higher purpose?

You know, many days I wake up and think it was all just a dream. I even imagine that I still have my hands, and then I realize they are not there.

I really think that there is a purpose to tragedies that befall us, because whatever happens to you in this world, it always has something to do with something else. In other words, as you say, it always has a higher purpose. You might not understand it right away, but definitely, things happen for a reason.

Being in a different country and a different situation, sometimes you have no choice but to endure these types of conflicts that have such tragic ends. But ultimately, it's something that God meant for you to experience, to learn from. If it wasn't for all of the tragedies that occurred in my life, I would never have been able to come to Canada to study or to start my foundation to help others.

What got you through your darkest times?

It was faith. I believe in God, and I also believe in destiny. I used to be angry. Even now, every once in a while, I am a little resentful. There come times when you think about events that have happened and things you have witnessed and you become infuriated. Then I draw back and realize that this happened to me and there are so many people out there that have even worse things happen in their lives and they survive and are able to go about their lives.

Do you feel free from your past? What has helped you to heal your emotional wounds?

We are human, we have feelings. There is nothing unique about that fact. It is only through faith – faith in God, faith in myself – that

I have been able to move forward. I can't just stay being a victim forever. I put the past aside and try to forget about what happened, although you can never truly forget. But still, I have moved on with life.

The thing is, I always believe that God is watching over me. I have been through so much and in my mind I feel there is nothing more I can experience that can break me. I feel I can get past almost anything now.

Do you believe your story and the inspiration it brings has an impact on the younger generation and encourages them to step up and act and make a difference in the world?

Some people think so. My hope and expectation is that I can inspire young people. I'd like to see more young people doing more for their world and helping others. If I can assist with that goal, then I'm happy.

What is your vision for the Mariatu Foundation?

I have already purchased the land (funded by private donations). The main vision right now is to build The Mariatu Foundation Home in Sierra Leone. This will be a home that focuses on aiding women and children, providing support for them and assisting them for the future. I want to help them to learn a trade or a skill that will make them self-sufficient. I'd like to have a little school for the children, a library, adult education, and counseling as well. I would like to provide courses in tailoring, soap making, hairdressing, and things like that. I'm also thinking of offering a course in agriculture. These are all useful skills that will enable them to become self-sufficient.

Do you feel that you have a responsibility to try to help children in abusive, dangerous environments?

I don't think of it as a responsibility. For me, it's just that I want so badly to do something to help, if even in a small way. I am determined to do my best to accomplish whatever I can, and I'm hopeful that it will make a difference in the lives of these people that have suffered so much.

How does one person step up and instigate change?

One person can always make a difference. Everybody has a story in this world, a tragedy or an event that changes them. Even if you feel helpless, there are so many things you can do to help. You can get involved in community work where you volunteer your own time. You can work within your community or work in an organization or raise funds or talk to your school or the people around you about issues that you feel passionate about.

In my experience, many young people want to lend a hand. After my presentations at high schools, there are many students who come up to me and ask how they can help. All they need is an increased awareness of what is happening and an idea of how to start. They really have the urge to assist other people.

You can do anything you want to in this world, as long as you put your mind to it and have faith and a positive attitude.

What words of inspiration do you share with people when you are a guest speaker, talking about your experiences?

I tell them that things happen, good or bad, for a purpose. You never know what lies around the corner. When something negative happens to you, it's true that you may never forget it, but you can forgive the person who wronged you and move forward. You have to learn to seek a higher meaning. Here's what I always say: Maybe

God took away my hands so that I can touch the world with my heart.

Empowering Orphans: An Interview with Neha Gupta

When American Neha Gupta was nine years-old, how harsh life could be for orphans became all too clear during a family visit to India. According to a time-honored tradition within her family, Gupta and her relatives would celebrate their birthdays by taking food and gifts to orphaned children in their hometown in India. From an early age, Gupta participated in this tradition. And each outing made Gupta realize that there was no one in the world who really loved these orphans.

These children had no money. They had no prospects. Furthermore, they could not get the education they needed to turn their impoverished lives around.

Gupta felt enormous empathy for the plight of these children. But she did more than just sit back and feel sorry for them. Gupta channeled that empathy into action, a decision that has changed the lives of the orphans, as well as enriching her spirit.

Determined to help this underprivileged group, Gupta set out to collect money for their cause. To date Gupta has raised more than $55,000 primarily by making and selling wine charms at community events. Gupta went door to door in local neighborhoods to find donations and enlisted family and friends to help her with her mission.

When children like Gupta take the initiative to care for other kids in need, huge vistas of hope are opened for the future.

Your actions and ideals definitely support the statement that "it only takes one person to change the world". Do you believe this to be true? What advice do you have for young people who are prompted to seek change in their communities and beyond?

Mahatma Gandhi once said 'Be the change you want to see in the world'. It is undeniable that just one person has the ability to make a positive change in the lives of thousands in his or her community. Becoming that 'one person' is quite achievable, if you make an active effort to convert your empathy into action.

Civic responsibility is a key component of what makes us human. Exposure to community challenges, a knowledge and understanding of global issues, and an appreciation of ethnic and social diversity all serve to enhance our civic awareness and the role each of us plays in the world we live in. It is my belief that it is never too early to gain this exposure, as civic responsibility begins with early childhood. It begins with sharing toys with siblings and other children, waiting one's turn, playing well with other children, and defending and protecting the weak against the playground bully. These civic experiences translate into adult life. They determine the types of friendships we forge and the relationships we have with co-workers, with a spouse, or with children.

My message to other young people is that getting involved with issues that affect the community and the world is a key component in their becoming responsible, well-rounded, and well-adjusted citizens. The fulfillment a person achieves in making a difference in the lives of others has no parallel to any other experience or material possession they might have.

In conclusion, becoming that 'one person' who is able to make a positive change in the lives of others does not mean that there is a one in a million chance of being that 'one person'. It means that every single person has the ability to be that 'one person', if they turn empathy into action. The difference between ordinary and extraordinary is the little word 'extra'. Everything in this world is attainable with determination and motivation. I would like to ask all young people to recall the story we heard as children, Watty Piper's *The Little Engine that Could*, and remember the wonderful motto from that story in their daily lives: 'I think I can, I think I can'.

The Empower Orphans logo is followed by the phrase, "empathy, opportunity, equality". What do these three words mean to you?

The goal of Empower Orphans is to motivate individuals to translate their *empathy* into action by providing orphaned and under-privileged children the *opportunity* to help themselves and so be treated with the *equality* they deserve.

How have your friends, family and community supported you and your mission to help orphans?

My efforts would have been to no avail were it not for my family and friends, the community (both in the US and in India), and the media. My friends accompany me in door-to-door selling and also in manning tables during craft shows and garage sales. The community has been tremendously supportive, both by purchasing wine charms and greeting cards and through their generous donations. The media has been greatly instrumental in facilitating my efforts by spreading the word. Articles published in print and interviews aired on radio and TV about Empower Orphans has led to people making donations and encouraging our efforts. I have also received funding through several grants that support social causes.

What are some of the more poignant life lessons you've learned as a young philanthropist and orphan advocate? What inspires you?

The experiences, fulfillment, and happiness which I have garnered by making a difference in the lives of orphaned and disadvantaged children are incomparable. They go far beyond any other experience I've had or gift that I've received.

I have gained confidence, the skill to effectively communicate with people, and marketing proficiency. In order to convince people to buy wine charms or greeting cards or to persuade them to join my organization and support it, I have had to make a compelling case, usually to complete strangers. I have also had to give interviews to professional media personnel. In the beginning, I was exceedingly nervous when I had to cold sell or speak with strangers about my cause. However, I've overcome my nervousness and am now comfortable with these activities.

Dealing with rejection and persevering despite it all has been one of the biggest lessons for me. I used to get discouraged when people turned me down, but now I know that success does not come easily and that a person has to have the tenacity to keep at it. I recall a time when my friend and I went around her neighborhood selling wine charms. We returned home after three hours, our bodies numb from the cold, with only $5 in our money box.

Gaining financial skills has also been part and parcel of the project. As a part of the process of making and selling wine charms and greeting cards, I have had to understand concepts like the cost of goods, profit and loss, etc. at a very early stage. I also operate a bank account for Empower Orphans with the assistance of my parents. As well, it is imperative that I organize and manage my time, juggling school work, sports, and social activities, along with activities related to Empower Orphans.

Civic responsibility is another area of growth for me. I am an only child and, within reason, I get what I want. However, working with the orphaned and disadvantaged children has opened my eyes to just how fortunate I am. As a result, I've become less materialistic since I started Empower Orphans. The poverty and the challenges faced by these orphaned and underprivileged children are unimaginable, and it is the responsibility of each one of us to give them a chance to improve their lives.

I can quote many stories of inspiration, but one recent one comes to mind. Last year, I donated sewing machines to older girls at the Shree Geeta Public School. When I went to India this summer, one of the girls invited me to her home, a single room shared among five people. She informed me with great pride and gratitude that her earnings as a seamstress allowed the family to get electricity in their house for the first time. This basic amenity that we take for granted allowed her to work at night and made it possible for her brother to study for and pass an exam which qualified him to become an electrician. Knowing that I had been able to make such a vast difference in someone's life gave me unquantifiable satisfaction.

How does it make you feel when you are able to help these children? Please tell us about one of your proudest moments as founder of Empower Orphans and your plans for the future.

I envision expanding Empower Orphans into a truly global organization, with children around the world helping other children better their lives. My short to medium term goal is to establish technical schools for orphaned and disadvantaged children. In India, once an orphaned child turns sixteen, they have to leave the orphanage and fend for themselves. With minimal education, these children are not equipped to earn a basic living and, as a result, the potential for their slipping into a life of crime or prostitution is high. To break this cycle, I hope to establish technical schools that will focus on teaching practical skills and trades to both the orphans and other disadvantaged children, allowing them to become electricians, mechanics, lathe operators, tailors, and seamstresses. Equipped with the skills needed to earn a decent living, these children will be able to stand on their own feet and hopefully become productive members of society.

At first, I simply felt empathy towards these children. However, once I turned my empathy into action, it opened my eyes to the fulfillment one receives in helping others. Being on the receiving end of smiles, hugs, and goodwill bears no comparison with anything else in the range of human experience.

The proudest moment for me has been to watch the first class of girls at the Sewing Center complete the course, establish their own businesses and begin to make a living. Beyond a doubt, to watch such a transformation occur made the tremendous effort that goes into Empower Orphans utterly worthwhile.

Do you believe in mentorship? If so, who are your mentors and why?

Mentorship is a critical ingredient of success. I've developed a mentorship program at the Sewing Center that we established at the Shree Geeta Public School. Older teen girls undergo free training that enables them to become seamstresses. They also receive a sewing machine at the end of the course, which allows them to start their own business. It is a basic requirement of the program that these girls give back in turn to the community by training other girls enlisted in the program and providing them with internships.

My parents serve as mentors for me, providing me with guidance and support. They recognized that I truly wanted to help the orphans and enabled me to translate empathy into action. They understand the lay of the land in India, as well as having the business experience and the connections to help implement and drive plans for Empower Orphans.

Generation Transformation: An Interview with Aitan Grossman

For 13-year-old Aitan Grossman the most important problem facing humanity today is climate change. Inspired by the documentary "An Inconvenient Truth" and the work of former U.S. Vice President Al Gore, Grossman set out to battle this impending danger to our world with a transformational voice comprised of a chorus of young people from around the world. In 2009, Grossman founded kidEarth, a children's environmental movement to inspire the kind of awareness society needs to help build a world that will last a hundred generations. And he's calling on all kids around the world to help get the job done.

Have you always been aware of environmental issues? What generated your interest and passionate concern for the earth?

As long as I can remember, I have been passionate about all living beings. I loved learning about animals, habitats, and insects in elementary school. My first pets were insects, two praying mantises I adopted from my backyard when I was six, because it was too cold for them to survive outside.

But I was completely oblivious to climate change until my ninth birthday, when my parents brought home the book version of *An Inconvenient Truth*. I read the whole book in one afternoon. It was unbelievable to me that adults had taken such poor care of our planet, and I felt so sorry for the animals whose lives depended on them. By the time I got to the back cover, I felt obligated and empowered to do something to save the planet.

Tell us about "100 Generations."

Music energizes me, and so I thought music might energize others to save our planet.

When I was twelve, I wrote and recorded a song about global warming called "100 Generations" featuring kids from all over the world singing the chorus and kids from my school recording the instrumentals. The voices of almost 100 children from five continents singing in four languages can be heard in the recording, some singing their own lyrics about the facets of nature in their countries that they hold dear.

We call ourselves kidEarth, and our song is on the kidEarth website. We want all the children around the world to sing it with us. Since we can't be in the same room at the same time, I've put the words, sheet music, and instrumental tracks on my website to make it easy for others to sing with us. They can sing my words or write their own.

I've taught my song to children in classrooms in the United States and overseas. I've spoken about my project and our message to almost 3,000 people at conferences, galas, community fairs and schools. iTunes rushed its release in time for Earth Day, helping me raise money for environmental nonprofits too.

It's working. Tons of people from all over the world (110 countries and counting) have visited my website and downloaded my song. And tons of adults from all over the world (including the United Nations and the EPA!) have helped by writing 100+ stories so more kids know that they can join in. It looks like our song will be around for awhile. A youth museum is being created for school children visiting the California state capital to show them how easy it is to improve the world. kidEarth is one of the examples of extraordinary projects they will be featuring. Cool.

My goal is simple – to find a way for frustrated kids like me to help. kidEarth raises awareness and creates one huge, loud, united, international youth voice to save our planet. When I visit classrooms with kidEarth, I also educate kids about the problem and discuss with them what else they can do to help. That's what kidEarth is all about.

Kids' future depends on the Earth and the Earth's future depends on kids.

Who are your mentors and what are the benefits of having a role model?

My role model and mentors are very different from one another.

My role model, Al Gore, inspired me to do my project. His books, speeches and slides educated me. His devotion to this cause inspired me. In Nashville, he stood on stage alone for an entire day telling us all what we needed to know about the climate. He didn't try to make it sound any different than what it is, important and urgent, with only two possible outcomes: good if we solve the problem and bad if we don't. I admired his honesty and directness.

His courage in presenting himself so boldly on an issue most people either ignore or deny was unbelievable to me. He was able to defy popular opinion and challenge the habits of Americans in order to convey a message that he believed deserved attention.

Mr. Gore showed us all how one person can change the world. I left thinking that I could be that kind of person too.

My main mentors have been my parents, who taught me how important it is to use what you enjoy to make the world a better place.

They also helped me with details I didn't even know would be needed for my project. There were lots of details. I didn't know much about mixing music, until my dad and I figured it out together on Garage Band. I didn't know anything about marketing, until my mom showed me how company names and logos make important first impressions. So I spent lots of time trying to come up with good ones. My project depended on lots of emails around the world to get it started too. Since my parents said I was too young to email strangers, they did that for me. And they still help a lot by making arrangements when I am asked to speak about my project so I can focus on being creative as well as doing my homework!

My teachers also helped me with the recording of my song, gave me advice on how to start my project, and encouraged me. Although a kid might be like me and have a big, ambitious idea of what he wants to do, kids are kids after all.

Find a mentor. They are great for encouragement which anyone at any age appreciates. They can introduce you to other people who can help you with your project, teach you things you didn't even know you needed to know and, if you're lucky, help you with the little stuff you're too young or too busy to do, because you're in school all day. Also, working with someone makes your project more enjoyable, and that person will help you when things get frustrating – which they will, trust me. But it's worth it!

Do you have any advice for young people who want to incite change in the world?

If you want to change the world, you should find what excites and motivates you the most and use it. In my case, I used my interest and talent – music – as a medium for change, so I could best portray my message. Take your passion, whether it be music, books, food, sports, etc, and make it into something creative. For example, my sister has a passion for books. So she organized book drives to start libraries in book-deprived African communities. My friend has a passion for sports. So he collected sports jerseys and money to buy "indestructible soccer balls" for poor communities. Do something for others that is meaningful to you.

Also, come up with a variety of ideas just in case your first one doesn't work out. Be creative – that's what gets people's attention – and use your age to your benefit, because when kids speak, adults listen.

And don't forget the internet and sites like Facebook. It's a free and easy way to publicize what you're doing and is an unbelievably great way to get your message to people you don't know, living in places you've probably never heard of before!

Are you currently involved in any special environmental projects or movements?

I was one of the youngest of 32 teens who were invited to an exclusive conference in Nashville, Tennessee last July to see the unveiling of the new *Inconvenient Truth* slideshow and learn from two days of presentations by environmental experts, including Al Gore. The group of teens call themselves Inconvenient Youth which is an organization Mr. Gore helped form that helps kids spread his message. I'm on Inconvenient Youth's Advisory Board.

I continue working on kidEarth. Each month I seem to do something different. This month I received the EPA's Youth Leader Award and was able to play my song and speak about the kidEarth project to an audience of 300 environmentalists in Los Angeles and meet Governor Schwarzenegger too (he was also an honoree). I'm always looking for opportunities and places to talk about my project, especially in front of kids.

At school I'm working on an independent study project with mentors from Tesla Motors, a Silicon Valley electric car company who are helping me understand alternative fuel sources for cars and helping me learn car design. I will be building a model car that gets its energy from one of those sources and answering questions about my research in front of my whole school in the spring.

What are your top three personal values?

Happiness – This has a completely different meaning than you might think. To me, happiness is not only the little enjoyable things that you look forward to, like video games or parties, but also the overall sense you have that you've led a good life because you've done things that make others' lives happier too.

Friendship – It's a lonely world without relationships. Life is about making others feel valued and important and about filling the world around you with people who support and value you and keep you company. Imagine all the things that you enjoy – eating, for example, or having a party – without anyone there to share them with. Imagine achieving something – writing a song, perfecting a piano piece, beating a video game – without someone to share it with. This is the importance of friendship.

Effort – Life doesn't have much meaning if you can carelessly breeze through everything you do without trying. You would experience a never-ending sensation of mushiness if you didn't put any effort into life. Imagine a life without school. You would quickly realize that you're on the dead end path of creating nothing for yourself or for the world. Success takes effort!

What are your plans for the future?

I want to continue to advocate for environmental awareness. Take care of the planet and it will take care of you. I will continue to promote kidEarth and visit classrooms, encouraging kids to use their own voices on this important issue. While there, I will bring Mr. Gore's slides and messages with me.

I'm not at the stage of picking a career quite yet, but for now my dream job is to start an environmental engineering company. I would love to use my creativity to design some sort of breakthrough technology that would help the environment and pay enough for me to buy a house (LEED certified) and car (electric, of course).

My hope is to go to Stanford and study innovation, environmental science, and entrepreneurship, all of which will help me when I start my company.

The Power of One: An Interview with Orren Fox

How could a 14-year-old boy from Massachusetts have such a powerful impact on the food industry? Orren Fox, author of the

Happy Chickens Lay Healthy Eggs blog, is an insightful tween, a committed vegetarian and a notable leader in sustainable agriculture who is making a difference in the world today by opening people's eyes, and he's creating quite a stir.

A project in the fifth grade was the starting point. Fox did research for a project on chickens and became shocked and dismayed when he discovered some unsavory facts on industrial chicken farming methods. This was followed last year by an essay called "Meet Your Meat", which was posted on his blog and which met with lengthy comments from the Head of Poultry Services in Canada. He has also elicited responses from Monsanto after posting an item on the controversial documentary, *Food Inc.*

Thanks to his interest in animals and agriculture, the Newbury, Massachusetts native has become an avid gardener. In 2007, he acquired his own chickens. That same year Fox joined the American Poultry Association and earned his Coop Tender Certificate. Fox is currently working on earning a Flock Tender Certificate. He also has 25 chickens, three call ducks, a rescue rabbit and he is planning on raising honey bees.

Fox is passionate about his birds and loves hearing them "talk." The teenager feels he can understand his chickens and that they are happy.

Through blog writing, fundraising, and social media, Fox has garnered much attention and has many supporters within the food industry. He hopes to help keep local farmers in business and says ethical eating is the environmentally responsible thing. Referring to soda pop as "death in a bottle," Fox's other mandate is to create an awareness that eating organic and locally raised food is also nutritionally sound.

According to this committed activist, children his age are interested in what he has to say, and many have changed their eating habits because of what he has taught them.

Every small, informed act creates a more sustainable world, says teen dynamo Fox. All people have to do is stop, listen, and think.

How did you develop an interest in our food system?

I think I got interested in fifth grade at school when we had to do a big research project. I became very interested in chickens that year and actually had some of my own. It was during the research for the project that I found out how horribly most chickens are treated in 'the food system'. I guess I never thought of it as a food system, when I was doing that project. All I knew was my hens were really amazing animals with personalities, with likes and dislikes, and I couldn't imagine them being crammed into a teeny, teeny cage with no opportunity to do the things healthy chickens do — take dust baths, perch, spread their wings, and eat bugs. Unfortunately, I didn't have to imagine it. This was happening in the factory farms just so we could all have cheap chicken meat and eggs.

What did you learn that surprised or shocked you, once you started researching further into the origin of our foods?

The thing that shocked me the most was how the big factory farms were treating the animals, the workers, and the land they were on. I guess I'm just not good with it. I know there are many opinions on this. I try to hear them all and consider other points of view, but, from what I've learned, it doesn't add up at all. I actually don't think it's sustainable.

You were quoted in a recent interview as saying, "We should be able to know what we are eating. We should know where our food comes from. Abuse doesn't have to be part of what we eat — abuse of the soil, abuse of the farm workers, abuse of the farmer, abuse of the animals."[54]

In your opinion, what actions are necessary to stop the vicious cycle you refer to? What can be done to educate and encourage kids to be pro-active and eager to make healthy choices and possibly initiate change within our food system?

In the movie *Food, Inc.* there is a really cool idea which is the notion that we all get to vote three times a day. At each meal we can decide what we'll eat and what we won't eat. If we don't want milk with rBGH (bovine growth hormone), GMO corn, HFCS (now renamed Corn Sugar), or chicken with growth hormones, then we don't have to buy it. When no one buys something, then the market won't sell it.

I know that, when you grow something yourself, like a tomato, it tastes different. It tastes great. You don't need much room to grow a tomato plant. So try it next spring. Honestly, I don't like the tomatoes from the market. They don't taste like anything. Once I grew some green beans, but they were ready to be harvested while I was at camp, and so my mom sent them to me. When they arrived, my cabin of ten boys went crazy eating them, because they tasted so great. They all said they were going to grow some the next year. Once you've had a real green bean, you never want to eat anything else. Kids like food that tastes good. Also, I have to say that you should add cheese. Cheese makes even Brussels sprouts taste good.

Some people say to me, 'But you live where you have space to grow things'. That's true enough. However, my friends at Eagle Street Rooftop Farm in Brooklyn are growing veggies, raising hens, and hosting bees on their rooftops! One of my heroes, Will Allen from Growing Power (a national nonprofit organization and land trust that helps provide equal access to healthy, high-quality, safe, and afford-able food for people in all communities) has a full farm in the middle of Milwaukee!

Are you surprised that what initially began as an interest or hobby for you has blossomed into a "mission" that has compelled you to take a stand and speak out on issues that affect our food chain? Do you ever get tired or over-whelmed by the challenge?

I don't view what I talk about or what I do as a mission. It isn't how I understand it in my head. I do it just because I'm really interested in it. I guess I just woke up that way. I never try to tell people what to think, but just let them know what I've discovered and let them make up their own minds. For example, I often take one of my hens (Susan or Sugar – they are really chill birds) to school and to our local farmers' market. Once people meet them and see how sweet they are, the next time they stand in front of the meat counter, they might ask the butcher how that chicken was raised before buying it, or they might try and find responsibly raised eggs.

I'm not overwhelmed by the challenge. I think it's exciting to think we kids could make the situation better. I feel that, if even one person asks to buy my eggs instead of factory-farmed eggs, that's great!

Some people say that everyone has the power to change the world in their own way. Do you believe in "the Power of One"? Do you think your generation embraces this notion?

Totally! I know for a fact that kids in my class think differently about eating chicken. I know that some people have read my blog and decided not to get backyard hens (which is great and really respectful of the animals). I think what we all feel is that little changes are just as important as big changes. Someone buying my happy eggs vs. factory-farmed eggs has changed the world. I would love for *everyone* to stop buying factory-farmed eggs. But that will take more than just me talking about it.

What advice do you have for kids who want to promote change in the world or in their community? How should they begin?

If you want to make a change, make sure you are really, really interested in the subject. I didn't wake up one morning thinking that I wanted to change the world. I woke up one morning thinking about those poor hens living in a cage no bigger that an 8.5 x 11-inch sheet of paper. That's not cool. Then I did more and more research. I talked to farmers. I visited farms and read everything possible. It didn't ever feel like work. It was what I wanted to know more about. Then I couldn't stop talking about what I had learned. I guess it's like someone who is really into guitar. They practice, practice, and practice. Then most likely they play for other people and, because they are good, they change the world. This may sound funny, but I think that's what happens. If you're interested in football and the environment, then find a local football stadium and set up recycling boxes for drink bottles. If you're into basketball and you and your friends outgrow your hoop shoes, give them to a local group that could use them. That's changing the world.

I believe in the importance of mentorship. Whom do you admire? Is there or has there ever been a family member, teacher, or other advisor that has become a mentor to you and guided you through this process of becoming an early-stage activist?

I have tons of mentors. It's funny. I don't think of myself as an activist. I don't really know what it means. Hold on. I'm going to look it up. Ok, here's the definition. 'Activism' consists of intentional action to bring about social, political, economic, or environmental change. Ok, I guess I am an activist, but it just isn't how I think about it. I'm trying to bring about change. But the reason I talk about the issue is for the birds, not for myself. I don't really care if I bring about change. I care that the way hens are raised is improved.

As for mentors, I count on them for information and I count on them for support. I just had a hen die and I was really, really sad.

So I reached out to one of my chicken mentors. She was really help-ful. In fact, she invited me to have one of her prize-winning hens! My family is also my mentor group. Just about every weekend, my family spends time with me helping me at the barn and with the hives.

And the really cool thing is: they let me lead.

TRY THIS

What is mentoring?

A mentor is someone who has knowledge and is willing to share it with another. The ideal situation is one where both parties in this exchange have an open mind, avoid a spirit of judgment, and enter-tain a genuine desire to learn from one another.

The role of mentor has traditionally been the domain of an older, wiser person who takes a younger, less experienced person under their wing. To my way of thinking, however, a real and powerful mentor-ship occurs when two people come together regardless of age or years of experience to coach, support and provide feedback to one another. In a number of instances, therefore, some of our "next gen" think-ers can mentor others from previous generations – Baby boomers, for example – particularly when it comes to certain aspects of new technology, such as social media. The whole issue is much more topic dependent than it is age dependent.

What makes it work?

Mentoring really works when there is a parity of respect between the two parties combined with a level playing field. This means that there is no grandstanding or power plays by the mentor and no feel-ings of intimidation or hesitation on the part of the mentee.

Tips for the mentor:

1. Be clear on the purpose of the mentorship. In other words, what is in it for you to mentor this individual? What would you like to get out of the relationship?
2. Be available as promised. When you and the mentee agree to meet on certain days and times, honor that commitment.
3. Be fully present and honest with your feedback and comments to the mentee. The mentee is there to learn from you and to grow in their capability. They can only do that if you are authentic and share your opinions and recommendations in all honesty.

Tips for the mentee:

1. Be clear on the purpose of this engagement. What is the goal of this relationship? What do you want out of the experience?
2. Show up on time and be fully prepared. If you were given homework, make sure it is completed prior to the session. The mentor is providing you with the valuable resource of time. So always fulfill your commitment and be grateful and appreciative of the mentor's time.
3. Think about how you can bring value to the mentor. In other words, is there a problem that the mentor is working on that you could provide assistance on? This can take the form of doing research on his/her behalf or providing information of interest like an article or news story or a new contact.

Social media is somewhat of a paradox. It powerfully connects us and yet, at times, it can distance us from the here and now. Like everything in life, it's all about balance. People can become addicted to social media as readily as they do any other addiction. The degree that such technologies are beneficial to others depends entirely on the underlying purpose behind the message, and the level of wisdom within the messenger.

Do not lose yourself in dispersion and in your surroundings. Practice mindful breathing to come back to what is happening in the present moment. Be in touch with what is wondrous, refreshing, and healing both inside and around you.

~ *Thich Nhat Hanh, "Fourteen Precepts of Engaged Buddhism"*

13

FOLLOW THE YELLOW BRICK ROAD

The Internet is becoming the town square for the global village of tomorrow.

~ *Bill Gates*

What's happened in the world in the last 30 minutes? Do you know? If you use social media networks and own a smartphone, tablet PC or some other form of portable technology, you likely have the answer. Social media users are usually the first to know about a major political event, business deal, local crime, or even incoming weather on the horizon.

Social media is not just a tool of web communication. It's not about what you ate for lunch or what you plan to do tonight. It's all about the generation and exchange of "User Generated Content" which, if used effectively, can change an event, promote a product far more effectively than advertising, save endangered species, or even assist a suicidal teen. Social media dialogues can sometimes spread more quickly and capture a wider audience than television, radio, or print.

While this new mode may have inherent issues and while a small percentage of social media addicts become as addicted as crack cocaine users (case in point: one couple updated their social media status during their own wedding), there's no denying the impact it's having on our modern culture.

Social media is not only affecting our opinions and buying decisions, it's also changing the way we do business and the way we live our lives. Some would say it's an extraordinary phenomenon. Others might say it's a scourge of modern living. One thing, however, is certain. Social media is growing in user friendliness and participation, cultural penetration, and business relevance. What's more, there is no evidence of it slowing down any time soon.

Social media, it turns out, isn't about aggregating audiences so you can yell at them about the junk you want to sell. Social media, in fact, is a basic human need, revealed digitally online. We want to be connected, to make a difference, to matter, to be missed. We want to belong, and yes, we want to be led.
~ *Seth Godin*

For social media users, sharing information and voicing their opinions on everything from politics and pop culture to commerce 24/7 is as natural as breathing. And, as any social media expert will tell you, business leaders who ignore this new reality do so at their own peril.

Thanks to Facebook, Twitter, and other online communities, today's social media users can exchange information whenever and wherever they like. Suddenly, opinions held by the "little guy" on the street are equally as important as those espoused by captains of industry. And customers' quick-time responses to everything from logo redesigns to corporate philanthropy cannot be disregarded.

The honest outpourings of consumers are altering business practices left, right, and center. In fact, it is no wonder that Facebook founder Mark Zuckerberg was named 2010's "Person of the Year" by *Time Magazine*. Just a few short years ago, Facebook was considered a tool for college kids to keep up on the campus parties. Fast-forward to today, and social networking has evolved from a personal communications tool for teens and 20-somethings into a powerful, transformative business vehicle that corporations are eagerly embracing, in order to build their brands for future renown. Thanks to social media, an interactive dialogue now exists between companies and customers such as never existed before, and the ongoing conversation is being heard by leaders of industry in a big way.

Marketing is no longer about the stuff that you make, but about the stories you tell.
~ *Seth Godin*

Suddenly, social media is helping businesses target specific demographics and reach consumers with personalized messages. Marketing dollars are shifting from big, expensive ad campaigns towards efforts to build content. Take for example PepsiCo's astonishing decision last year to forgo its usual big-ticket Super Bowl ads in favor of social networking.

More impressive still, consider the extraordinary benefits Old Spice gained when it launched its online video response campaign during the 2010 Super Bowl Weekend. Over three days, a team of creative directors, digital strategists, developers, and producers filmed 180 videos around the clock, responding directly to fans and celebrities in near real time to forge what is now known as the best social campaign ever to have been created.

On day one, the campaign achieved almost six million views. That's more than Obama's victory speech. On day two, Old Spice had eight of the 11 most popular videos online. On day three, the campaign had attained more than 20 million views. Facebook fan interaction went up 800 per cent. Old Spice's Twitter followers increased 2,700 per cent, and, within the first week alone, Old Spice had more than 40 million views. But here's the real bottom line: This daring new campaign using social media increased Old Spice sales by 27 per cent over six months and turned it into the No. 1 body wash brand for men. If that doesn't gauge the power and opportunities inherent in social media, what does?

For this reason, *Harvard Business Review* writer Bill George has called social networking "the most significant business development of 2010, topping the resurgence of the U.S. automobile industry."

In his article "How Social Networking Has Changed Business" (December, 2010), George outlines the growth of this phenomenon with striking statistics. More than 600 million users worldwide are active on Facebook. Remarkably, the most rapidly growing demographic is people over the age of 40.[55]

More impressive still is that approximately 200 million people are active on Twitter, and another 100 million use LinkedIn. These are mind-boggling numbers, especially when one considers that at the beginning of this decade none of these social networking tools existed.

Love it or hate it, social networking has charmed Apple's Steve Jobs, Microsoft's Steve Ballmer, IBM's Sam Palmisano, and countless other heads of corporations, universities, and governments. In the end, social media's lure and reach have been too irresistible to ignore.

"Emerging media is about two-way communication; it's not just another advertising alternative or push marketing tactic," says American social media expert, Sarah Evans. The way this acclaimed specialist sees it, businesses cannot merely sign up for a Facebook account or occasionally Tweet to customers and expect to enjoy social media's benefits. "They have to listen and learn how to engage their audience and become part of their conversations," says Evans.

Thanks to social media's reach, today's businesses can communicate authentic, real-time messages to millions of users in seconds. A brand's philosophy or a corporate vision can be shared with social media users with an efficiency and creativity previously unheard of. The payoff from this two-way dialogue is immense and can build mutually beneficial relationships, where both parties can learn from each other. But this new reality has shifted the traditional business paradigm for all time.

You can't tiptoe into social media. You have to jump into the pool. People have a natural fear of it. But the scary part is not being there. Your customer is already there.
~ *Dave Saunders, madisonmain.com*

Dr. Natalie Petouhoff has been a champion of the importance of social media for business for many years. As a Senior Analyst with Forrester Research, she is well known for her specialist insights into the realms of social media and customer service. She has a particular expertise in social CRM (Customer Relationship Management), which combines the notions of customer service and relationship management as found in a traditional model of enterprise with the emergence of social and customer networking tools. I asked her to weigh in on how social media is changing business.

How has social media changed the face of customer service?

Customer service conversations used to be between the customer service agent and the customer. Now the conversations are between the customer and the company with millions of people watching.

That there is now a 'witness' to how a company will respond has changed the way that companies respond. This witness factor means that the dynamics of the interaction are changing, not because it's the right thing to do, but because someone is watching. Customer service has suffered from the Rodney Dangerfield effect for a long time, which is to say that customer service and customers don't get enough respect. The long held belief that customers are easily replaceable or that customer service doesn't impact the bottom-line —these myths really don't make sense upon authentic examination.

Now that there is a witness, many companies are cleaning up their act in terms of their treatment of customers.

What are some of the challenges of delivering exceptional customer service through social media?

First, you have to understand what it is you need to do. When I was working as an analyst, I found that some people wanted me to just cover customer service without the social part — as if somehow social media were separate from customer service or any other part of business. I saved those emails because I found them fascinating. There is no separation between social and 'regular' customer service or between social media and marketing and PR. Social is now a way of doing business. Ten years ago, the authors of a book called *The Cluetrain Manifesto* said that there would come a day when the customer would be in control of the message and there would be an enabling technology. Guess what? They were right, and we are in the nascent stages of that prediction with no turning back.

Customer service has its challenges because it wasn't done well to begin with. Now you shine a light on it with social media, and you've exposed an area of business that most companies have not done very well with. Why? It's complicated. It takes a village. The technology required to do it well requires that most companies do a major overhaul of their systems, their databases, their customer records. It requires that somebody care enough to spend enough money on the software and hardware to provide the agents and the self-service portals with the right capabilities. We've not outgrown the myths yet.

How would you convince skeptics that they must deploy social media to enhance their company's customer service performance and brand recognition?

I predict that in, say 5 to 10 years, companies that did not take social media seriously won't be in business, while those that did will thrive. Why? It's common sense. But I'm not the first person to give this advice. It goes back to experts like author and consultant W. Edwards Deming, who urged that you should listen to your customers and listen to your employees. Take the information you glean from them and integrate it into your company. If you do, you produce better products while at the same time making your customers and employees happier and more loyal. That's what social media is: a *big* enterprise feedback mechanism.

Traditionally, if a customer had a complaint, they wrote a letter or made a phone call. Now customers have the ability to go public with their complaints instantly, with one click. How should companies deal with negative comments on social media sites and blogs?

They should start by monitoring the social web. Listen and then watch how other companies that are doing it well are responding. Then start interacting. Then audit your brand. Figure out where your brand is in the social media maturity continuum.

How should business leaders unify a company's traditional customer service platform to work in harmony with their social media customer service practices?

Get real about what is. Get real that you want to make a change. Then change the things that are not working. Get advice from the outside and follow it. Use organizational change management to stop the internal mental constipation that stops most companies from making progress.

Businesses have to be hyper-aware that unpleasant customer service experiences can quickly turn into a social media driven PR disaster. In my mind, PR is customer service and customer service is PR.

What does the future of social media look like in terms of customer service?

In the future I believe customer service won't be called customer service, marketing won't be called marketing, and PR won't be called PR. All those functions will be merged into one, and they will all co-exist under the umbrella of service to the customer.

Listening, engagement, trust, transparency — these are words often used in social media circles. Has social media helped us shift toward a more empathetic and responsible world?

Yes, I believe it has. If you look at the fact that news anchors are picking up stories by scanning Twitter, it is evident that the world is changing. I have clients who say, 'Our customers are not on Twitter, so we don't need to be there'. I say that may or may not be true, but the press is there, and they are lurking and looking for stories. When you see anchors like Anderson Cooper and Wolf Blitzer go after companies that have clearly not treated customers well, you know that times have changed and there is nowhere to hide.

Of course, active engagement in social media dialogue is not without its dilemmas. With so much riding on real-time engagement, social media takes time away from our off-line lives. This has many people asking: are we living virtually or are we only virtually living?

"The web has become nearly inextricable from the fabric of our lives in a relatively short time," says writer Steve Silberman.

In his 2010 article "Did You Get the Message?", Silberman says consumers "work and play online, stay in touch with loved ones, follow the news, track investments, and plan journeys in the offline world using GoogleMaps". All of this online time has its consequences. As Silberman says, "It's getting hard to tell where the virtual world ends and the actual world begins."[56]

Remember the pre-web era, when people read a novel to relax or went outside for a quiet, undisturbed walk in the countryside? For die-hard social media fans, pastimes like these are becoming somewhat passé.

Silberman makes the following observation: "This constant stream of titillating ephemera can pose challenges for people who are trying to live in a more conscious way. The effort of settling the mind in the here and now often requires reducing the amount of input and taking a friendly attitude toward boredom....Nowadays, we rarely allow ourselves to be refreshed by boredom. Restorative intervals of silence and solitude have become an endangered species of experience. As thankful as I am for the invaluable gifts that the internet has brought to my life, I also miss the slower pace of the pre-web era, the spacious, uninterrupted hours spent turning the pages of a novel with snow sifting outside the window. It's hard not to wonder if all this connection and convenience is driving us crazy".

Amid the information overload of the 24/7 news update, tweet, and ping cycle, our ability to stay focused and on task – and even our ability to focus on each other – has come under increasingly heavy challenge. New scientific research, moreover, indicates that the constant lure of online distractions and what scientists refer to as "inattentional blindness" resulting from multiple distractions may not bode well for the next generation of social media users. Scientists wonder what effect the short bursts of news and information we receive and send into the void will have on our brains.

In "Growing up Digital, Wired for Distraction," an article written in 2010, writer Matt Richtel asserts that today's constant stream of online stimuli may pose a profound challenge for the human brain in terms of concentration and learning.[57] Researchers also believe that young people may become more habituated to constantly switching tasks and less able to sustain their attention thanks to today's online technologies.

"Their brains are rewarded not for staying on task, but for jumping to the next thing," says Michael Rich, an associate professor at Harvard Medical School and executive director of the Center on Media and Child Health in Boston. As he tells Richtel, "The worry is we're raising a generation of kids in front of screens whose brains are going to be wired differently." And the effects of all this could linger for a long time.

Mark Bauerlein, professor of English at Emory University, wrote a book on the effects of web obsession, called *The Dumbest Generation*. The tag line for the companion website is "50 Million Minds Diverted, Distracted, Devoured." Despite the unease, schools around the world are embracing digital age diets. Day-in, day-out, this new breed juggles emails, texts, tweets, and other bursts of information at lightning speed. In fact, in 2008 researchers at the University of California estimated that people consumed three times as much information each day as they did in 1960. Such nonstop interactivity has marked one of the most significant shifts in the human environment in mankind's history.

But what does that mean for the human brain, an organ which requires downtime, just as the body needs sleep, to rejuvenate itself and function? It's too soon to tell how all this will shape the minds and lives of tomorrow's social media users. But as University of California neuroscientist Adam Gazzaley says, "We are exposing our brains to an environment and asking them to do things we weren't necessarily evolved to do. We know already there are consequences."

That concern may not play well in today's wired world, where constant online stimulation is here to stay. But any worries have not stopped global business leaders from embracing social networking as the means to a bright future and better bottom line. And, says Sarah Allen, social media is "the new state of being" in the 21st century world. It has changed the way people across the globe conduct business. It has democratized the corporate playing field, giving greater control and a louder voice to consumers. In future years, social media could propel mankind forward in ways that outshine Neil Armstrong's first steps on the moon in the 1960s. And, as Allen says, it is something brands and companies "must embrace or risk being left behind."

I have an almost religious zeal – not for technology per se, but for the Internet, which is for me the nervous system of mother Earth, which I see as a living creature linking up.
~ Dan Millman

The Shape of Things to Come: An Interview with Sarah Allen

Visionary social media strategist Sarah Allen has been helping small businesses, organizations, and non-profit groups engage successfully with online communities since January of 2009. Over the last few years her company, Sarah Allen Consulting, based in Sydney, Australia, has realized considerable success providing social media workshops to clients who wish to socialize their brand online and tap into the power and passion of web users. Allen's rise has as much to do with word-of-mouth feedback exchanged by her online followers as with social media considered as a phenomenon in and of itself. Allen's message is simple: embrace social media now or be left behind in the dust.

How would you describe social media to someone who has never heard the term or seen it in action?

Social media is quite simply about people having conversations online. They give people ways to connect globally and in real time. So for brands, the traditional marketing approach no longer applies.

Being social online is no different from socializing face-to-face. There are courtesies, certain etiquette, and ways of interacting with others. I often liken it to dinner party conversation. No one likes to be spoken 'at' or get stuck talking to that one person who takes themselves too seriously. We tolerate it for a while, and then we switch off!

For me, the online social network has revolutionized my business and my life.

Through active participation on Twitter and other forms of social media, I transformed my business from a traditional marketing consultancy to that of a social media consultant and trainer, taking my marketing, communications, and public relations background to its full potential. Along with my training workshops, I sit on a number of boards, providing thought leadership to organizations on how to become more social media savvy. I enjoy speaking about socializing brands online, and I try to provide sage advice by way of my blogs and other forums.

My life has been enriched by the people I've come to know online. There are business associates with whom I share knowledge on a daily basis, heads of online communities, bloggers, marketing masters who have been so generous with their time and thinking, forward-thinking clients, and passionate comrades. In fact, my ongoing connection with one client, Media 140, came about by way of a 140 character tweet. I have contacts that in 'traditional' business would be considered competitors, but online are true collaborators. Even the dear friends I have made on Twitter, whom I refer to as my baby son's 'Twitter Aunties', request updates on my darling boy.

These opportunities all came along by my wholehearted participation within online communities, and I love every aspect of my new business life. Granted, it can feel a bit like chasing your tail, this challenge of constantly trying to use and evaluate emerging trends, but it's always fast moving and totally engaging.

I run my business this way, because it's my life. I want to enjoy it, have great conversations, come up with fresh ideas, give rein to a sense of fun, and, ultimately, help others in my small way.

Social media has rapidly changed the way we communicate and conduct business. Do you think companies that ignore social networks will be left behind?

I reckon it's like this: if your customers, target market, or prospective markets are socializing online, then chances are they're having conversations about your industry and your brand. Now that we have the ability through social media to listen to that conversation, wouldn't you want to join in?

One beauty of social media is that it happens in real time. So, if you have the capacity to be reactive and creative and you're prepared to relinquish some control, you can have success, fun, and even the oft-yearned-for return on your investment.

Once a brand decides they want 'in' on social media, they'll want to talk about means of measuring success, such as the number of positive conversations about their product, increased traffic to their website, increased subscriptions to their blog, and improving sales figures.

But I'd bet my last bottle of Bollinger that they'll be more surprised by the results they hadn't envisaged: the new product lines their customers are asking for, the strength and reach of advocates who spread the good word on their behalf, the way any perceived wrongs are addressed by tackling the issue head-on, and a renewed ability to position themselves as a leader in their field, enhanced by their willingness to share knowledge and be generous with their experience and time.

The best approach is one that doesn't put social media in the marketing department, but instead takes an integrated whole organization approach to becoming more social, thereby combining marketing and public relations, legal and compliance departments, business development and sales efforts – the whole kit and caboodle.

We're all aware of the recent revitalization of Old Spice's brand and product line, which took the Old Spice Man viral through one-of-a-kind video content on their YouTube Channel and was supported by TV advertising, a PR campaign, and in-store point-of-sale marketing, not to mention an innovative second wave campaign featuring a truly responsive, real-time Facebook and Twitter presence. This resulted in 1.4 billion campaign impressions and a sales spike in excess of 100%.[58]

So, yes, those companies who ignore social media do so, sadly, at their peril. It's the equivalent of putting your head in the sand. You're missing opportunities to build your brand and discover untapped markets. As people flock to social communities in the millions, brands must recognize this shift and start to meet and talk with their customers there.

Thought leaders, small businesses, and community-minded people have found a platform of their own through social entrepreneurship. Do you think this trend has forced big business to stop and take notice and so rethink their company values and marketing strategy?

Social media is the perfect platform for social enterprise. For a start, both contain the word 'social' for a reason! It's no surprise that social enterprise, whose premise is that people are inherently good, relies on the grassroots movement, word of mouth, and networks to spread their message. Such an approach has brought success and global reach to this concept.

I love to spread the good word of my favorite social change-makers by sharing their content with my networks.

One, 'charity:water', takes a simple message combined with compelling imagery and videos to bring about the provision of clean and safe drinking water to one billion people in developing nations. They've had phenomenal success, funding 3,196 projects and having already helped close to 1.5 million people get clean water for the next 20 years.

Another, 'Improv Everywhere', is not technically a social enterprise, but rather partly flash mob and partly breath of fresh air while at the same time being an inspiration to social organizations and big business alike. Created in 2001 by New Yorker Charlie Todd, Improv Everywhere has the ability to use social networks in such a way as to take their scenes of 'chaos and joy' global. They are guardians of a 'brand' (though not a brand in the traditional sense) for which there is much affection, taking a fresh approach with a strong network of 'agents' and supporters, a sense of shared identity and great content. If that isn't a winning combination, I don't know what is.

These are just two examples I use when talking to brands about jumping on the Twitter train. Watching the video of Improv Everywhere's agent Rob giving out 2,000 'high fives' on a New York subway escalator shows how unexpected fun can form a vital part of your brand values and company culture.

Likewise, seeing charity:water founder Scott Harrison eloquently tell the story of his organization and convey his vision that everyone on the planet should have access to clean drinking water would bring shivers to the spines of even the most experienced marketing managers and business owners. So our sense of humanity still has an integral part to play in organizations everywhere, especially those with a strong social media presence.

Do you think social media has changed the face of customer service?

Social media has returned power to the people. As consumers, the conversations we have in this space with our friends, families, colleagues, customers, and other brands have immediate advantages. Our likes and dislikes are amplified, while conversations travel fast and gain momentum quickly, meaning there is potential for our comments to be heard, magnified and dealt with in a very short period of time.

This democratization of influence strikes right at the heart of what social media is about: the ability to have a voice again, to be heard, and to regain control.

While many brands and companies are fearful of this new state of being, it's something they must embrace or risk being left behind. After all, every piece of bad feedback is really an opportunity to turn dissatisfaction into a positive customer experience.

The fact is, we have had conversations about brands for years and we will continue to do so in kitchens and lounge rooms, at water coolers and boardrooms, in cars and on public transport. The difference is that brands can now start listening to that feedback, flex their customer service muscles, take a deep breath, and either acknowledge the positive feedback and engage in conversation or else tackle the issue head on with humility, promptness, professionalism and transparency.

So yes, social media has turned previously accepted models of customer service on their head, forcing brands to stop hiding behind their corporate façade and become more accountable, more responsive. In doing so, the social media phenomenon has created a level playing field for consumers.

Social media practices are frequently hyped as a "miraculous formula" that can literally transform a company, its customers, its culture and the bottom-line. As a result, a considerable number of "social media experts" have surfaced. How should one wade through all the professional advice that is readily available?

Clearly I'm a big fan of this emerging discipline of social media and online communities. I see so many trailblazers online who have fabulous knowledge, experience, and ideas and who are prepared to share it. They are people who are well regarded, produce quality content, demonstrate thought leadership, share knowledge, and are well-networked amongst other leaders in the field.

Equally, I'm all for what will soon be coming, namely a suite of internationally recognized qualifications along with a training framework as a way to regulate the industry.

When seeking out the advice of a social media 'expert' I strongly recommend you do your homework, both online research and offline.

A social media expert may talk the talk, but do they walk the walk? If you're not sure, Google them. Check to see if they are as active in their social media channels as they say they are. Look at their reach and audience and evaluate the content they distribute on their social media channels both in terms of quality and quantity. Add bonus points if they share their knowledge openly and are generous with their time. Check their LinkedIn profile to review any other sectors they have worked in. Do they have a good number of glowing recommendations?

Equally, check to see if they are selling a product or if, rather, they are having genuine conversations with people. Are they well regarded by their peers, included in Twitter lists and other compendiums online?

Some other attributes to look for are whether or not you have similar values, are like-minded, and whether your ideas bounce off theirs. This can be gleaned through a phone conversation, Skype, or a coffee catch up, not to mention a few well-placed calls.

What does the future of social media look like? Do you feel the leaders of the next generation will dramatically reshape the way we work in the future because of their core values and newly available technology?

Social media has already changed the way we do business by revolutionizing the way we connect with others, socialize, and engage with brands. As engagement with social media increases, some of their characteristics such as being virtual, reactive, real-time, hyper-connected, and fast-moving will feed back into the way we run the offline component of our lives.

It's interesting to see how, when new media are introduced into wider society, we work through issues such as trust (How do we verify new online contacts?), privacy (How do we protect ourselves online?), etiquette (What are the accepted ways of communicating online?), and workflow (How do we find an online/offline balance?).

I used to feel that the process of drafting a formal letter or email to new contacts, following up with a phone call, and arranging a meeting to discuss the proposal was so time consuming! The tech-nologies I've grown up with −phone, television, computer, mobile phones − have dictated the speed and style of my own interactions, and the way I now do business is perfectly suited to my generation. For me, microblogging and online social networks are the ultimate ice breaker, sidestepping all the awkwardness of traditional business introductions and replacing them with a nifty 140 character limit that forces us to get to the point.

As for the next generation?

Mobile devices are now being used to tap into our social net-works (last time I checked, there was a 350% increase in this type of activity), and this mobile trend is set to continue with internet con-nectivity in our televisions, cars, smart goods, portable technological devices, and even our clothes.

User-generated and user-driven content is going to continue to gain momentum. Previously, brands bought television advertis-ing because they knew the family would be gathered in the living room watching that top-rating program together. Now we find fami-lies under the same roof watching a program online or a YouTube clip, talking or texting or socializing via Facebook on the mobile, researching a school project, college essay, or recipe online, typing up a business paper on the laptop, or Skyping an overseas mate on their PC. We search out entertainment and information ourselves. No longer 'glued to the box', we take technology where we go and use it in a multitude of ways. Likewise, brands will evolve to be more interconnected, user-driven, and mobile themselves.

One thing's for sure: I can't wait to see the manner in which social media will continue to affect the way we do business, the way we act on behalf of brands, and how we run our lives.

As a social media influencer, do you believe the boundaries of your on-line and off-line lives have merged? Do you ever feel the need to unplug?

My husband probably wishes I would un-plug more often, but, when time is at a premium and there are only 24 hours in the day, I multitask. It's not just my online and offline realities, but also the boundaries between my private and professional selves that are just about irretrievably merged.

You need to be absolutely true to yourself in social media, in order to have a seamless transition between your online persona, which is in effect your personal brand, and your offline self. But once you're active in social networks online, the idea that you have distinct online and offline lives can seem faintly ridiculous. They are, after all, one and the same.

But, as a new mom running a business, I'm thankful for my 'social enablers' – my iPhone and iPad – that make it easy to have conversations, as well as create and share content on the go.

I check into Twitter at least twice a day but I know I can't possibly 'listen' to everything that is being said. On Facebook, I tune in at least three times a day, because I get plenty of questions via my business page. Plus I'm interested to see how organizations and companies are using their pages to communicate. I'm also documenting my son's first year of life on my Facebook personal page (probably much to his dismay, once he grows up). And blogs? I subscribe to many blogs, vlogs and audioblogs, so a look to the subject line and a quick scan means they're read, explored, or stored. Talk about economy of attention! So no, I don't really unplug for more than a day at a time.

Having said that, it's my business to stay up with the Joneses of the internet. So I don't advocate everyone be so hyper-connected. Instead, it's absolutely achievable for all creatures great and small to develop a workflow for their social media presence that enables content to be developed in blocks, scheduled out by the week, checking in twice daily and measuring success month-on-month. It takes time, a solid strategy, and planning, but when done well has game-changing results!

Do you get the sense that social media is a significant tool for change?

Within our social networks are active communities of people connecting in real and important ways online, talking about how we can solve some of the big issues of our time and make our planet a safer place. So social media has become a platform for change as individuals, brands, and multinationals join an exciting grassroots movement, led from the bottom up.

What this has shown us is that change is possible on an individual, local level and that it can be heard and gain support in such a way as to have far-reaching, global consequences.

I always look to the leaders who are trailblazing, sharing information and ideas, teaching others, connecting people, and, through their own influential social networks, starting a wave and making change happen.

And every day I remind myself of some wise words, pinned to my noticeboard: 'What would you do if you knew you couldn't fail?'

The mind is naturally radiant and pure. The mind is shining. It is because of visiting forces that we suffer.
~ *Sharon Salzberg*

A highly developed mind is empty of the fears, anxieties, attachments, discriminations, judgments, and other limited modes of thinking. These negative states arise within the mind naturally, but the length of their stay and the intensity of their impact depend on whether we hold onto these "visiting forces." Kensho is an advanced state of consciousness in the Zen tradition, reflecting a highly developed quality of the human mind, including an ability to operate with focused concentration, equanimity, and tranquility.

14

NEURO-WHAT?

The human brain is the last, and greatest, scientific frontier. It is truly an internal cosmos that lies contained within our skulls. The more than 100 billion nerve cells and trillion supporting cells that make up your brain and mine constitute the most elaborate structure in the known universe.

~ Leon Kass

When we think of the dazzling complexities of the brain with its billions of nerve cells called neurons tangled in an intricate web, it is difficult to imagine how we could even begin to understand such an immense jumble of circuitry. From thought patterns to emotions, every facet of human expression is to be found within the extraordinary capacity of our grey and white matter. How does this mysterious three pound organ hold such sway over the matters of life, death, consciousness, perception, sleep, and so much more? And more importantly, are we born with a brain that achieves its optimal state and then fails, little by little, as each year passes?

Answering these questions has sparked all manner of fresh new debate and at least one major scientific breakthrough. It seems the human brain may be more capable of changing, growing, and re-wiring itself than was ever dreamed possible in the 20th century.

Welcome to the age of *neuroplasticity*. If you're not familiar with this term, then you may not, happily, be "of a certain age" or you may simply not have been exposed to one of the most fascinating discoveries of our time. Neuroplasticity refers to the structural and functional changes that occur in the brain through training and experience. Arguably, the most exciting element of this discovery is that we now know that our brains are capable of ever-evolving potential. If you are under the age of about thirty-five, this may not be something that catches your atten-tion, but to many in the throes of middle age or to many suffering from neurodegenerative disease, the idea that we can now transform the mind by changing the brain is compelling, to say the least.

Neuroplasticity has arguably become the catchphrase of the last decade. Adult brains are now thought to be more adaptable, more capable of reprogramming themselves than was once thought. This could have exciting and far-reaching implications for our physical and mental health.

How? It's all correlated with ongoing intellectual stimulation and the learning of new tasks. When we develop new interests and activi-ties that we are passionate about or we perform specific brain exer-cises, we enhance our brain's ability to become more proficient, while at the same time enhancing our memory. If we engage in activities that utilize our minds, we build up our "cognitive reserve".

Mark Fenske, an associate professor at the University of Guelph, Ontario, explains neuroplasticity this way:

One of the key discoveries is that focused practice at specific tasks can lead to changes in the function and physical structure of the brain throughout our lives. Such adaptability is known as experience-dependent neuroplasticity.

Consider the drivers of London's elite Black Cabs. Their experience memorizing city routes and landmarks has been associated with size increases in regions of the hippocampus, a part of the medial temporal lobe involved in spatial navigation and memory.[59]

⧼✦⧽

With modern parts atop old ones, the brain is like an iPod built around an eight-track cassette player.
~Sharon Begley

Brave New Brain: An Interview with Dr. Sandra Bond Chapman

Sandra Bond Chapman, Ph.D., is founder and chief director of the Center for BrainHealth, Dee Wyly Distinguished Professor in BrainHealth, and Professor in the School of Behavioral and Brain Sciences at The University of Texas at Dallas.

As Chief Director of the Center for BrainHealth, her vision is for the Center to become an international focal point for new discoveries in brain health by applying the latest in brain research to treatments that are faster and more effective than anything that has come before. On the new frontier of brain research, Dr. Bond Chapman is collaborating with scientists across the country and around the world to solve some of the most important issues concerning the brain and its health.

Dr. Bond Chapman is dedicated to making her leading-edge research serve as a national public health road map both in terms of discovering ways to maintain cognitive health into late life and building critical thinking and reasoning skills in today's youth. I asked her to weigh in on current brain research and her work with the Center for BrainHealth.

You champion the message that the brain is one of the most modifiable parts of our whole body. Can you expand upon this statement?

Years ago, science and medicine held that our brain was unalterable, operating much like a computer with a fixed memory and processing power. But now, science has reversed these beliefs that were once widely held. Our brain continues to grow, change, and repair itself throughout our lifetime, forming new, complex connections throughout our lives. We have considerable control over our own brain function, since much depends on experience and how we use our brain. Brain plasticity refers to the brain's ability to be changed, modified, and repaired. The changes can consist of building new brain cells, forming new connections, or strengthening old ones. Our brain changes moment to moment in response to each new experience or new process of learning or even an intensified application of our existing areas of expertise.

Tell us about the cognitive assessment offered at the Center for BrainHealth that you often refer to as the "neck up check up" (officially known as the BrainHealth Fitness Checkup). Is this type of "brain physical" something that companies should be offering their leaders and employees to identify personal strengths and areas of improvement with the end in mind as well of sustaining productivity?

Based on more than two decades of Center for BrainHealth research, the BrainHealth Fitness Checkup is a unique two-hour cognitive assessment and one-hour feedback session that examines vital brain functioning abilities and establishes a benchmark of cognitive reserve in pivotal areas of higher-order mental functioning, such as integrated reasoning, innovative thinking, strategic learning, and mental flexibility. Many companies would benefit from offering their employees the opportunity to take the BrainHealth Fitness Check-up. Businesses spend millions of dollars to improve job specific technical skills and encourage physical fitness and health. Yet at the same time meager resources are directed to the brain's health and fitness, even though it is the most complex yet dynamically modifiable part of our body, one that offers the highest return on investment of time and energy. In fact, our brain is the most important aspect of our health and should be assigned a role of the highest importance at the very focal point of our attentions.

In a recent "Harvard Business Review" blog, David Rock, founder of the NeuroLeadership Institute wrote, "I believe that neuroscience research will be a significant factor in reshaping how we define leadership, select leaders, and design leadership development programs."[60] What are your thoughts and experience regarding neuroscience research and how it relates to corporate leadership?

At the Center for BrainHealth, our research encompasses the entire human lifespan. One of the main areas of study that we focus on is the teenage brain. The brain goes through more changes in the teenage years than at any other point in development except the first two years of life. Our research has shown that emphasis on mechanistic, rote fact-learning, rather than reasoned thinking makes classroom learning less engaging for students and less conducive to their achieving their highest level of cognitive potential. Based on a recent economic forecast, every year that we fail to train youth in strategic thinking and advanced reasoning, we fail in effect to invest in the future of our human cognitive capital and thus fail to produce more well-prepared leaders.

As things stand now, we are not preparing our youth for a workplace where information is constantly changing. Success should be defined by the ability to flexibly engage the mind in solving new problems and even identifying problems that do not exist yet. Corporate leadership should be developing training programs that foster leaders and should be seeking individuals who are not frustrated by change, but rather are inspired and challenged when moving from the known to the unknown. We have found that knowledge is not by definition power in the workplace of today or tomorrow. At the Center for BrainHealth, we are, in fact, training people to move from being knowledge seekers to being strategic thinkers.

In your blog, "Tips to Improve Brain Health For Every Generation", you state: "The lure of technology is rewiring our brains in detrimental ways, leading to weakened focus, shallower thinking, a reduction of creativity and forward thinking, and a diminished ability to shut out irrelevant information, all decreasing our brain's potential."[61] How can we effectively combat the negative effects of information overload on the brain?

Our brain is capable of processing 400 billion pieces of information in a minute, but at great cost. In this day of information overload, individuals are rapidly losing critical aspects of brainpower due to impaired strategic attention. An individual's capacity to sift through information effectively is diminished, and this prevents them from blocking unnecessary and less relevant information. To combat information overload, it's important to laser focus on a task for brief intervals, block extraneous details, and efficiently manage the wealth of information at your fingertips. For example, turn off your email notification or silence your cell phone when thinking strategically or focusing on a task at hand. We must constantly build a brain that knows when to block and stop information seeking.

The emphasis on brain-fitness is evident in your work and research, which ultimately maximizes cognitive function in both people with healthy brains and those with brain injury or disease. What are some examples of brain-fitness activities that will boost lasting brain health?

a) Limit multitasking. Multitasking diminishes mental productivity, elevates brain fatigue, and increases stress.
b) Sleep. Make sure you regularly get 7-8 hours of sleep. Information is consolidated in the brain at a deeper level of understanding during sleep.

c) Exercise. Get 30 minutes of aerobic exercise 3-4 times a week to improve memory and increase attention and concentration and brain blood flow in the memory brain area.

d) Construct bottom-line messages from task assignment reading, training seminars, articles, the movies you see, or the books you read. Abstracting novel ideas versus remembering a litany of facts builds a brain that has an enhanced long-term memory for global ideas and the ability to retrieve fundamental facts.

e) Laser focus on important tasks. Block out information that is relatively unimportant. Limiting the intake of information is a key brain function associated with brain health.

f) Stay motivated. A motivated brain builds faster and more robust neural connections. Identify your passion and learn more about it.

What type of brain fitness programs do you personally employ to instill clarity and balance in both your own private and professional life?

I push my brain never to accept the status quo and to keep thinking of better ways to advance brain health. I am inspired mentally by creating new avenues for the application of ideas, by learning new things all the time, and by critiquing my own work and seeking the same from others.

Every man can, if he so desires, become the sculptor of his own brain.
~ *Santiago Ramon y Cajal*

In the following interview, Chief Scientific Officer Dr. Michael Merzenich of Posit Science explains why brain health is receiving increased attention and also highlights neuroscientific breakthroughs and the potential ramifications of these advances.[62] Posit Science is a company comprised of a global team of scientists who build scientifically validated, non-invasive programs for improving brain health. These practical tools act on breakthroughs in the science of brain plasticity – the ability of the brain to change itself at any age.

For years we've received advice on the importance of having a healthy heart. Recently, we have been receiving similar advice about brain health. Why is the brain getting more attention recently?

Well, the heart is a vital organ and deserves the attention. But brain health is equally important. The brain grows and sustains our human abilities, and its problems are expressed as our disabilities. The brain defines us, after all, as the person that we are. Have you ever witnessed the slow deterioration of a loved one with Alzheimer's? If so, you have watched the person that you knew and loved slowly fade away, even while their body may have remained relatively healthy.

Scientists used to believe that the brain developed all of its major functionality – that is, the 'wiring' of the brain that supports hearing, seeing, feeling, thinking, emotions, and the control of movements – in early infancy. The 'mature' brain was thought to be unchangeable, like a computer with all its wires permanently soldered together.

Recently, however, there has been a revolution in our thinking. We now know that the brain is constantly revising itself. Physical brain change occurs every time we learn something new. This new finding – that adult brains are malleable – has far-reaching implications for our understanding of brain fitness. We refer to this capacity for continuous physical, chemical, and functional brain change as 'brain plasticity' or 'neuroplasticity.'

How does neuroplasticity, or the brain's ability to rewire itself, relate to brain health?

In the case of aging, the plasticity of the brain can have negative consequences. The brain of the average mature adult actually shrinks, as the brain machinery supporting hearing, seeing, feeling, thinking, emotion, and movement control degrades over time. These changes occur to a large extent precisely because mature individuals are less likely to use their brains in the specific ways that are required to sustain our cognitive abilities. In the case of other neurological and psychiatric conditions such as schizophrenia or Parkinson's disease, large-scale neuroplasticity actually plays a powerful part in distorting the brain's chemistry and ability to function. On the brighter side of the equation, the breakthrough in neuroplasticity research has revealed strategies by which we can restrengthen the brain's functionality.

What types of strategies can we use to restrengthen the brain's functionality?

We need to constantly use and develop our brain's machinery through learning. This does not mean academic learning (although that is always useful). It means practicing targeted activities that engage the senses and our memories and that involve the production of refined movements. By applying the breakthroughs in neuroplasticity to the development of brain health tools, scientists can help people maintain – and possibly restore – their cognitive abilities.

What types of activities can engage the senses and memory?

To keep our senses and memory healthy, it is very important that we spend time each day in intensive, effortful learning that requires our close attention. Under these conditions, our faculties can remain remarkably well preserved. For example, professional musicians can sustain their craft at the highest level of ability until the end of life, but only if they practice almost every day, using an intensive and closely attentive learning strategy. Their careful listening, precision of movement, accurate reading, and complex recourse to memory are essential for sustaining their great skills. If a violinist in an orchestra does not practise intensely over the period of just a month, other musicians around her will begin to ask, 'What's wrong with her?'

Are you saying, in essence, that we need to exercise our brains?

Absolutely! Maintaining a healthy brain requires that we all have to work hard to sustain the crucial abilities that define what we can and cannot do, that support the person that we are.

The Beautiful Brain: An Interview with Noah Hutton

These last ten years have ushered in a new era of scientific research into the brain that is based on the theory of neuroplasticity. Scientific data dating back any further than the year 2000 is now considered to be knowledge of "historical" significance only and is discounted within the confines of current research endeavors as an outdated representation. fMRI data has set the stage for a renaissance in brain research, and the scientific community is delving eagerly at full throttle into uncovering the untold capacities of the mind.

With this rekindling of hope in brain revitalization comes a myriad of scientific missions dedicated to understanding the brain and the mysteries of the mind. One such undertaking which, if successful, will represent a scientific breakthrough of almost biblical proportions, is called The Blue Brain Project.

The Blue Brain Project is a collaboration between the École Polytechnique Fédérale in Lausanne, Switzerland, and IBM. The purpose of the project is to reverse engineer a human brain, using supercomputers and a biologically accurate model of neuronal activity. Neuroscientist Henry Markram, the leader of the project, is attempting to demystify the innumerable cellular connections in the brain and how they link together. "There is still so much that we don't know about the brain," he says. "The Blue Brain Project is about showing people the whole."

Enter documentary filmmaker Noah Hutton who sheds further light in the interview that follows below. For the next ten years, Hutton will be working on a documentary about The Blue Brain Project in Lausanne, Switzerland.

The son of actors Timothy Hutton and Debra Winger, Hutton is a graduate of Wesleyan University, where he studied art history and neuroscience. He began his ten-year journey with the Blue Brain project in the fall of 2009. He is also the Founder and Contributing Editor of *The Beautiful Brain*, a webzine that "explores the latest findings from the ever-growing field of neuroscience through monthly podcasts, essays, and reviews, with particular attention to the dialogue between the arts and sciences."

How would you describe the field of neuroscience and how did you become fascinated by it?

The field of neuroscience is one of the last bastions of scientific inquiry on this planet. Together with quantum physics, neuroscience represents some of the most daunting, unanswered questions in all of science. How can we account for the complexities of human thought through what appears on the surface as the firing of a limited amount of cells between our ears? We find ourselves looking into the brain as if we were the great explorers of the 15th and 16th centuries, poised to discover new lands that will radically transform our idea of the world. This century will truly be the century of the brain.

I became fascinated by neuroscience when I read a book by cognitive scientist Andrew Newberg called *Why God Won't Go Away* which presented his research into the brains of monks, nuns, and other religious people who claim to have transcendental, out-of-body experiences while meditating or praying. He presented fMRI data after putting these subjects under a scanner that correlated their

out-of-body experiences to a drop in activity in the posterior parietal lobe, an area that has been tied to our ability to orient ourselves
in space. I knew then that this was a field that had the potential to
answer some of our deepest questions. There is no loss of awe in
doing so. If anything, there is the sense of wonder that millions of
years of evolution have shaped such a beautifully complex organ.

*The on-line magazine you founded, "The Beautiful Brain" encapsulates "the art
and science of the human mind". Could you tell us more about your concept for
the magazine and what you hope to achieve through this medium?*

I started the magazine and podcast because I had been looking
for something like it and couldn't find anything. I studied art history
and neuroscience in college and starting *The Beautiful Brain* was originally my way of staying engaged in this dialogue between the brain
sciences and the arts, even while I provided content to our readers
and listeners that they hopefully have found interesting. Since starting the magazine, we've grown quickly to a point where we're receiving around eight hundred unique visits a day and have thousands of
subscribers to our podcast.

The concept for the magazine is to humanize the sciences which
often feel far too cold and overcomplicated. Our aim is to beautify
the brain for our readers and listeners, both by presenting the work
of artists who are inspired by the brain and by presenting reviews and
essays that expound on the beauty of this wonderfully complex organ
and all its various functions and processes. The overall goal, in fact,
is to open the doors onto neuroscience for those who would otherwise never pay attention. A secondary goal is to further the dialogue
between the arts and sciences, to encourage crosstalk between disciplines, and foster an understanding that science and art are equally
valid ways — and equally beautiful ways, I might add — to understand
ourselves, this world we find ourselves in, and the people we find
ourselves around.

You are filming a documentary that will span the course of the next ten years and is called the Blue Brain Project. Could you tell us more about this and briefly describe the project for us?

For the next ten years, I will be taking a trip once a year to Lausanne, Switzerland, to document the progress of The Blue Brain Project, one of the most ambitious undertakings in modern neuroscience. Using IBM supercomputers to model each and every neuron in the brain, Henry Markram has estimated that the project will have a full simulation of a human brain built in ten years. Whether they succeed or not, a film should be made to document this pursuit, one of the holy grails of modern science. I will be interviewing Markram every year and filming around his lab, and every year I will post a short video update of the project on The Beautiful Brain website. I posted the first one early this year, and it spread very quickly around the internet, with the website Boing Boing posting it on their frontpage. My hope is to create an audience for the film year by year with these updates, so that in ten years there will be a built-in audience for the film release, that is to say, the thousands of people who have watched a film come together over the course of a decade.

This is such an astounding scientific undertaking. Do you get the sense that you are involved in something unmatched in terms of ground-breaking neuroscience research? What was it like visiting the Blue Brain lab in Switzerland?

The Blue Brain Project is certainly unmatched in its scope and in its goals. Whether or not a human brain is successfully simulated, the project will begin to yield results within a few years that will have significant impacts on a wide range of brain diseases and injuries. The Blue Brain Project is comparable to the Human Genome Project in its scope and in the potential of its findings to dramatically affect modern science, as well as the public's conception of the human body.

When I visited the Blue Brain lab this past fall, I had the feeling that I was stepping into a shrine of modern science. For those who grasp the scope of this project, there is an awesome sense of the future unfolding before us. It was like stepping onto a bridge that's being built in front of your eyes.

This research has the potential to help so many people in terms of studying disease, medicine, and brain function, but do you think there will be any trepidation or backlash from religious groups or others concerning the ethics of building a human brain model?

I do anticipate significant backlash if we approach a functioning model of a human brain. It's difficult to predict the nature of a backlash that's probably a decade or more in the future, but there will certainly be groups of people who fear this development and speak out against it. But the findings have the potential to cure many neurodegenerative conditions and help millions of people around the world. It won't be the findings themselves that people should fear. It will be the manipulation of those findings. If people use a brain model for purposes of harm, that's a reason for trepidation. The achievement itself should not be condemned. It's part of the awesome march of science in the annals of progress, and its results can and will certainly be harnessed for the betterment of humanity.

Do you feel that your knowledge of neuroscience and an understanding of the nuances of brain function allow you to observe life through a different lens?

I believe that, since I began to seriously study neuroscience while I was in college, my worldview has significantly changed and I live life differently. One must penetrate the hard science to truly grasp the complexity of the brain. Having done so, I find that its complexity is the source of a deep and humbling awe in my life. It is also empowering. I now understand that, as I move through each day, I have an active hand in shaping my brain and its thoughts. From taking in hand decisions on what I should dwell on, what I should eliminate, and what I should improve, I've come to feel more ownership over my own life. Understanding that the brain is plastic is another key. We always have the ability to change. Even the most deeply ingrained habits and patterns of behavior can be changed.

Then there is the intellectual relationship a student of science has with the brain, which is akin to an architecture student stepping into a gothic cathedral. Evolution is the ultimate artist, shaping organisms through chance mutations, environmental adaptations, and a range of other factors, having left us with this three-pound organ that is the seat of each of our personal universes.

It is interesting that you have chosen a career path with a media production company that enables you to document other people's lives and scenarios. In a way it's like getting inside someone's brain to paint a picture of the way they observe and experience life. Do you feel that there is an integration of art and science in your work?

I'm not sure how scientific my actual film work is. But I do hope to make films about science and to open the door to an appreciation of science for others. I consider the documentary filmmaking I'm currently engaged in as a a kind of research for the narrative films I hope to make in the future. I'm learning about humanity. I'm documenting people, places, and projects that interest me, and many of these have to do with a dialogue between the arts and sciences. I believe that the most fulfilling experience of this world comes from an understanding and appreciation of both science and art, and it is that experience which guides my work.

Who or what inspires you in your work?

There are some heroes I think of often for inspiration. Henry Markram is certainly one of them. The principle that motivates me the most is the entrepreneurial spirit, be it in science or art. It's the idea that you shouldn't wait for permission to do something. If you feel moved by something, if you feel a passion to create, you must do it. I strive to spend less time talking myself out of doing something and more time giving it a try.

TRY THIS

Use It, So You Don't Lose It

You've probably heard the phrase "use it or lose it." But how can you "use it" effectively?

The story in brief: Keep learning. Activities you have already mastered, even if you found them challenging at one point, won't do your brain much good.

Based on their detailed understanding of the brain, neuroscientists suggest you choose activities that fit these criteria:

1. They should teach you something new. The brain is a learning machine. To keep it strong, you must continually develop new skills.
2. They should be challenging. Activities should command your full and close attention, in order to drive chemical changes in the brain.
3. They should be progressive. You can begin a new activity at an easy level, but you should continually challenge yourself to stay at the edge of your performance abilities, at your "threshold", so that you improve. This goes for older, longer-standing activities you enjoy too. Pushing yourself to improve will help your brain.
4. They should engage your great brain processing systems. Tasks in which you must make fine distinctions about what

you hear, see, or feel and in which you must use that information to achieve complex goals drive the brain to change its abilities on different levels.

5. They should be rewarding. Rewards amplify brain changes, leading to improved learning and memory. They turn up the production of crucial brain chemicals that contribute to learning, memory, and good spirits.

6. They should be novel or surprising. New, positive, and surprising experiences exercise that part of the brain's machinery that makes you bright and alert.

On the face of it, it might sound hard to find activities that meet all of these criteria. But the truth is that many new activities you undertake will meet most of them, whether it be learning to cha-cha, improving your Spanish, taking up juggling, or whatever you choose. If you put in the right level of effort, they will all fit the following criteria:

They will challenge your brain (i.e. prompt the comment, "It's hard!").

They will get progressively harder (i.e. cause you to move on from Lesson 1 to Lesson 2).

They will engage several brain systems (i.e. your motor skills, as well as your ability to listen and your visual system).

They will reward you (i.e. elicit satisfaction, so that you end by saying, "I can finally do that!").

They will fill you with surprise (i.e. bring on the question, "What comes next?").

(Reprinted with permission from www.positscience.com, 2010)

Escapist activity takes us away from our path of awakening, and away from nature to be joyful toward ourselves and the people in our lives — our family, our friends, our co-workers, our neighbors — people who truly matter and for whom we make a difference.

Let me respectfully remind you
Life and death are of supreme importance
Time swiftly passes by and opportunity is lost
Each of us should strive to awaken...
Awaken!
Take heed!
This night your days are diminished by one.
Do not squander this gift of life.
~ Traditional Zen Buddhist Evening Gata (prayer)

15

DISTRACTIONS AND DOGMA

You don't exist if you aren't famous.
~ *Teenage Paparazzo, HBO Films, 2010*

Do you remember the 1997 movie *Wag the Dog*? The movie, a dark comedy, begins with a major White House scandal. Just a few weeks before an election, the President is accused of inappropriate behavior with a young girl visiting the Oval Office. By all accounts, he is guilty, and that's when the duplicity and the unraveling of all moral parameters begin.

White House spin-doctor Conrad Brean (Robert De Niro) is called in to troubleshoot. He engineers a plan to divert the public's attention away from the scandal. Brean does this by hiring a Hollywood producer named Stanley Motts (Dustin Hoffman) to create a fictional war that can distract America's voters and allow the President to get back to protecting the free world.

This appalling sleight of hand is pulled off by computer geeks and actors working in front of blue screens. A former psychiatric patient becomes the fake campaign's war hero. In no time at all, the country's voters buy into this prefabricated madness, and the scandal is forgotten.

Even across the decades, the ironic message of *Wag the Dog* continues to resonate.

From local news stories to an entire TV channel devoted to the subject, "wag the dog" scenarios play out today in politics, on Wall Street, in the judicial system, and in other realms that exercise their attraction on the volatile interest of the public. But all of this pales in comparison to the prevailing allure of America's culture of celebrity.

Day after day, it seems that celebrity "journalism" is increasingly replacing more traditional stories on TV, in print, and on the internet. The end product is "news" that is increasingly more entertainment focused or titillating. Thanks to the media, celebrities have been elevated to near-mythical status, whether they deserve the accolades or not. Although this phenomenon is not new, the powerful reach of internet sites devoted to celebrity gossip has morphed this fixation into obsession. Whether it be marital infidelities, criminal investigations, embarrassing public brawls, shopping sprees, diet secrets, or fashion and beauty tips…it's all fair game. It has also become a very lucrative business.

Hollywood TV is the latest destination of online celebrity news seekers. Within their first year, Hollywood TV shot up to a top five celebrity gossip website with an average of a million views per day and growing. As the foremost supplier of celebrity content to all the major TV networks as well as the owner of their own branded, syndicated TV show, Hollywood TV is seen in 270 countries and by over one billion viewers.

❦

...it's time that we start making movies about this weird culture that we now live in. People think they have access to people, or they idealize people that are absolutely destroyed inside, but look great from the outside...and how hopeless that is.

~ *Gemma Arterton*[63]

In his critically acclaimed documentary *Teenage Paparazzo*, actor/director Adrian Grenier goes behind the lens of 13 year-old Hollywood paparazzo, Austin Visschedyk, and explores the heroes and villains of our tabloid-crazed society.

"It's a symptom of what's happening in our culture," Grenier comments, "with technology taking over...and all of us taking pictures... of taking pictures. I think, in a lot of ways, celebrities represent the American dream. We're perceived to have more money... more fun...which may or may not be true...and to indulge without the consequences, although that's not true."[64]

When you have the paparazzi hiding in the bushes outside your home, the only thing you can control is how you respond publicly.
~ *Portia de Rossi*

"Paparazzo", the singular form of the word "paparazzi", is taken from the Italian word for mosquito or "buzzing insect". It's easy to make the comparison.

This hunter-gatherer of sorts has gone from a mere annoyance to a dangerously defiant risk-taker in recent years. We all remember one of the most tragic events involving celebrity photojournalists: In August of 1997, Lady Diana, Princess of Wales, was killed in a car accident while being chased by the paparazzi in Paris.

No one can argue that the root of the paparazzi's relentless pursuit stems from the fact that there's a profitable payday for these photographs.

Recently, the state of California passed a law attempting to quell some of the madness. In the summer of 2010, the legislature passed a bill that punishes reckless photographers with harsh penalties, including possible imprisonment.[65] Under the new law, photographers who break traffic laws or interfere with the operation of a celebrity's car could receive a maximum $5,000 fine and one-year imprisonment.

The line between fiction and reality is getting blurred.
~ *Adrian Grenier, Teenage Paparazzo*

As a celebrity-obsessed culture, are we the ones feeding into this spectator sport of attention and diversion by our insatiable desire for more?

Psychologists have come up with a term to describe our obsession: para-social relationships. Para-social relationships occur in a somewhat alienated and dysfunctional society. It means in fact that we begin to believe we have a bona fide relationship with a celebrity, merely because we know so much about them, even though we've never met them. Simply put, it's a superficial connection with an image emanating from a screen. Adrian Grenier describes it as "a weird, one-way relationship, where we don't actually know the people on TV but we feel like we do."

Is it a dangerous fixation or simply escapism? I asked the journalists who cover celebrity culture to weigh in on this issue.

"So long as media platforms transform and expand, so, too, will our coverage of celebrity culture," says American novelist and celebrity writer Malina Saval.

"Celebrities and entertainment have always been a means of escape for many people in our society," she says.

"Our world can be a toxic place full of unhappy news and unfortunate life circumstances. Fixating on celebrities and movie stars is a way by which we can dissipate some of this pain and focus our attention on people and things that from our perspective are not really grounded in reality.

For example, we can read about a celebrity revealing some of her own personal struggles in an article and identify with her experience to the extent that it makes us feel better about our own personal issues. It's classic Schadenfreude," says Saval.

It's also a perfect defense mechanism against our own day-to-day problems. "If a movie star is going through a rough time in life, then we can suddenly feel better about ourselves," says Saval.

"Many of us would love to be wealthy, well-known, beautiful, and befriended by other beautiful, rich people.... On the other hand, we refer to movie stars as a way of self-reflection. We identify with certain celebrities because their upbringings mirror ours or they've experienced something in life that we have. For example, when celebrity sisters squabble with their mother, we relate to it. When we share any similarity with a celebrity, it makes us feel as though, in a tiny way, we're just as good as they are and they're just as hum-drum and normal as us," she says.

That desire to be like Hollywood's rich and famous has escalated to extremes in recent years, particularly in terms of the number of women and men who undergo plastic surgery to look like their favorite stars.

"That," says Saval, "can be deeply detrimental to our levels of self-esteem."

Saval is certainly not the only person who holds this opinion. Talk show hosts like Dr. Phil have tackled this subject numerous times on daytime television. And Dr. Phil's point of view on this topic is unmistakably on the mark. Americans *are* obsessed with celebrities. They *are* fixated on entertainment magazines and TV shows. Sadly, this excessive infatuation with their favorite celebrity's life, loves, and travails is wreaking havoc on the self-esteem of millions of North Americans.

To combat this obsession, Dr. Phil has adopted the motto, "Don't be a sucker."

As Dr. Phil points out again and again, we as a society have allowed ourselves to be duped by a marketing machine. And the price we have paid for that is our self-esteem.

Perhaps the greatest irony of all is that celebrities themselves are getting in on the action, updating fans with a wide variety of information on Twitter, Facebook, and blogs.

Certain celebrities are using the medium to bring attention to altruistic causes but other stars repeatedly send out frivolous or mundane updates into the ether. Their pet fell ill. They shopped for new clothes. They're jetting off to a private island to de-stress. They tell why they walked away from a bad romance. And readers lap it up.

"I can't speak for society 30 or 40 years ago, but inarguably today we have much more sophisticated means of tracking celebrities: TMZ, Twitter, Facebook, and blogs. Not only are we stalking celebs. They are alerting us via status updates and tweets on their daily goings-on," says Saval.

Do we care if these news flashes are true? Not really, says Saval. We care "as long as it's a good story."

That said, each day news wires are full of momentous news stories that have nothing to do with celebrities. Rather they touch on the economy, ecology, wars, and world hunger, for example. There are a myriad of real issues that news outlets and audiences should be focusing on. Some may argue that this is all just part and parcel of our need for escapism. Others, however, may view this fixation with celebrity as a red flag.

"Without that juicy daily fix of who's dating who and who wore what, our world spins in far less interesting ways, so millions of people believe," says Constance Droganes, movie critic for CTV. ca (Canada's major TV network) and former contributor for People Magazine.

"That's no big surprise, really," she explains. From the days of Roman spectacles in the Coliseum to the mega-shows produced by P.T. Barnum, audiences have bought into these amusing distractions to lessen their dull, daily grind. And certainly, no one can blame a person for wanting a good laugh or a pleasant distraction.

"But the world changes.

"This is the big question I think we all need to consider: what qualifies as 'real', well-researched entertainment news and what is merely tabloid junk? Our tabloid culture is growing stronger, faster, and as many would argue, less responsible than ever especially in the internet age.

"As a result, our feverish consumption of celebrity gossip has escalated to the point where breaking news about a Hollywood star's hair may seem more attention-worthy to some people than the crash on Wall Street.

"I'm not saying that everyone is guilty of this," continues Droganes. "Not at all. But it's a dangerous skew, and one that continues to blur the lines between what is news and what is merely fluff filling air time. The fact that many people cannot see the difference is vastly disturbing to me.

"Once the world huddled around radios and listened transfixed, as Winston Churchill and Franklin Roosevelt spoke of looming war. People watched their televisions in the 1960s, listening as John F. Kennedy and Martin Luther King Jr. delivered inspirational messages of change.

"Fast-forward four decades and what do we find?" she says. "The war in Iraq rages on. North Americans struggle to find jobs. Oil spills and other eco-disasters have wreaked havoc on our environment. The threat of terrorism is everywhere.

"Even as Africa's poor die from hunger and Japan lies in ruins after a devastating earthquake, some seemed more concerned about a celebrity's fashion faux pas than the gravity of lives being lost around the world.

"This is the monster that the media has helped create over the last 10 years. In its wake, a generation of insatiable, 'quick-time' news consumers exists that prefers the light and trite above all else. They live it. They breathe it. Sadly, that preference is only making us far less informed," says Droganes.

"Looking ahead, it is hard to gauge where this passion for celebrity will lead, especially as technology and the means to access news speed up. As always, the onus is on us to discern true news from marketed hype."

As Droganes concludes, "I think there will always be a place in this world for wonderfully-written exposés on a real talent, as well as thoughtful, well-researched pieces that shed new light on the entertainment industry. If this sort of balance remains, the public should see the other distracting kind of celebrity buzz for what it is."

The Star Effect: An Interview with Anna David

Pop culture author and reporter Anna David has spent years working in the entertainment industry. The changes she has seen in it are enormous. But nothing compares to the combination of technology and tabloid journalism that has shaped a new generation of ardent celebrity devotees.

In your article "Sometimes Stardom Sucks", which appeared in "Cosmopolitan" in 2005, you quote Elayne Rapping, PhD, professor of American Studies at the University of Buffalo, as saying: "We used to admire them from afar, but now we want to feel like we know celebrities personally, as if they're our neighbors or friends. We want to know the intimate details of their lives..."

Do you feel our society's obsession with celebrity culture has escalated in the last five years? Have we gone overboard?

I think our obsession with celebrity culture has grown in exponential leaps and bounds. When many celebrity magazines went to a weekly format, the 'write-around', which is to say, pieces that didn't require the celebrity's participation for them to be published, became the norm. As a result, the people who cover Hollywood started digging their nails in. I believe that it's the personal publicists who are at fault in this scenario, as many of them played power games with journalists and were naïve enough to think they could control the story if access to the celebrities was limited. The media soon tired of these tactics and began going to other sources who were willing to 'dish dirt' rather than trying to get the story from the subjects themselves. The launch of Perez Hilton and TMZ took this phenomenon even further.

At the publication where I worked as a journalist covering celebrities in the late 90s, there was a certain code you complied with. It was forbidden, for example, to 'out' someone as gay or write about an extra-marital affair. Now these things are considered not just fair game, but news the public actually feels entitled to.

It's a chicken and egg situation. As the public becomes more obsessed with celebrity culture due to the proliferation of entertainment news, it follows that the media are asked to pursue more and more stories. And the more outrageous these are, the better.

As a reporter and writer working on celebrity pieces, do you feel you have to "dig for dirt" to get the upper hand on your competitors or to please your editors?

I know I felt that way when I was on contract with celebrity publications in the past. I couldn't turn something in that wasn't 'dishy', and that meant that I had to ask things I wasn't comfortable with. I remember one of my bosses calling me one day and asking me to stand outside a restaurant all day stalking celebrities who might show up. That was the day that I said, 'I got a college degree for this? No more.'

Do you feel celebrity stories often distract us from the "real" hard news stories of the day? If so, what does this reflect about our culture?

I must confess that I'm the first person to allow celebrity stories to distract me from the hard news stories, which I guess is the point. If you're not interested in a celebrity scandal, you're not going to click on those stories online.

The fascination with celebrity news is a form of escape that has been prominent for decades. In the 40s, Walter Winchell's gossip column purportedly reached 90% of the American public. It may sound off-putting, but it feeds our guilty pleasure to read about people who have more money and adulation than most of us will ever dream of having and to see that their lives are just as messed up, if not more so, than our own. In a sense, it's all very reassuring.

TRY THIS

So what are we to conclude from all this? I think it makes sense for us to be aware of the very natural temptation we have to idealize celebrities whom we really don't know, putting many of them on pedestals when in fact they're human beings who must rise to the challenges of life just like the rest of us. The pitfalls that await us at the other extreme, however, can be just as daunting. A preoccupation with hard-hitting news, political dogma or catastrophic events doesn't necessarily serve us any better. Being bombarded by negative messages that further fuel our fears and dash our hopes is no less detrimental to our achievement of a sense of wisdom and balance as we regard the bittersweet spectacle of life with all its tragedies and triumphs. We need to be informed, yes, but watching negative events on television, as broadcasters continually play the same footage over and over again is not helpful in fostering a proper appreciation of the mystery and wonder of what it means to be human, especially when such events are beyond our control.

The lesson to me in all this is that we should be aware of the intoxicating pull, the desire, perhaps quite unconscious, to escape. We would gain far more in the way of equilibrium and insight into the human condition if we turned our focus inward instead. We need to come to terms on a deeper level with the fascination that the celebrities hold for us, our rapt absorption with their lives, just as we need to be aware of the distorted attention we pay to all the negative news events in the march of current affairs. This can only be achieved by working on the inner void, by taking a long close look at our lives and asking ourselves where our interests truly lie even as we watch the beguiling drama of life unfold.

*Even as a mother protects with her life
Her child, her only child,
So with a boundless heart
Should one cherish all living beings:
Radiating kindness over the entire world
Spreading upwards to the skies.*

~ from the Karaniya Metta Sutta

16

A GIVING SPIRIT

You give but little when you give of your possessions. It is when you give of yourself that you truly give.
~Kahlil Gibran

It is currently estimated that 30 million people in the United States practice yoga on a regular basis. In fact, if you asked most yoga die-hards, they would tell you that there is nothing like the combination of stretching, breath control, and meditation to revitalize the mind and body in response to the rigors of 21st century living.

The roots of yoga date back some 5,000 years. Yet the current impact of this age-old practice on our attitudes towards health and spirituality has been profound. People are looking for answers these days. Life moves too quickly much of the time, taxing our nervous system and overwhelming our immune response. As a result, we often feel burned out, anxious, and disconnected from ourselves and others. We long for the means to find true inner peace. These feelings have much to do with yoga's boom in recent years, and it's becoming the most rapidly growing health movement of our time.

The whole of us is so much greater than the sum of our parts.
~ *Sue Jones, Founder, yogaHope*

An organization called yogaHope is taking the practice of yoga one step further. This non-profit yoga outreach program, founded by Sue Jones of Boston, is dedicated to bringing the practice of yoga to underserved women in recovery or life transition. Jones and her team bring the benefits of yoga to prisons, drug and alcohol treatment centers, homeless shelters, and homes for battered women, as well as running programs for women transitioning from hospital treatment for eating disorders.

The practice of yoga has been shown to produce positive motivational change by helping women regain their vital center of energy, satisfaction, and stability. It also teaches mindfulness, impulse control, interpersonal relationship skills, and discernment in decision-making, as well as patience and acceptance of self and of the surrounding world. The practice of yoga can help reduce low self-esteem and poor body image and greatly improves a woman's sense of personal empowerment.
~ *yogaHope website, 2010*

We've all heard statistics regarding yoga's numerous benefits: reduced blood pressure, better sleep, lower heart rate, and increased strength and flexibility... but yoga can do much more than just improve fitness levels and restore frazzled nerves.

Take the story of Amy for example. The 27 year-old practitioner at the yogaHope centre in Boston had been coping with depression and drug addiction for years, but found the route to rehabilitation through yogaHope.

"By February 2007 I was completely strung out. I weighed 95 pounds. My skin was grey. The only time I was awake was to do drugs and I wanted to die. Out of desperation I checked into treatment on February 13, 2007. My life completely changed while I was in treatment. I was introduced to yoga through yogaHope. Because of yoga I found true happiness, love, and serenity. I have managed to stay sober since February 14, 2007 with the help of yoga and a 12 step program. Now I am a student at yogaHope and I hope to someday teach yoga, so I can give to other addicts and homeless people what was so freely given to me, the gift of yoga."

Through her intense research Jones discovered that trauma experienced either in childhood or later in life was a common denominator in those her programs served. For that reason Jones set out to treat trauma and in that way help women recover. Yoga has the inherent power to do this.

"It's not what's outside that's being changed; it's what's inside," says Jones.

When we commit to the yogic path through the physical asana practice, we are doing much more than just exercising our bodies. Although it is slowly becoming more accepted in the West, it is much more common in Asian thought to recognize the inseparability of the body, mind, and emotions. Chinese doctors insist that our organs are linked to our emotions, which affects our overall health, while Indian Ayurvedic doctors and yogis inform us of the interconnection between our state of mind, our breath, and our bodies. So, it naturally follows that the emotional impact of our experiences are imprinted into our bodies, affecting the balance of our vital energy and the harmony (or disharmony) of our whole system.
~ Sarah Powers, Yoga Journal website 2010

Clearly, yogaHope's therapeutic programs are enabling these troubled women to make profound, permanent changes in their lives.

The act of healing carries enormous weight, even while it is tempered with great optimism. Sue Jones' yogaHope program proves that we can learn to transform the "me" philosophy of years gone by

into the emerging "we are one" philosophy of our times. From scholarship programs to volunteer training, yogaHope exemplifies a new
desire to merge a call to healing with a charitable, spiritual attitude.

As the ancient yogis have espoused for centuries, when the mind
and body are aligned to a true purpose, all manner of positive changes
can occur in your world, even if that world is limited to your own
back yard.

Making the Mind-Body Connection: An Interview with Sue Jones

Sometimes you come across an individual who inspires you not
only on account of the work they do, but also because of their ability
to rise above their own strife and come out the other side triumphant.
Sue Jones is one of those people. The founder and executive director of yogaHope is a passionate advocate of integrating mind-body
practices in therapeutic settings to help survivors of trauma and those
suffering from depression, anxiety, and PTSD (post traumatic stress
disorder). She is currently developing a therapeutic approach called
Trauma Informed Mind-Body Programming, which is specifically
designed for women in crisis. I wanted to learn more about Jones'
altruistic work and her inspirational story.

What is yogaHope's mission statement?

Our mission is to provide rehabilitative yoga programs in facilities for women in acute crisis situations or life transformation. This
would include women undergoing treatment for substance abuse and
those in homeless facilities, as well as domestic violence survivors.

How many volunteers do you have now?

We have approximately twenty-five actively teaching volunteers
and four hundred volunteers who step up whenever we need them,

whether it be for an event or assistance with grants or donations. We have all kinds of volunteers on our list who do all sorts of things that go above and beyond teaching.

What areas do you serve?

We serve women in acute crisis situations that occur in a range of scenarios, from substance abuse treatment centers and homeless facilities to domestic violence safe houses. As we move forward with more trauma-focused programming that we are developing, we will be looking to expand our services to rape crisis centers. The thing that we discovered through this very intense research initiative was that the common denominator in the populations we serve is trauma, both early childhood trauma and trauma that occurs later in life. So it is that our programs are becoming more specifically designed for the treatment of trauma and helping women recover from it, which yoga does inherently. We have a limited time frame within which to help these women and we need to have openly stated target outcomes to prove that we are achieving them.

Yoga is a lifelong practice. The objective of the program is to give these women new, active, coping strategies for the stresses of life that they are going to encounter once they get out of their 'false living environment'. I say this, because in a residential facility there are therapists and social workers to help these women who are dealing with addiction or abuse and other issues. When they leave the facility, they go back to the boyfriend who is in prison and the mom who is the addict. This means they have to integrate coping strategies and find very different ways of being in their own self, of sitting in their bodies in the face of these outside stressors. That's why yoga is so exciting and effective. It's not what's outside that's being changed. It's what's inside. What I believe in is intuition and creating space to listen to where you should be going, not where you think you should be going. If you already have an entirely full cup, your mind is made up and you have no room for anything new. You have no room for anything else to come in.

What parts of the country do you serve?

Right now we are based in Boston. Once we launch our new program, we will integrate a 'teach the teacher' model, combining our program and our information about trauma – what it is and how it affects women – with a strategy about how to work in the context of this program with trauma survivors. We want to take it to different parts of the country and lead training for teachers or social workers or anybody who wants to bring this program to their facility. We would provide training, manuals, and ongoing support. Our goal is to reach more women. If we teach ten or twenty social workers who are all going to take this program to as many facilities, then suddenly we are reaching one hundred or two hundred women.

How did yogaHope get started?

Several years ago, I had gone into a very severe depression as a result of leaving my husband. I guess you could say I had a mid-life crisis and felt completely in a place where I didn't know who I was any more. I felt utterly 'stuck'. After we separated, I went into this downward spiral. During that time I had very serious suicidal thoughts. I had started taking yoga again, right before I made the decision to leave, which doesn't surprise me. Yoga will often shake up people's lives. Yoga was the only thing that allowed me to get through that dark time by allowing me to be okay with where I was and to put some space between where I was and what decisions I felt I needed to make. Within the sanctuary of my yoga practice, I was able to just sit and not make any rash decisions, particularly about whether to take my own life or not. I often say that yoga saved my life, and I really think that it did.

Through yoga, I slowly started the process of rediscovering who I was and loving that person. And then I started to move forward from there. Once I was out of my own acute situation, I went to a teacher training in Hawaii simply to see what it was like. But I had no intention of becoming a yoga teacher. It was a very intense experience. Often, yoga trainings are very powerful on a personal level, because there is a lot of self-investigation and self-discovery that happens along with that training.

I wanted women to use yoga as a tool to help them learn how to navigate through those devastating experiences with a sense of spaciousness and grace. I wanted them to see that, by not making rash decisions and by beginning to see themselves for who they really were, they would thereby begin to know and love themselves.

It started as a seed of an idea. And right away I knew that I would need support. I thought: What if I get sick, or what if my kids are on school vacation and I can't come and teach this class? My immediate thought was that these women were in need, and I didn't want to let them down. I put out the call to every yoga teacher I knew in Boston, and it just grew from there.

What were the most difficult setbacks that you experienced when you first started yogaHope?

In the last couple of years we had two major setbacks. One of them was personal and one of them was professional. The personal one is that about two years into the history of yogaHope I had gone back to my husband. I had decided that I could go back, that I could make my marriage work, and that I could exist in that marriage as the person I had discovered which was really the person I wanted to be. About two years later, I discovered that my husband had been living a double life for fourteen years and that he had had dozens of extramarital affairs, including one with my midwife and many of my friends. It was obviously a devastating discovery. My son started talking about suicide. I was totally debilitated by the emotional upheaval and couldn't work. I had to pull way back and take care of my son and try to keep him safe. It was extremely difficult. The only thing that got me through the experience was the yogaHope women and teachers and community. They absolutely buoyed me through the process. It seemed to me at the time that somehow the universe knew that I was going to need to create this support system because something 'big' was going to happen.

Up until that point, I was basically the only fundraiser for the organization. I did have a board, but the board was very inactive and fragmented. The organization went into a very serious financial crisis. I had to call the board and ask for help. To their credit, they all rallied and everybody did everything they needed to do to get the organization back on solid financial footing. It was wonderful.

The other area of setback has come in the form of professional challenges. I would say that in this respect the biggest challenge for me would have to be lack of patience. I'm a visionary. I'm someone who wants to go full steam ahead, because I see what I'm doing as something that can be transformational. I believe so passionately in it, but I must answer to a board.

I'm not the kind of person who sits back and says, 'But what if this happens and what if that happens?' I say, 'Let's do this. Let's see what happens, and we'll take it from there.' The board is the other way around. They're accomplished people with professional credentials. They range from attorneys to business professionals in various sectors and as such they're more practical because their ways of thinking are different. Working with my board meant that I had to slow down and present the information to them and demonstrate why it made sense.

What do you find empowering about this experience?

For me, the big empowering piece is being able to say to women that I found my heart. I went back to a marriage that inevitably didn't work any more, because I didn't buy into my husband's negativity toward me. When you're in an abusive relationship, whether emotional or physical – and this is a common situation for women – you think so poorly of yourself that you feel lucky that you have this man to love you. It's very empowering to have lived through all this negativity and then rediscover the basic truth that your abiding nature, the real you, in fact, is a person of beauty, love, and trust.

Who inspires you? What motivates you?

In order to inspire, you must first be inspired. What inspires me is humanity and everybody who surrounds me. Every exchange I have with someone, even if they are showing signs of resistance or anger, inspires me, as I know that resistance is always rooted in fear. It inspires me to have that human interaction and be able to say, 'Ask yourself what you might be afraid of. Ask yourself where the resistance is coming from, and together we can approach this place in you that feels free and pure and open and light.' This is where I get the most inspired. It's just that level of human interaction and being able to see it in every single person I come across, even if it's not on the surface. In my workshops, I try to help people see that they have this beauty inside them. That is just so inspiring to me, because I believe that it's the essence of life. It's where every single one of us connects.

Where do you see yogaHope in five or ten years? Do you have a vision of that?

Through my work in conjunction with other yoga non-profits that are popping up around the country, I believe that together we are going to create a new way for society to look at mental health recovery. Organizations like yogaHope are all starting to bridge the gap between the mental health community and the yoga community. I was asked to give a talk on yoga for trauma recovery at a conference for clinicians recently. The conference was about ending sexual assault and domestic violence. I feel that yogaHope is headed towards a close, cooperative relationship with these other remarkable organizations so as to make a difference. If someone calls me and says, 'I work with incarcerated youths. I want to get a yoga program,' then I can refer them to the right person.

Our yogaHope programs are for women, but we are all empowering each other, because as a whole we are so much greater than the sum of our parts.

In your opinion, how can one person begin to make a difference with regard to the social injustices or tragedies that we are facing in the world today?

What you have to do, if you want to make a difference, is regard what you're doing as seed planting. You may not be able to change an entire society of people. You may not be able to single-handedly rebuild a whole city. You can't really think of it that way. The way to think of it is that you are planting a seed and that, just as it is when you plant a garden, those little plants are small at first. Over the course of years, that garden starts to grow and thrive, and there are 'plants of opportunity' that spring up. That's how we make a difference. It's not necessarily the wealthiest or most powerful person that can make a difference. In the beginning, yogaHope was just me going into one place and teaching six women, and then calling some friends who had other connections that were able to help, and having them come on board.

The important thing is to be open to new ideas and 'seeds of change'. I used to own a restaurant and when I sold it, everybody asked me, 'What are you going to do now?' My answer to that was, 'I'm not going to go and find what I'm going to do. I am going to let it find me.' Using your intuition and creating space to listen to where you should be going, not where you think you should be going, is important. If you have an entirely full cup, then you have no room for anything new. You have no room for anything to come in.

You will lose enthusiasm if you set your long term goals at too lofty a height. You need to pull back and remember that you're a seed planter. I never could have imagined that this was what I was going to do.

Plant the seed, watch your idea expand, nurture it, and be sure to keep an eye open for opportunities, so that they may 'find you' as you grow.

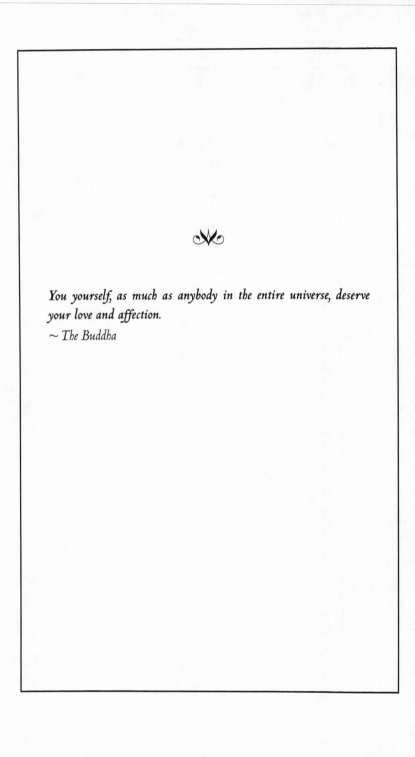

You yourself, as much as anybody in the entire universe, deserve your love and affection.

~ *The Buddha*

17

LIFE: A LOVE STORY

*When the grass looks greener on the other side of the fence, it may
be that they take better care of it there.*
~ *Cecil Selig*

In my 2004 book, *Heart Centered Leadership*, one short phrase summarized my belief regarding the path to personal fulfillment. It was a
concept that was expressed by two simple words: Know thyself.

Self-reflection is not an easy task. It requires honesty, integrity,
and the motivation to take the time to focus internally and to let go
of blaming others for the circumstances of our lives. To make a shift
of focus from external frustrations towards assuming full responsibility for whatever is happening in your life is not an easy task.

As many experts and psychologists affirm, it is only as we begin
to look in the mirror and take ownership of who we are including the
good, the bad, and potentially the ugly while still showing compassion and empathy for ourselves that we are able to discover our capacity for love and compassion for others. The depth and quality of the

authentic union between you and your inner, loving self ultimately determine the success of your relationships.

We can never obtain peace in the outer world until we make peace with ourselves.
~ *Dalai Lama*

Why should we strive for a solid foundation of self-awareness and self acceptance? Because authenticity of self is the currency of meaningful relationships, and self-reflection can be a springboard for positive change in our lives. And since true loving relationships begin with the relationship you have with yourself, pursuing such a path may be the only way to be truly happy.

Yet with so many external factors bombarding us day in day out, taking a few moments to reboot and realign our inner selves might seem impossible. It's a challenge, to be sure. But if we don't commit to this inner journey of exploration in order to truly assess who we are and how we present ourselves in the world, much unhappiness can follow. It is a waste of time to put our focus on the outside, for the only thing that we can really control is what we do and say. Therefore it's an "inside job". Much time and energy are wasted by wishing others could "only be different". Again, this is an external focus. Instead, observing and reflecting on our thoughts and how they create our feelings which in turn create our behavior is the only way we can truly achieve happiness and peace.

In a December 2010 entry in her blog, *The Best Brain Possible*, author Debbie Hampton points out that, "When people take the time to connect with the rhythm of their breathing and their true feelings, a powerful source of wisdom and information can suddenly be accessed. All one has to do is tap into and unleash an unlimited supply of trustworthy tools that can be used to navigate through the many challenges of our world.[66]

"Our awareness of another person's state of mind depends on how well we know ourselves. If you do not allow yourself to feel and sense your own internal state, you're not going to be very good at reading others," continues Hampton. "We cannot begin to know or understand others until we first begin the process with ourselves," she says.

This process of self-examination requires courage, honesty, and the willingness to operate from a level of truth too many people often ignore, whether by circumstance or preference.

"Alone time is when I recharge and go back to my center," TV titan Oprah Winfrey told fans back in 2005. A strong supporter of pursuing the journey within, Winfrey said that distancing herself at times so as to be tranquil and reconnect with herself has helped her tune out the clattering voice of the world around her and hear her own voice with more clarity.

Winfrey feels that time spent in quiet reflection is synonymous with peace of mind. "It's when I consciously count my blessings, take a deep breath, and try to absorb the wonder and glory of all my experiences."

Some may see this practice as narcissistic. But nothing could be further from the truth.

"People who are vain or conceited have a lot of self-hate covered over by a layer of 'I'm better than you'," says Louise Hay, the renowned author, speaker, and founder of Hay House Publishing.

Turning one's gaze within to focus on both strengths and weaknesses makes a person powerful. It liberates them from fear. It is, without question, the place where the false self ends and the real self emerges. And when this transitional passage occurs, it is not merely for our own benefit.

"When a person connects within and learns to truly appreciate the miracle of who they are, they can never hurt themselves or another person," says Hay. The ripple effect of that awareness is huge. The compassion that it inspires in the human heart is also astounding.

There are also those like Hay, for example, who wholeheartedly believe that connecting with the self and tapping into self-love can eradicate disease. Long before the mind-body connection became popular book-club fodder, Hay's first book *You Can Heal Your Life* which appeared in 1976 asserted that humans created their own disease through limiting thoughts, emotions, and beliefs. By urging them to look within and counseling the use of daily affirmations, Hay showed millions of readers around the world how to tune into themselves, clean up their mental clutter, and become the people they were born to be. But the process required commitment. Anything less meant a person was not serious about the pursuit of their own happiness.

According to Hay and other self-love theorists who have followed, loving who we are, warts and all, lies at the foundation of any kind of fulfillment or success. As Hay said at the pinnacle of her career, "When someone comes to me with a problem, whether it be poor health, lack of money, unfulfilling relationships or self-esteem issues – I don't care what the problem is – there is only one thing that I ever work on, and that is loving the self. I find that when we really love, accept, and approve of ourselves exactly as we are, then everything in life works."

And so it does.

From nurturing one's body to cultivating respect for oneself and others, filling up on self-love is the first step towards vanquishing old fears and unloading many of the inhibiting burdens of society's expectations.

To love oneself is the beginning of a life-long romance.
~ Oscar Wilde

"It takes courage to stand up to the world's expectation," says Jack King, a leadership consultant committed to building a world of "we" through love and service. "When we focus on the imperfections, we miss the beauty that resides within," adds King.

It takes courage to accept our imperfections with grace and balance. But what some may see as imperfections others may view as positive traits.

"Sally Fields put it this way," continues King. "'It took me a long time not to judge myself through someone else's eyes.' I think it important to...refrain from judging ourselves through any eyes. Instead, we need to look within our heart on the beauty of our own particular circumstances of life. Only then can we clearly see...and unconditionally love even our self."

Only then can people fully embrace themselves as they are in the present moment. Only then can they claim their happiness instead of putting it off. For one to accept the alternative is to deny oneself the fullest expression of one's personhood, as well as any chance for real happiness down the line.

⚜

Seven Essentials of Self-Healing

1. **Self-awareness:** includes awareness of our bodies, emotions, and thought patterns, as well as the spiritual dimension of ourselves

2. **Knowledge:** includes knowledge of our body, the role that our emotions and beliefs play in the functioning of our bodies, and the ways to bring greater health to all these levels of our being

3. **Motivation:** a strong enough desire to strive after greater health and well-being as a motivation for us to take action

4. **Self-love:** the ability to be receptive to ourselves and care for ourselves with kindness

5. **Courage:** the courage to move out of our comfort zone and experience the feelings we undergo as we change

6. **Self-authority** (or self-responsibility): being responsible for our own decisions regarding our self-care as opposed to relying solely on the opinion of authorities

7. **Self-care:** taking the practical steps that are essential to healing, while not forgetting that, without the first six essentials we won't do this in an effective, consistent way[67]

"It's okay to make mistakes. Mistakes are our teachers – they help us learn," says John Bradshaw, who founded the concept of "the inner child" years ago.

When people get back to that powerful, Zen-like state that all children share, says Bradshaw, the ability to harness the power within at any time, anywhere, becomes unshakeable. Suddenly creative channels open up that enrich our lives and those of family, friends, and coworkers. Restrictions on lives dissolve. The process does not happen without its trial and errors. But the journey itself is the reward.

As Bradshaw says, "It is a mark of soulfulness to be present in the here and now. When we are present, we are not fabricating inner movies. We are seeing what is before us."

Plant your own garden and decorate your own soul, instead of waiting for someone to bring you flowers.
~ Veronica A. Shoffstall

◦✷◦

Let Love Lead: An Interview with Dr. Jack King

Jack King has over thirty years of leadership experience and has worked with a variety of thought leaders. He is the President of Walnut Ridge Consulting, LLC, and he has served as an academic dean and a senior consultant serving the public sector in the National Capital Region. In addition, he created, built, and now manages the non-profit organization NorthFork Center for Servant Leadership.

How would you describe "self-love", and why is it necessary to cultivate it?

Self-love, for me, is like opening a window on your heart, a window that allows one life to brighten the path of another. Teilhard de Chardin said, 'We are not human beings having a spiritual experience, we are spiritual beings having a human experience.' Self-love plays off the same script.

A problem arises when we place restrictions, usually associated with time, matter, and space, on love. It is these self-imposed restrictions that highlight our imperfections. When we focus on the imperfections, we miss the Beauty that resides within.

What are some of the ways we can examine our personal strengths and weaknesses within the context of self-love?

Humans share a highly emotional, innate sense of wanting to belong. We want to matter. And we are willing to make most any sacrifice to build a relationship, even a bad one. We want to be cared about and we want that care to be openly expressed.

In short, we want acceptance; we'll do practically anything to have another show just how much they care and just how much they will forgive our trespasses, our stumbles and staggers, and our failures. We seek esteem and we seek to avoid situations that diminish us, particularly in the eyes of those we want to love us. Why? Because we think it is their love that sustains us, failing to realize love has been with us all along. It is only when we look within that we can find the light certain to illumine our journey. In finding it, we find self, we find a greater reason to love, and we find a greater joy in being love.

In your opinion, how do our "life stories" as young children affect the way we live in the world as adults?

Storytelling transforms lives. Every culture exists, in part, because of the stories people needed to tell. Storytelling opens our minds to new horizons, to the realm of possibility comfortably nestled deep within the dominion of the impossible. Storytelling invites the listener to develop an intimate awareness. It nourishes the imagination. It honors life, grooms connection, and builds relationships. The stories we tell embrace a level of power that befits kings, a power that transcends time, matter, and space.

A personal example may be helpful. Much of my uniqueness was shaped in my early years. As a child, I was involved in an auto accident that came perilously close to taking my life. Essentially, I recall every detail. At a young age, the fragile nature of life was indelibly imprinted on my soul. I came to appreciate our inherent obligation to make the very best of it. As time progressed, I became more aware of my existence, my life's story, and, more importantly, my connection with humanity. Soon, simply making the best of my life was no longer enough. I had to do what I could to help make life better for others. I learned to step out of my comfort zone and step headlong into the comfort zone of others. It's not enough to find the voice behind our story. We must use it to tell our story.

It has been said that lack of self-love is the "problem behind all problems". As someone who is committed to nurturing servant hearts in young and emerging leaders, how can we, as parents, mentors, teachers, and society in general, foster self-love in our young people?

Each of us possesses a unique work in life and only with exceeding effort can we begin to encompass our innate yearning to share it. It is to that end we must find our voice and be ourselves. Like a good wine, however, we cannot rush the process. Margaret Atwood tells us, 'We can only find our own meaning in our own time.' Let no one mislead you. It is much easier to talk about finding our voice than it is to actually unearth and share it. A battle rages deep below the surface, pitting our desire to be liked, accepted, and esteemed with an inconvenient calling to serve, to speak out for those who have no voice of their own. Luciano Pavarotti said, 'The rivalry is with our own self. I try to be better than is possible. I fight against myself, not against the other.' This is an important point. Oftentimes, we are left with little choice but to set aside all we stand for, as we search the furthermost reaches of our being for our true self. In the subtle convergence of time and space, we are surprised to learn that our voice, grounded in authenticity and personal truth, finds us. In so doing, it gives our life a rich intonation. It also gives us the courage not only to open a new door in our life, but to walk through it, to cross a threshold to newfound freedom, a freedom that looks to our childhood for clues on how to courageously face our world as adults.

Courage, however, can be elusive, but it is necessary all the same. You see, not every door will open to self-actualization. Many will present unexpected challenges, repeated trials, and sweeping tribulations that cause us to shake in our boots. Others will cast a light on our greatest fears: isolation, loneliness, or despair. Nevertheless, through the doors we must proceed.

Our voice finds us because we are the only one in all of Creation who can use it for the good of humanity. It finds us, because our life's story is part of the larger whole, and it needs to be told. You see, when you zero in on the heart of the matter, our voice really isn't ours at all. It belongs to humanity, and it wants to be heard. And those around us need to hear it.

You have said, "Leadership without love is no leadership at all." Please explain why this statement is so important to you.

Many believe love is a feeling that overcomes them when they least expect it. Others look at it more as an obligation, a duty if you will. But love is so much more. So much more, in fact, that the ancient Greeks devised four words to help capture its immensity. 'Eros' is the love that gets our fires burning. 'Storge' is the love warmly shared by a parent and child, a familial love. 'Philia' is a love most often associated with great friendship. Hence Philadelphia, for example, is the city of 'brotherly love.' What's common about these first three classes of love is their reflection of deep, emotional attachment. Paul, a first-century Roman citizen and Hebrew Pharisee from the Mediterranean city of Tarsus, describes the fourth kind of love, 'agape', in his letter to the residents of the cosmopolitan city of Corinth some 2,000 years ago. In this letter, we learn that:

'Love is patient, love is kind. It does not envy, it does not boast, it is not proud. It is not rude, it is not self-seeking, it is not easily angered, and it keeps no record of wrongs. Love does not delight in evil, but rejoices with the truth. It always protects, always trusts, always hopes, and always perseveres.'

'Agape' is a love that not only loves, but also gives... because it wants to. 'Agape' gives without expecting anything in return. 'Agape' is other-centered. It is about self-denial for the sake of another. Alan Redpath describes this love as 'the actual absorption of our being in one great passion.'

I personally like what Martin Luther King Jr. has to say about the matter: 'Love is the only force capable of transforming an enemy into a friend.' How does it do this? Quite simply, it bears all things. You see, love nudges us in but one direction: to continually look for the good in others. Why? Because we are certain to find it. Isn't that what leadership is all about?

The Circle of Compassion: An Interview with Dr. Marsha Lucas

A licensed psychologist and neuropsychologist, Dr. Marsha Lucas, Ph.D. has a great deal to say about the importance of self-love. Lucas has been studying the brain-behavior relationship for nearly twenty years. A former faculty member at the Emory University School of Medicine, Lucas now practices in Washington, DC. Much of her research today is devoted to understanding how mindfulness stimulates the brain to grow new, more integrated circuits. In this growth, says Lucas, may lie the secret of true human well-being, as well as society's new appreciation for greater empathy and connectedness in today's world.

Self-love is a topic that is not often openly discussed. Is there a stigma attached to self-love and self-acceptance? How can we encourage people to have authentic conversations about self-love in all facets of life?

You're absolutely right. There is a ton of negative press about self-love and self-acceptance.

'Self-love' has come to be shorthand for being self-centered, self-involved, selfish, and/or self-indulgent, maybe even narcissistic, all of which are aspects of the shadow side of self-love, self-love run amok, irresponsible self-love.

Why all the shots fired at poor old self-love? Because these distortions of healthy self-love threaten the well-being of the community or culture as a whole. In terms of evolution, everyone in the cave had to share the rations, so that the clan (and their DNA) could survive and reproduce. Selfishness put everyone in danger. The shadow side of self-love rolls together three of the seven deadly sins – greed, gluttony, and worst of all, pride – into one terrible mass of toxic glop.

I'd also say that the shadow side of self-love creates many of the challenges we face in our culture. We are, indeed, too selfish and self-centered. This causes things like an overconsumption of limited, shared resources, a sense of entitlement, and letting atrocities go unchallenged simply because it isn't happening to you, to name just a few problem areas. Unfortunately, the list goes on and on. As comedian Bill Maher has said, 'We have the Bill of Rights. What we need is a Bill of Responsibilities.'

As for self-acceptance, it has been distorted in a slightly different way. Many people misuse it as a cop-out to resist the idea that they need to be responsible to others, whether in intimate relationships or the culture at large. 'That's just who I am, take it or leave it' is a phrase I hear all too often coming from someone who is terrified, consciously or unconsciously, at the prospect of taking responsibility for self-examination and for making necessary, grown-up, 'growthful' changes in how they consider others and respond in relationships, even their relationship with themselves.

No wonder we've stigmatized the whole thing from top to bottom indiscriminately, but that's throwing out the baby with the bathwater.

How to change all of this? Short of a sudden, earthquake-like, cultural shift, encouraging people to have authentic, productive conversations about self-love and self-acceptance is slow work. To really love yourself in an authentic and healthy way, you need to actually know who's in there – good, rotten, and in-between. You have to do an honest inventory. That can be pretty provocative intense work, especially if you've been successfully hiding from yourself for thirty, forty, fifty or more years. You can't love someone else just based on what you see in the first layer or two of their outer self. The same is true for an authentic, healthy, balanced love of yourself. And if your habit of hiding those less-than-savory parts of yourself came about because you also have the habit of shaming yourself for not being perfect, or out of fear that, if you're not good enough, you'll be rejected, then self-acceptance is going to mean a lot of heavy duty practice at self-compassion and letting go of the 'safety' of beating yourself up.

As with many challenges in life, it is often difficult to identify problem areas and solutions when we lack the ability to look inwards with discernment. How can we genuinely gauge our level of self-love?

This may sound flip, but one relatively simple place to start is to listen in on the voice in your head. In terms of just everyday stuff, what do you hear? Keep a count of many times a day – even how many times an hour or a minute – you say something judgmental, cruel, or harsh to yourself.

I'm not suggesting that the path to greater self-love is to tell yourself a bunch of Stuart Smalley-style affirmations. Rather, take a measure of how much compassion you show yourself. How much contempt do you hold over your own head? If I get lost while driving (which I'm phenomenally good at doing) and I feel my gut get tight, I check to see what I'm saying to myself. My automatic reaction used to be to berate myself in a way I'd never speak to a friend ('What were you thinking? Why do you always have to get lost? This is your own neighborhood, for crying out loud!').

Now some people think that then the thing to do is just stop saying those things to yourself, to literally or metaphorically put a rubber band on your wrist and snap it hard whenever you catch yourself doing it. That, unfortunately, just keeps the same patterns going: 'Oh, man, there I go again with a mean message about myself. What the heck is wrong with me?!' <Snap goes the rubber band.>

The answer is more along the lines of creating a new path – quite literally, new pathways in your brain – for how you relate to yourself and how you might better love yourself. And it does take practice, compassionate practice. As Henry David Thoreau said,

As a single footstep will not make a path on the earth, so a single thought will not make a pathway in the mind. To make a deep physical path, we walk again and again. To make a deep mental path, we must think over and over the kind of thoughts we wish to dominate our lives.

I'd like to say something about the development of those unhealthy pathways and the role they play in how we do or don't love ourselves or others. This is also known as our attachment style. Our attachment style is learned and pretty solidly established when we're quite young, by age three according to some estimates. And that's pretty much it for the rest of your life, unless you do something about it. The way you perceive and respond to others in the world – your family, your co-workers, your boss, your friends – is established very early on. If you don't know what your attachment style is, you end up with all of those repeated, knee-jerk reactions, which often don't have much at all to do with the current situation. Rather, they're the result of the attachment pathways that you were 'wired with' when you were a baby and a toddler.

Our attachment style – an anxious-to-do-well-and-please style, for example, or an overly-rational-with-no-room-for-feelings style – shows up not just in how we engage in our relationships with others, but also in how we love ourselves. And the extent to which we love or don't love ourselves gets smack dab in the way of how or even whether we can love and be loved by others in healthy ways.

So how do you fix something that was set down before you were in kindergarten? The clue to an answer is best illustrated by the way a parent helps his or her child develop a healthy attachment style: practice attuned, contingent communication. 'Attuned' means that your parent showed (and you felt) that they 'got' you, that they could tune in and understand, and also help you understand, what all of those rich, complex feelings were inside of you without at the same time losing their own awareness of themselves. 'Contingent communication' is best understood by looking at the times when your parent was able to tune in and 'get' you and so was able to respond in a way that actually had to do with you and your needs, even while not unduly losing themselves in the process.

Like many of us, I didn't get enough attuned, contingent communication when I was a young child. That's why I offer my deepest thanks to attachment pioneer Mary Ainsworth for teaching me about these things. She opened a path to my being better attuned and contingently responsive to myself. This led to a healthy interpersonal attunement that rippled out and enabled me to do the same with others in my life including my child when he was born.

Loving and being loved, is that really what we're all truly seeking? Would you agree that a happy, complete life begins by accepting and loving the self?

I see that having a happy life begins anywhere on the circle of compassion, but if you exclude yourself from that circle, it goes nowhere except perhaps to emptiness, exhaustion, resentment, and/ or sadness.

Is there a way that we can we re-wire our brain to generate feelings of self-love?

For me, these last two questions mesh beautifully together. As I talked about earlier, our capacity for healthy self-love depends in large part on what we learned when we were very young. The extremely good news is that your brain has the capacity to grow new pathways, and even new neurons, throughout your entire life. What prompts the brain to do this? That's the role of your experiences, including your thoughts.

Whenever you ask your brain to do more of something, it will commit more resources to building better, faster pathways to accomplish it. If you practice piano, for example, it builds more pathways in the sensory-motor cortex, the part of your brain that controls your hands and finger movements. If you practice driving around a major city center, the pathways for your visuospatial skills bulk up and get more efficient. So you have to practice being more attuned to yourself, as a parent attunes to a child, and reacting to what you find within yourself in contingent ways. As a result, you'll have beefier, more luxuriant brain pathways, allowing you to achieve a healthier, more loving attachment to both yourself and others.

There is a rapidly growing body of scientific research on how the brain changes in response to meditation, and I encourage everyone to learn more about this work. I take great pleasure in writing about the research in 'real English for real people' and posting it on my blog, so that many more people can understand how their brain works and learn how to rewire it to achieve great well-being, a concept that includes, most fundamentally, their capacity for healthy self-love.

Can you suggest a simple exercise that may assist us in boosting our feelings of self-love?

Here are a couple of simple exercises although they're not necessarily easy. So be kind to yourself as you practice them:

1.   Basic mindfulness meditation: There are many great resources for how to practice mindfulness meditation which is a practice of attention to the present moment as you experience it. It's a very well-developed system, refined over the course of 2,500 years in the Buddhist tradition, but I hasten to add that no religion is required. You also don't need to be able to 'clear your mind' or get rid of all thoughts. It's the noticing of the thoughts we naturally have and then gently bringing our attention back to the moment that seems to bring about the rewiring we're after.

2.   Metta (loving-kindness) meditation is another simple practice for increasing self-love. It is a practice by which you

progress from yourself, for example, to a mentor, then to an acquaintance, then to a person whom you find to be difficult, on to a community of people, and then back to yourself. For each of these, you practice generating love and compassion by focusing your thoughts on statements of compassion, such as 'May I know peace!' or 'May you be safe!' Again, there are excellent resources on how to practice metta meditation.

Do you believe that, when we authentically acknowledge and accept the soul, the result is a more fulfilled, connected, and enhanced relationship with the world around us? In other words, does a healthy self-understanding allow us to feel more connected on a broader scale?

Absolutely! Although our terminology might differ, I agree. When you have a greater capacity for healthy self-love (and self-understanding is a necessary ingredient for this), you have the authentic capacity to love others and to more deeply experience the reality that we're all in this together. You make better decisions and choices about how to engage with the people around you, both locally and globally. To paraphrase Plato and mash him up with Buddha: We're all on a challenging, often painful journey. Be kind to yourself and others along the way, and you'll find we all suffer less.

TRY THIS

21 Ways to Feel Good about Yourself, by Rick Hansen, PhD

1. Do the right thing. The bliss of blamelessness. Practice the virtues that are the foundation of any psychological growth or spiritual practice.
2. Tend to the causes of accomplishment; do the things that will legitimately earn you success. All you can do is feed the

fruit tree; you can't make it give you an apple. Take initiative, be "ardent, diligent, resolute, and mindful," and be at peace with whatever happens. As Meher Baba said: "Don't worry. Be happy. Make efforts."

3. Love. Practice loving-kindness for everyone, including (especially?!) neutral and difficult people. Feelings of love neutralize feelings of shame.

4. Do things that ground you increasingly in a sense of your own beingness, always already awake, benign, and contented. For example, meditate, spend time in nature, cuddle your children (or sweetie), do yoga, etc.

5. Relax "self." Take things less personally. Give up trying to perfect yourself; that's like trying to polish Jell-O.

6. Accept yourself as you are. You are what you are, and you cannot change how you are in this instant, though you can create the causes that will develop you in the future. But at any moment of now, there is nothing you can do besides accept it and act to improve it. In particular, try to accept the vulnerable or not-so-pretty parts of your self. Everyone has these; for example, it is not bad to be anxious, sad, or needy.

7. Accept where you are in the four natural, unavoidable stages of learning and getting better at anything: unconscious incompetence, conscious incompetence, conscious competence, unconscious competence. The second stage — conscious incompetence — is the hardest one, and it's where people are prone to quit, but keep going toward growing competence, which will support your sense of worth.

8. Serve the world. Donate to charity. Tend to your friends and family (including animal companions). Be nice to strangers.

9. Exercise your capacities. If you have talents lying fallow, start using them. "The most expensive piece of equipment is the one not making any money."

10. Reflect on your accomplishments and good qualities each day. Perhaps take brief inventory before going to bed each night, answering questions like these: What did I get better at today? How did I act with good character? What have I gotten done? In what ways did I help others?

11. Be in reality about the facts of who you are, and what you have done in your life (the good and the bad). See yourself as a mosaic with a hundred tiles, and tell the truth about what is actually there; it's always mostly good.

12. Be fair. You would want to be fair in your judgments of others; why do you, another human being like them, deserve any less?

13. Take in the evidence of your own contributions, skills, accomplishments, loveableness, value to others. Fill that hole in your heart so that you become less hungry for "narcissistic supplies" over time.

14. Spend more time with people who like you. Perhaps even identify a kind of "go-to" or support team of key people who are major and credible validators of you, and deepen your involvement with them. Spend less time with people who are neutral, indifferent, or negative toward you. If people are critical, it can help to reflect on the myriad factors that led them to treat you that way, which can put it in context and make it feel less personal. If appropriate – and not just getting sucked into wrestling with the tar baby – stick up for yourself. If appropriate, ask others to stick up for you, too.

15. Ask for appropriate positive feedback. It is a lot more useful to know what you are doing right than what you are doing wrong, since the latter only tells you that you're missing the target, not where it is or how to hit it.

16. Get a sense or image of internal nurturing and encouraging figures, such as the loving eyes of your doting grandmother,

a guardian angel, or simply a clear voice of reason about your good qualities. Build up the realness of those internal "nurturing parent," "protector," or "guide" figures, and listen to them more often.

17. Sort criticisms about you into four piles — "not valid," "valid but to heck with it, I'm not going to change that one," "not a moral fault but worth putting in correction from now on," and "deserves a healthy wince of remorse" — take maximum reasonable responsibility for the third and fourth piles, make the appropriate changes sincerely and diligently (perhaps even specific amendments or expiations for serious wrongdoings), and move on.

18. Forgive yourself your past misdeeds and your present faults. This does not mean letting yourself off the hook for them, but means instead not berating or whipping yourself over and over for them. In a way, self-flagellation is a kind of avoidance of responsibility; when we take true responsibility, there is a kind of forgiveness, an honest facing and then a moving on. If you like, write out sentences like, "I forgive myself for _____." Or imagine others forgiving you, like the other people involved, or beings who have a powerful meaning to you (e.g., a teacher, Jesus, the Buddha).

19. See the empty nature of both your good qualities and your bad ones. They are all compounded from smaller parts, they're the result of ten thousand factors (give or take a few), and they arise and disappear interdependently with the whole wide world; therefore, they have no inherent static independent existence. They are simply qualities, some good, some bad. The good ones are worth encouraging, and the bad ones worth discouraging — for the sake of yourself and all beings — but none of them is worth identifying with.

20. Stick up for yourself within yourself. Talk back to irrational or self-critical thoughts. Classic examples: comparing

yourself to others (especially unfair comparisons); equating the worth of who you are with the success of what you do.

21. You should treat yourself as if you matter. Listen to your innermost hopes and dreams, don't dash them, don't rain on that parade, but encourage them in realistic ways. Give yourself empathic attunement – which may have been in short supply when you were a child – for your own feelings, being mindful of them, friendly toward them, and accepting (meditation is great for developing this ability). Let yourself let down sometimes; drop the load, put your feet up, and relax; maybe you need a good cry, for real; build in routine times for rest and respite; take more long baths, long walks, long lovemaking, long board games with the kids, long chats with good friends.

Whoever judges hastily
does Dhamma not uphold,
a wise one should investigate
truth and untruth both.

~ The Dhammapada[68]

18

GOING MENTAL

A belief is like a guillotine, just as heavy, just as light.
~ *Franz Kafka*

We are born into this world knowing nothing. But infants become children. Children grow into men and woman. And every one of us carries within all that our parents, as well as life, have taught us to believe.

That exchange of information can be one of the most positive experiences we humans can share on this planet. But, along the way, what we are told to believe may not always fit with what we know to be true about ourselves or the world around us. Many times, as we were growing up, the well intentioned adults in our lives imposed their beliefs on us at a time when we were young and impressionable. Therefore, because of our youth at the time, we didn't really have a say or choice as to what we believe.

Ask yourself this question: what do I believe?

Have your beliefs helped you acquire a positive view of the world and your place in it? Are your beliefs rooted in negative thoughts that hold you back from real happiness? If the latter is true for you, you're not alone.

Over a lifetime, we accumulate memories and experiences that can do one of two things. They can be a comfort to us and propel us on in this life with hope. Or else they can hold us back and prevent us from achieving real happiness.

Just think of it as "mind junk," says author and counselor, Edward B. Toupin. It just keeps getting in the way whenever we attempt to move forward in our lives.

It's as if people "feel that they have to deal with each and every disassociated memory lying on the floor of their brains," says Toupin. "But sometimes it is necessary to reinvent your belief system and redefine your values, so that you can see more clearly and be able to achieve the fulfilling life that you desire."

It's not easy to redefine what we believe. The very act brings into question all we think, feel, and are. But without such housecleaning done at regular intervals throughout our lives, we can never know ourselves or the route to real happiness.

The greatest weapon against stress is our ability to choose one thought over another.
~ *William James*

"A thought is harmless unless we believe it," says author Byron Katie. And yet, so many of our beliefs can be shadowed by negative emotions and memories that we have long outgrown.

"When you're operating on uninvestigated theories of what's going on and you aren't even aware of it, you're in what I call 'the dream.' Often the dream becomes troubling. Sometimes it even turns into a nightmare," says Katie.

Confronting that nightmare requires courage. But such a reexamination is essential if we are to live our lives with joy and authenticity.

In 1986, at the bottom of a ten-year fall into depression, anger, and addiction, Byron Katie woke up one morning and realized that all suffering comes from believing our thoughts. She realized that, when she believed her stressful thoughts, she suffered. But when she questioned them, she didn't suffer.

This is true for every human being.

Today, Byron Katie is the author of six books (including *Loving What Is, A Thousand Names for Joy* and *Tiger-Tiger, Is It True?*) and has one primary mission: to teach people how to stop suffering. She guides people through her simple yet powerful process of inquiry called The Work. The Work helps them to uncover stressful beliefs about life, other people, or themselves and prompts a radical shift in thinking that has the power to set them free.

Katie has been bringing The Work to millions of people around the world for more than 20 years, starting when people in her hometown knocked on her door because they had heard she could help. Katie has presented The Work in prisons, hospitals, churches, veterans' treatment centers, corporations, universities, and schools. Her free public events, weekend workshops, nine-day School for The Work, and 28-day residential Turnaround House have brought freedom to people all over the world.

"An unquestioned mind is the only world of suffering," says therapist Lise St. Germain echoing Byron Katie.

A belief system gives us a core set of values to live by. Those values define how we think, how we act, and how we expect others to act towards us.

Those values are defined in turn by what we hold dear in our lives. Family, friends, our work, our health...the list is endless. But each one imparts structure to our lives, our minds, and our sense of human morality.

These things flood into our lives as easily as we breathe. But collecting all this information and keeping a firm handle on it in our conscious minds requires commitment and clarity.

As Edward Toupin says, "Our conscious mind takes these rules and shaves off the sides, planes the ends, and polishes the exterior to make it easier to process and store in our subconscious."[69]

That process makes us the keepers of our own story. But it's a story that can change on the turn of a dime.

Death, divorce, illness, financial setbacks – outside influences like these can turn our lives upside down without warning. When that happens, looking inward and practicing the art of cognitive reappraisal can be an anchor in the storm.

"Practicing cognitive reappraisal is a way of training yourself to catch the small droplets before they become a flood," says leadership consultant and writer Bruna Martinuzzi. "Use it as a tool to help you stay cool under fire."

Reexamining our beliefs makes our minds healthier, says Martinuzzi. That, in turn, gives us the focus to become better parents, leaders, friends, and people.

Here's the good news. Each of us has the potential to overcome such confusion. All it requires is a little time and the willingness to look at who we are, where we've come from, and how we wish to move forward in our lives. As American psychologist and philosopher William James once said, "The world we see that seems so insane is the result of a belief system that is not working. To perceive the world differently, we must be willing to change our belief system, let the past slip away, expand our sense of now, and dissolve the fear in our minds."

The secret is to believe in our potential, to be fearless about discarding the old, limiting beliefs that imprison our minds and to hang on to the beliefs that empower us and set us free.

When I work with clients, we uncover their particular belief system. Your prevailing beliefs, or what I call your mental models are there, waiting to have light shed on them. Only by examining them, fully understanding them, and becoming conscious of them, do you have any real chance to change them. And you can change them! The process involves first identifying the beliefs that you hold and then discerning how these beliefs serve you for good or ill. If at that point you establish that your beliefs have not been helpful, you need to reshape and reframe them until you achieve a proper and comfortable fit. Finally you have to start to practice the behaviors that will help you step into a new frame of mind and assimilate new structures of belief, where you can begin to live according to the adjustments you have made.

Belief in the truth commences with the doubting of all those "truths" we once believed.
~ *Friedrich Nietzsche*

The Belief Key: An Interview with Lise St. Germain

For 23 years Lise St. Germain, a Toronto-based therapist, has been unraveling the causes of people's negative belief systems. As she has learned over the years, the route to healing and nurturing people's psyches and beliefs would not be possible without noting their unconscious patterns and hurts and giving them expression. Whether it be through dream work, inner child work, or working with life patterns and other modalities, finding the true expression of a person's belief system begins by addressing their physical, mental, emotional, and spiritual state. When all these facets of our identity come under close and truthful examination, says the author of *Catch You Later*, our "inner healer" can emerge and begin to bring real harmony into our lives.

American psychologist and philosopher, William James, once said, "Believe and your belief will actually create the fact". Do you concur with this statement?

I do concur with this statement, provided we assume that James meant that beliefs, properly understood, enjoy a congruence through all levels of consciousness, that they're grounded in consciousness and understood as a multi-layered, integrated whole. At the superficial level, conscious belief is not, in and of itself, powerful enough to create fact. The surface statement of belief must be in accord with the unconscious material for it to become fact. (For the purpose of coherent argument, the term unconscious is used here interchangeably with the term subconscious)

Here's a short allegory that illustrates the relationship between our beliefs and the realm of the unconscious. We are standing on a dry floor on the second storey of our home. There is a flood in the basement. Someone coming from the basement tells us that, as a matter of solid fact, there is water below. We choose not to believe this and continue with unshakeable conviction to believe that the basement is dry. We can persist in our belief, but that in no way negates the fact that there is water in the basement. When the water reaches the second level and is consciously confirmed by our sense perception (through visual, auditory, tactile, olfactory and/or gustatory stimuli), the preexisting fact adjusts or alters our reality and therefore our belief. Our belief and the underlying reality, literally speaking, achieve a congruence. They are no longer disconnected.

Always, it is the unconscious belief (i.e. the underlying water of our allegory) that will manifest itself and actually create the fact.

Here's an illustration with more immediate relevance. Let's say that I consciously believe and affirm the following propositions: I am rich. I have lots of money. I will win the lottery. I experience only affluence and abundance. Every day in every way I get richer and richer.

In spite of all this, the financial reality is: debt and debauchery, piles of bills and odd ills, poor me!

The problem is that there may be unrecognized unconscious beliefs that are creating the existing financial reality, irrespective of the conscious affirmations, beliefs like the following: Money is evil. Rich people are selfish. I have no earning power. No matter how hard I work, it's never enough. Money slips through my fingers.

Positive thinking and affirmations are useful, but they are not sufficient to change an unconscious belief.

An excellent practical way to test the congruence of beliefs is Robert Williams' 'Psych-K'.[70] 'Psych-K' is a remarkably simple and efficient tool to change limiting beliefs rooted in the subconscious.

In her book "Loving What Is," Byron Katie makes the statement that thoughts are harmless, unless we believe them. Why would we buy into a "reality" that is hurtful and/or harmful?

Thoughts are harmless, unless we believe them, and part of the reason we continue to believe certain harmful thoughts is because of our emotional investment in them.

For example, take the statement: "That person is unkind." Without the emotional overlay, this is merely an observation. On the other hand, "that person is unkind, because he or she just insulted my pride, so that now I am angry, feeling belittled, and need to remedy this internal turmoil" creates my personal reality.

Healthy human beings do not consciously buy into hurtful or harmful reality. Unfortunately, they tend to believe the hurt and harm IS their reality.

How do you help your patients move past mental models that do not serve them?

The first step is to identify limiting beliefs. Limiting beliefs reveal themselves in repetitious, painful thoughts such as: 'I'm not good enough.' (that's a very popular one). 'No matter what I do, I can't get ahead.' 'Everybody is so selfish and uncaring.' 'The world is a cold and dangerous place.' 'I'm invisible.' 'No matter how hard I try, I can't effect change.' If we don't know that we're actually thinking those thoughts, we cannot change them.

Some of those thoughts may be conscious. That is to say, they can be identified throughout our daily mental awareness, observations, and activities. Those are the statements we exclaim in exasperation such as: 'See, I knew that would happen!' 'I always mess up.' 'Things never turn out well.' 'People always reject me.' 'It's their fault.' 'What do you expect?' (Meaning of course what do I expect? When we put statements in the second or third person, we're keeping their real meaning and the emotions attached to them at a distance to avoid pain) These broad generalizations and absolute statements give us a clue that something painful is brewing underneath them. When we pay attention to them, we are actively identifying limiting beliefs.

The beliefs that are still unconscious are the ones most likely to cause the most pain because they manifest themselves in our lifestyles, our habits, our actions, and our reactions without our consciously understanding why and where they come from. In therapy, we work together at gently allowing unconscious beliefs to surface gradually and safely. It's like peeling an onion. We peel and heal one layer at a time, and then the next level of healing surfaces, and so on.

Example:
Conscious belief: 'I can't do public speaking.'
Possible unconscious beliefs: 'I'm stupid.' 'I'm invisible.' 'Nobody listens to me.' 'Nobody hears me.' 'I'm not valued.' 'Nothing I do is good enough.' 'People don't "get" me.' 'I feel like a phony.' 'I'll be exposed.' 'Everyone will know who I am.' 'Everybody always judges me.'

Possible emotions to be released: fear – of failure, of ridicule, of humiliation, of success. Sadness – at being hurt, targeted, incapable, repressed, unexpressed. Anger – at all of the above, at self, at specific others, at others in general, at the world!

Once the hurt is exposed, the repressed emotions attached to it can be expressed. Emotional expression is release, and release is freedom of expression. Once the emotional release is complete, understanding follows. In this way, the trauma is neutralized. Then, and only then, we can consciously choose a belief that promotes growth and serves development.

What is important to note is that complete healing includes emotional release. Intellectual understanding is not equivalent to experiential 'knowing', nor is it sufficient to achieve full resolution of any hurt.

I believe that grown adults are really babies in big bodies, still trying to heal, unconsciously perhaps, all the things in the past that hurt them. How do we become a "grown-up"?

We are an active, alive, vibrant culmination of the totality of our past experiences. Our beliefs differ about where we actually begin. Do human beings begin at conception? In gestation? At birth? When they can think? Speak? Or when they're potty trained or socialized? It doesn't matter one way or another because, to be sure, all adults had to have been born and experienced a childhood. Therefore, each of us carries an inner child within. It cannot be otherwise. A healthy, curious, playful, content, needs-met child will be reflected in a well-adjusted, independent, secure, productive, flexible, spontaneous adult self. No work to be done with those fellow humans! How many of those have you met?

It is the frightened, hurt, uncertain, angry, sad, needs-unmet and/or lost little child who needs healing. Working with this inner child directly brings immediate and in-depth healing when done effectively, thoroughly, and with gentle love for self.

When an external event or an inner thought charged with emotion triggers the little child within us, we are temporarily catapulted into becoming 'the person in pain'. That is the part of us that requires immediate attention and healing if we are to resume our capable and resourceful adult functioning.

When we realize that we were in fact helpless because we were only little children, we are then able in the here-and-now to release associated emotions which could not be articulated or were not permitted to be expressed at the time of original pain. These emotions include the fear of being helpless, for example, anger, sadness for the little child, or any other associated feelings.

Why is this tremendously healing? Because feelings don't know time. When a feeling is born, it has only one of two ways to go: expression or repression. Which is to say that it's bottled up, waiting for an opportunity to be expressed.

We become a grown-up when we acknowledge that the little child that we were is still very much alive within us. We become a healthy grown-up by embodying an inner ideal parent with the capacity and willingness to nurture our inner child whenever the need arises.

An excellent resource for inner child work is John Bradshaw's *Homecoming*.[71]

Would you agree that what we criticize in another is what we dislike in ourselves? How can we identify these patterns and work through these emotions?

The notion that what we criticize in another is what we dislike in ourselves aptly defines the Law of Mirrors. Every person we meet is a potential mirror, gifting us with insight into our self. Much as hairstylists are likely to first notice somebody's hair and dentists usually zero in on teeth, whatever our current and immediate concerns are will be what we focus on in others, consciously or unconsciously.

For example, a person-struggling-with-yet-another-diet comments on somebody else's body weight, body shape, or choice of food in unfriendly, unkind, and ungenerous ways because struggle is usually paired with pain in equal measure. That is, the bigger the struggle, the deeper the pain. Harsh judgment, criticism, ridicule, debasement, sarcasm, shunning, or belittling are expressions of unresolved pain. So when we feel attacked, if we can just as quickly remember that attackers are telling us their own story (after all, they know nothing about ours), we put ourselves in a better position to offer understanding, compassion, patience, and good will.

Identifying the patterns of our own hurt in ourselves is truly very simple. It means paying attention to our thoughts and our comments about others. Any time we have an unkind or critical thought about another in any way, shape, or form, it applies to self. We are mirroring in another our own displeasure with that part of our self.

Here are some examples of mirroring thoughts:

'Gee, I wonder where that person learned to dress'.
Translation: I feel insecure about my sense of fashion. My clothes don't fit well. Nothing suits me. I always dress inappropriately. I look awful.

'Think that idiot got a driver's license legally?'
Translation: I feel inadequate and fear that I have bad judgment in general. I feel stupid, so others are stupid, I feel lacking in something so I ascribe a deficiency to others.

'Too bad there aren't any parenting manuals. See how that parent is ruining the life of that poor child?'
Translation: I am a bad parent. I am angry at my parents. I don't like children and feel guilty about it. I wish I had children. My inner child is screaming inside, as I summon up memories.

It's the old adage: Some people make themselves feel taller by cutting off others' heads. Ouch!!

Our belief system is based upon our evaluation of something. When we reevaluate ourselves and, in turn, our beliefs, I believe we can break free of pain and suffering. Some say we can actually activate certain brain cells that make us "lighter" and more positive. Would you agree?

When we reevaluate our beliefs, we can break free of pain and suffering, provided our reevaluation and our approach to healing reach down to the roots of our limiting beliefs. Being consciously aware of specific beliefs that cause pain and suffering is a good beginning. Investigating the origin of those beliefs is essential, but an intellectual understanding alone is not sufficient to change the belief or bring resolution. Emotional release frees us to broaden our overall understanding and enables us to reevaluate the truth or validity of our beliefs as they apply to our current development. Undoubtedly, our beliefs are rooted in our biology, and changing our beliefs alters our biology. An excellent scientific resource on this subject is Bruce Lipton's *The Biology of Belief.*[72]

Harness The Work: An Interview with Byron Katie

What causes us to create and attach to a mental model or belief system?

We don't need to know what causes us to create or attach to our belief systems. The only important thing is to be aware of what are our stressful thoughts – the thoughts that cause all our suffering – and then to write them down and question them. This is how the truth sets us free.

A thought is harmless unless we believe it. It's not our thoughts, but the attachment to our thoughts that causes suffering. Most people think that they are what their thoughts tell them they are. One day I noticed that I wasn't breathing. I was being breathed. Then I also noticed, to my amazement, that I wasn't thinking, that I was actually being thought, and that thinking isn't personal. It's not as if you wake up in the morning and say to yourself, "I think I won't think today." It's too late: You're already thinking! Thoughts just appear. They come out of nothing and go back to nothing, like clouds moving across the empty sky. They come to pass, not to stay. There is no harm in them until we attach to them, as if they were true.

No one has ever been able to control his thinking, although people may tell the story of how they have. I don't let go of my thoughts. I meet them with understanding. Then they let go of me.

Thoughts are like the breeze or the leaves on the trees or the raindrops falling. They appear like that, and through inquiry we can make friends with them. Would you argue with a raindrop? Raindrops aren't personal, and neither are thoughts. Once a painful concept is met with understanding, the next time it appears, you may find it interesting. What used to be the nightmare is now just interesting. The next time it appears, you may find it funny. The next time, you may not even notice it. This is the power of loving what is.

I often use the word 'story' to talk about thoughts, or sequences of thoughts that we convince ourselves are real. A story may be about the past, the present, or the future. It may be about what things should be, what they could be, or why they are. Stories appear in our minds hundreds of times a day — when someone gets up without a word and walks out of the room, when someone doesn't smile or doesn't return a phone call, or when a stranger does smile, before you open an important letter, or after you feel an unfamiliar sensation in your chest, when your boss invites you to come to his office, or when your partner talks to you in a certain tone of voice. Stories are the untested, uninvestigated theories that tell us what all these things mean. We don't even realize that they're just theories.

Once, as I walked into the ladies' room at a restaurant near my home, a woman came out of the single stall. We smiled at each other, and, as I closed the door, she began to sing and wash her hands. 'What a lovely voice!' I thought. Then, as I heard her leave, I noticed that the toilet seat was dripping wet. 'How could anyone be so rude?' I thought. 'And how did she manage to pee all over the seat? Was she standing on it?' Then it came to me that she was a man, a transvestite, singing falsetto in the women's restroom. It crossed my mind to go after her (him) and let him know what a mess he'd made. As I cleaned the toilet seat, I thought about everything I'd say to him. Then I flushed the toilet. The water shot up out of the bowl and flooded the seat. And I just stood there laughing.

In this case, the natural course of events was kind enough to expose my story before it went any further. Usually it doesn't. Before I found inquiry, I had no way to stop this kind of thinking. Small stories bred bigger ones. Bigger stories bred major theories about life, how terrible it was, and how the world was a dangerous place. I ended up feeling too frightened and depressed to leave my bedroom.

When you're operating on uninvestigated theories of what's going on and you aren't even aware of it, you're in what I call 'the dream.' Often the dream becomes troubling. Sometimes it even turns into a nightmare. At times like these, you may want to test the truth of your theories by doing The Work on them. The Work always leaves you with less of your uncomfortable story. Who would you be without this story? How much of your world is made up of unexamined stories? You'll never know until you inquire.

I have never experienced a stressful feeling that wasn't caused by attaching to an untrue thought. Behind every uncomfortable feeling, there's a thought that isn't true for us. 'The wind shouldn't be blowing.' 'My husband should agree with me.' We have a thought that argues with reality, then we have a stressful feeling, and then we act on that feeling, creating more stress for ourselves. Rather than under-standing the original cause, i.e. a thought, we try to change our stress-ful feelings by looking outside ourselves. We try to change someone else, or we reach for sex, food, alcohol, drugs, or money, in order to find temporary comfort and the illusion of control.

It's easy to be swept away by some overwhelming feeling. It's help-ful, therefore, to remember that any stressful feeling is like a compas-sionate alarm clock that says, 'You're caught in the dream.' Depression, pain, and fear are gifts that say, 'Sweetheart, take a look at what you're thinking right now. You're living in a story that isn't true for you.' Caught in the dream, we try to alter and manipulate the stressful feel-ing by reaching outside ourselves. We're usually aware of the feeling before the thought. That's why I say the feeling is an alarm clock that lets you know there's a thought that you may want to do The Work on. And investigating an untrue thought will always lead you back to who you really are. It hurts to believe you're other than who you are, to live any story other than happiness.

If you put your hand into a fire, does anyone have to tell you to move it? Do you have to decide? No. When your hand starts to burn, it moves. You don't have to direct it. The hand moves itself. In the same way, once you understand, through inquiry, that an untrue thought causes suffering, you move away from it. Before the thought, you weren't suffering. With the thought, you're suffering. When you recognize that the thought isn't true, again there is no suffering. That's how The Work functions. 'How do I react when I think that thought?' There's the hand in the fire. 'Who would I be without the thought?' Now it's out of the flames. We look at the thought, and it's as if we feel our hand in the fire. Then we naturally move back to the original position. We don't have to be told. And the next time the thought arises, the mind automatically moves from the fire. The Work invites us into the awareness of internal cause and effect. Once we recognize this, all our suffering begins to unravel on its own.

In the Introduction to "Loving What Is" your husband Stephen Mitchell, writes about the "interpreter" in the brain (in the left cerebral hemisphere) that is prone to fabricating verbal narratives. He highlights the fact that our brain is literally "wired" to tell us lies in order to keep our personal story together. What if a story is so deeply rooted in the mind that it's difficult to identify?

Well, that doesn't matter, thank goodness. When you unravel one story, you begin to unravel all stories. People who have been doing The Work have reported to me, hundreds of times, things like, 'I did The Work on my mother, and smoking quit me', or 'I did The Work on my boss, and my marriage improved.' It doesn't matter what stressful thoughts you start with. They're all interconnected. We're not dealing with people here, but with concepts.

That's why I recommend that people write Judge-Your-Neighbor Worksheets which bring up all sorts of judgments about a person you dislike or worry over, about a situation with someone who angers or frightens or saddens you, or about someone you're ambivalent or confused about. I invite people to write their judgments down just the way they think them.

Don't be surprised if you find it difficult at first to fill out the Worksheet. For thousands of years, we have been taught not to judge. But let's face it, we still do it all the time. The truth is that we all have judgments running in our heads. Through The Work, we finally have permission to let those judgments speak out, or even scream out, on paper. We may find that even the most unpleasant thoughts can be met with unconditional love.

I encourage you to write about someone whom you haven't yet totally forgiven. This is the most powerful place to begin. Even if you've forgiven that person 99 percent, you aren't free until your forgiveness is complete. The one percent you haven't forgiven them is the very place where you're stuck in all your other relationships, including your relationship with yourself.

If you are new to inquiry, I strongly suggest that you not write about yourself at first. If you start by judging yourself, your answers come with a motive and with solutions that haven't worked. Judging someone else and then inquiring and turning it around is the direct path to understanding. You can judge yourself later, when you have been doing inquiry long enough to trust the power of truth.

If you begin by pointing the finger of blame outward, then the focus isn't on you. You can just let loose and be uncensored. We're often quite sure about what other people need to do, how they should live, whom they should be with. We have 20/20 vision about other people, but not about ourselves.

When you do The Work, you see who you are by seeing who you think other people are. Eventually, you come to see that everything outside you is a reflection of your own thinking. You are the storyteller, the projector of all stories, and the world is the projected image of your thoughts.

Since the beginning of time, people have been trying to change the world, so that they can be happy. This hasn't ever worked because it approaches the problem backward. What The Work gives us is a way to change the projector, i.e. the mind, rather than the projected. It's like when there's a piece of lint on a projector's lens, and we mistakenly think there's a flaw on the screen. In the same way, we try to change this person or that person, whoever appears to be carrying the flaw that's been projected. But it's futile to try to change the projected images. Once we realize where the lint is, we can clear the lens itself. This is the end of suffering and the beginning of a little joy in paradise.

People often say to me, 'Why should I judge my neighbor? I already know that it's all about me.' I say, 'I understand, but please trust the process. Judge your neighbor, and follow the simple directions.' Here are some examples of people you may want to write about: mother, father, wife, husband, children, siblings, partner, neighbor, friend, enemy, roommate, boss, teacher, employee, co-worker, team-mate, salesmen, customers, men, women, authorities, God. Often, the more personal your choice is, the more potent The Work can be.

You have been quoted as saying: "There are no physical problems, only mental ones". How do we distinguish between the actual physical issues and the attach-ment to the fear we experience when we are suffering?

All suffering is mental. It has nothing to do with the body or with a person's circumstances. You can be in great pain without any suffering at all. How do you know you're supposed to be in pain? Because that's what's happening. To live without a stressful story, to be a lover of what is, even in pain — that's heaven. To be in pain and believe that you shouldn't be in pain — that's hell. Pain is actually a friend. It's nothing I want to get rid of, if I can't. It's a sweet visitor. It can stay as long as it wants to (And that doesn't mean I won't take a Tylenol).

Even pain is projected. It's always on its way out. Can your body hurt when you're not conscious? When you're in pain and the phone rings and it's the call you've been waiting for, you mentally focus on the phone call, and there's no pain. If your thinking changes, the pain changes.

I have an Israeli friend who is paralyzed from his neck to his toes. He used to see himself as a victim and he had all the proof. The mind is good at that. He was certain that life was unfair. But after doing The Work for a while, he came to realize that reality is just the way it should be. He doesn't have a problem now. He's a happy man in a paralyzed body. And he didn't do anything to change his mind. He simply questioned his thinking, and his mind changed.

The same kind of freedom can happen to people who have lost their husbands or wives or children. An unquestioned mind is the only world of suffering. I was once doing The Work with some maximum security prisoners in San Quentin, men who had been given life sentences for murder, rape, and other violent crimes. I asked them to begin by writing down their angry or resentful thoughts. 'I'm angry at such and such a person because of such and such a thing', for example. Then I asked each of them in turn to read the first sentence he had written. One man was shaking with rage so uncontrollably that he couldn't finish reading his sentence which was, 'I'm angry at my wife because she set fire to our apartment and my little girl was burned to death.' For years he had been living in the hell of his anger, loss, and despair. But he was an unusual man, who really wanted to know the truth. Later in the session, after he read another statement he had written — "I need my daughter to be alive" — I asked him The Work's second question: 'Can you absolutely know that that's true?' He went inside himself for the answer, and it blew his mind. He said, "No, I can't absolutely know that." I said, "Are you breathing?" He said, "Yes," and his face lit up. And eventually he discovered that he didn't need his daughter to be alive, that beneath all his rage and despair he was doing just fine, and that he couldn't even absolutely know what the best thing for his daughter was. The tears and laughter that poured out of him were the most moving things in the world. It was a great privilege to be sitting with this amazing man. And all he had done was question his own beliefs.

TRY THIS

Judge-Your-Neighbor Worksheet

Fill in the blanks below, writing about someone (dead or alive) you haven't yet forgiven 100 percent. Use short, simple sentences. Don't censor yourself — try to fully experience the anger or pain as if the situation were occurring right now. Take this opportunity to express your judgments on paper.

1. Who angers, confuses, saddens, or disappoints you, and why? What is it about them that you don't like?

I am _____ at (Name) _____ because _____

_____

_____

_____

(Example: I am *angry* at *Paul* because *he doesn't listen to me. He doesn't appreciate me. He argues with everything I say.*)

2. How do you want them to change? What do you want them to do?

I want (Name) _____ to _____

_____

(Example: I want *Paul* to *see that he is wrong.* I want *him* to *apologize.*)

3. What is it that they should or shouldn't do, be, think, or feel? What advice could you offer?

(Name)_____ should/shouldn't_____

_____

_____

(Example: *Paul* should *take better care of himself. He* shouldn't *argue with me.*)

4. What do they need to do in order for you to be happy?

I need (Name)_____to_____

_____

(Example: I need *Paul* to *hear me.* I need *Paul* to *respect me.*)

5. What do you think of them? Make a list.

(Name)_____is_____

_____

(Example: *Paul* is *unfair, arrogant, loud, dishonest, way out of line, and unconscious.*)

6. What is it that you don't want to experience with that person again?

I don't ever want to _____

_____

(Example: I don't ever want to *feel unappreciated by Paul again.* I don't ever want to *see him smoking and ruining his health again.*)

The Four Questions

1. Is it true?
2. Can you absolutely know that it's true?
3. How do you react, what happens when you believe that thought?
4. Who would you be without the thought?

Turn the thought around (original thought: *Paul doesn't listen to me.*)
a) to the opposite (*Paul does listen to me.*)
b) to the self (*I don't listen to me.*)
c) to the other (*I don't listen to Paul.*)

And find three genuine, specific examples of how each turnaround is true in your life.

One-Belief-at-a-Time Worksheet

On the line below, write down a stressful concept about someone (alive or dead) whom you haven't forgiven 100 percent. (For example, "He doesn't care about me" or "I did it wrong.") Then question the concept in writing, using the following questions and turnarounds. (Use additional paper as needed.) When answering the questions, close your eyes, be still, and go deeply as you contemplate. Inquiry stops working the moment you stop answering the questions.

Belief: _____

1. **Is it true?** _____

2. **Can you absolutely know it's true?** _____

3. **How do you react, what happens when you believe that thought?**

_____

_____

a) What emotions happen when you believe that thought? (Depression, anxiety, etc. If needed, an Emotions and Reactions List is available on www.thework.com)

_____

_____

b) Does that thought bring peace or stress into your life?

_____

_____

c) What images do you see, past and future, when you believe that thought?

_____

_____

d) Describe the physical sensations that happen when you believe that thought.

_____

_____

e) How do you treat that person and others when you believe that thought?

_____

_____

f) How do you treat yourself when you believe that thought?

\
\

g) What addictions/obsessions begin to manifest when you believe that thought? (Alcohol, credit cards, food, the TV remote?)

\
\

h) What do you fear would happen if you didn't believe that thought? (Later, take this list of fears to inquiry.)

\
\

i) Whose business are you in mentally when you believe that thought?

\
\

j) Where and at what age did that thought first occur to you?

_____

_____

k) What are you not able to do when you believe that thought?

_____

_____

Belief you are working on: _____

_____

_____

4. Who would you be without the thought? Close your eyes, and observe, contemplate. Who or what are you without that thought?

_____

_____

Turn the thought around.

(Example of a statement: *He hurt me.*)

Possible turnarounds:

1. To the opposite
   a) *(He didn't hurt me.)*
   b) *(He helped me.)*

2. To the self *(I hurt me.)*

3. To the other. *(I hurt him.)*

Give at least three genuine, specific examples for each _____

_____

_____

_____

_____

❧

Among the heedless, heedful,
among the sleepy, wide awake.
As the swift horse outruns a hack
so one of good wisdom wins.

~ The Dhammapada[73]

19

MINDFUL MASTERY

❦

It's no secret that stress can drain us of joy and wreak havoc on our bodies and spirits. Are we really meant to live like this?

Some may see this as the price we pay for life in the Internet Age. But consider this the next time you multi-task and do several stress-inducing things at the same time. According to an international study, people who are unable to effectively manage their stress levels have a 40% higher rate of death from all causes than their non-stressed counterparts.[74]

In the U.S. alone, over 300 billion dollars, or 7,500 dollars per employee, is spent annually on stress-related compensation claims, reduced productivity, absenteeism, health insurance costs, direct medical expenses and employee turnover. And medical researchers estimate that stress is now the underlying cause of over 80% of all illnesses.[75]

With so much to contend with, maintaining a healthy lifestyle or even a healthy state of mind may seem impossible. Faced with such challenging times, people are more likely to put their need for rest, rejuvenation, and reflection on the back burner as their "to-do" list overtakes them.

The answer may be to master the transformational art of mindfulness.

Postdoctoral researcher Philippe Golden of Stanford University's Department of Psychology describes "mindfulness" as having the capacity to be fully and completely present in the moment.

All of us do daily activities without giving them much attention...since our minds are mostly off thinking about something that happened yesterday or making plans for later today. We might give most of our available attention to the person we are talking to on our cell phone, leaving little left over for the car we are driving. We might be only "half listening" during a conversation with a friend because at the same time our minds are mostly drawn to thinking through our upcoming to-do lists. "Automatic pilot" is a term we like to use to describe this process. Most everyone has the ability to run on automatic pilot. In many ways, having this ability, and not having to be fully present for such tasks as brushing our teeth or having a conversation can be most useful. Life would be incredibly burdensome if we needed to give our full attention to everything. Yet, on the other hand, having a hard time being present in the moment and placing our attention to the future or past can make life incredibly burdensome as well.

More then anything, mindfulness is about cultivating an ability to be fully present in a single moment. All of us come into the world with this capacity, but most of us spend very little time "here and now." So how does this happen, and why should we care? In short, we think that in many ways our culture unintentionally "deprograms" us from being present in the moment by heavily rewarding us for not being here. For instance, we get rewarded for multi-tasking, or doing several things at once, since it helps us accomplish a great deal. We also get rewarded for focusing on the future and the past, since doing either can make us better prepared and help us avoid repeating past mistakes. What is the big deal if we do not spend much time in the moment? Unfortunately, the habit of ignoring present moments in favor of others yet to come or those already passed inevitably creates problems. Overly attending to either of these can make people feel very anxious, stressed, worried, sad, guilty, and "out of touch." It can unnecessarily spoil present moments, making it all the more difficult to be effective right now. The truth is that there is only the present moment. The past is already gone and the future is pure imagination. Being present in a moment is a skill that the practice of mindfulness cultivates. Having the skill puts us in a position to take charge of our attention. Instead of making decisions automatically, being able to get into the moment gives us the opportunity to consciously choose whether it is more effective to focus on the moment, or to instead allow our attention to focus on the future or the past. Without this skill, people tend to make decisions out of habit and often unconsciously rather than based on what is most effective for them.[76]

It is estimated that more than 25% of all prescriptions written in the US every year are for controlling drugs such as tranquillizers, anti-depressants, and anti-anxiety drugs. Remarkably, one of the most effective means to combat such modern-day stress does not come in a pill. It lies in the power of our ability to focus and calm the mind – and in the way we breathe.

"We have become the land of multi-taskers," says Michael Tompkins, the General Manager of the world-renowned Miraval Spa in Arizona. "Information can't come to us fast enough or in large enough amounts. Because of that, people have become conditioned to moving at a pace that is not natural to the human body. They lose track of who they are, who they want to be, and oftentimes they lose track of something as simple as their own breath which, as we all know, is the connection to life."

The only way to break this stressful cycle and re-energize our lives is through mindfulness, which is the core of Miraval Spa's philosophy. Being mindful is all about living in the present moment. It is about understanding how to de-clutter your mind at any given time, so that you can regain a more healthful, powerful equilibrium between the mind, body, and spirit.

Mindfulness is not necessarily meditation. Mindfulness is a conscious effort to be aware of all things around you at any given moment, so that you can appreciate the beauty of the here and now. That may sound too difficult for most of us to accomplish. Yet the path to such grounded calm and long-term illumination is as simple as allowing mindful elements such as patience, trust, and non-judgment to pervade our awareness.

When was the last time you were caught up in the moment? When time stood still and nothing else mattered than your awe of nature or deep connection to another human being? How do we access that all-encompassing beauty, simplicity, and stillness of being in the moment?

The single most effective relaxation technique I know is conscious regulation of breath
~ Dr. Andrew Weil

Indeed, just the benefits of a simple breathing technique can have an impact on the body.

That seemingly insignificant yet life-altering remedy is one of the core practices taught at Dr. Andrew Weil's groundbreaking Integrative Health & Healing program, which has been delivering a unique approach to mind, body, and spirit wellness at Miraval since 2005.

"I saw, through the Andrew Weil Wellness Center at Miraval, that breathing training helps you focus on your breath and brings you back to being in the moment," says Tompkins. "But at the same time, over a period of time, it will lower your blood pressure and your stress level."

The Breath of Life: An Interview with Dr. James Nicolai

Dr. James P. Nicolai, a board-certified family practitioner and a graduate of the Integrative Medicine Fellowship at the University of Arizona in Tucson, was handpicked by Dr. Weil to lead Miraval's acclaimed Integrative Health & Healing program. I interviewed him about the importance of stress reduction and mindful breathing techniques.

"Breathing is one of the few things human beings can do either consciously or without having to think about it", explains Nicolai. "Breath connects our physical bodies with the involuntary nervous system – the same system that is responsible for activating the fight or flight response on one hand and the relaxation response on the other hand."

Simply by retraining ourselves to breathe, we can reach that state of calm. As Nicolai says, "We have unconsciously trained ourselves to breathe in such a way that our default mechanism falls in the direction of anxiety and panic."

Mindful breathing can be done anywhere and at any time. It can create a sense of calm and more clarity of thought, when we stop, breathe, and become mindful of the present.

Breathing in this fashion allows us to be more aware and to foster a deep sense of connection with the world around us, one that we might not have experienced before. Mindful breathing shifts our attitudes and our focus from anxiety to the awe and power of the moment.

That, says Nicolai, provides every human being with an opportunity to shift their nervous system to a setting "that is much less wired for the constant survival mode that stress often creates."

Would you agree that stress is a major contributing factor to many of our illnesses and wellness challenges of today? How can we begin to make significant, mindful changes when it comes to dealing with stress and our coping mechanisms?

Absolutely! Stress hurts and is killing us.

According to the American Institute of Stress, which rates stress as America's number one health problem, 75 to 90 percent of visits to primary care physicians are for stress related issues.

As a matter of fact, ninety percent of all illness is either caused or worsened by stress. Studies show that people who live in a state of high anxiety are 4.5 times more likely to suffer sudden cardiac death than those who are more calm.

A sense of feeling disconnected and out of control can take our health to dangerous places. Some studies show that simply belonging to a group of any kind can reduce all-cause mortality and increase longevity regardless of health risk.

The question is, how do we effectively reduce our stress reactions? We can begin to make small changes both in our internal and external environments to reduce these dangerous levels of stress and the harmful effect it has on our bodies. We offer an integrative approach that teaches people to deeply relax their mind and body, learn about foods that dial-down the stress-response, and take stress-busting nutritional supplements and medicinal plants. We show guests exercise programs that can be feasible and fun, help with reframing limiting beliefs or attitudes, and create a community that can foster connection.

These are the skills we want to train guests to acquire as they venture back into their stress-filled lives.

The Integrative Wellness Programs at Miraval incorporate many breathing techniques that support a comprehensive wellness plan. What are some of the health benefits of mindful breathing?

Mindful breathing activates the relaxation response, creating a sense of calm, connection, and clarity of thought. This state decreases stressful hormones like adrenaline, norepinephrine, and cortisol, each of which can contribute to a host of unhealthy diseases from obesity, heart disease, and high blood pressure to panic attacks and depression. Breathing in this fashion allows an individual to be aware of the present moment as opposed to being focused on what has gone before or what might happen in the future. This mindful state can foster a profound sense of connection with people and the world around us that we might not have experienced before.

Aside from the personal benefits, dialing-down human stress levels through greater mindfulness can be a good investment in your place of business.

If organizations were more mindful of what they were doing within their organizations, leadership competencies would shift in extraordinary ways.

In her 2010 article, *A Call for Mindful Leadership*, author Ellen Langer argues that mindfulness – or the simple act of noticing new things – would produce corporate and world leaders who felt more responsible to society, not merely to themselves.

"In more than 30 years of research, we've found that increasing mindfulness increases charisma and productivity, decreases burnout and accidents, and increases creativity, memory, attention, positive affect, health, and even longevity. When mindful, we can take advantage of opportunities and avert the dangers that don't yet exist. This is true for the leader and the led," says Langer, a professor in the Psychology Department at Harvard University.

In an increasingly complex world, where work cuts across all types of institutional boundaries, the inclination may still be there to trust our leaders to know it all. They can't, says Langer. Nor can we.

"When leaders keep everyone in their place with the illusion of knowability...and we 'obey'...the cost is that they create lemmings. Their mindlessness promotes our own mindlessness, which costs us our well being and health. Net result, the leader, the led, and the company all lose," she says.

The visionary leaders of tomorrow will become more mindful of their own actions in the workplace. They will encourage their colleagues and employees to do the same. It may take time to achieve such a universal model. But as Langer puts it, "We need leaders whose major, perhaps only, task is to promote mindfulness in those around them. By learning how to exploit the power of uncertainty, maybe all of us will wake up."

So how do we move toward mindfulness at work?

The Energy Project: An Interview with Tony Schwartz

For more than ten years, Tony Schwartz, the President and CEO of The Energy Project, has been challenging corporate leaders to recognize the emerging "energy crisis" in the workplace. Schwartz and his team members have developed a set of simple principles and highly actionable practices for more effectively managing energy by harnessing the science of high performance and teaching mindful work performance techniques.

I asked Tony to give me some insight into how we can become more mindful in the way we work.

You champion the message that it is more effective for an organization to manage their people's energy rather than manage their time. Could you expand on this concept?

Time is a great resource, but it is finite. There are 168 hours in every week. There will never be more hours than that, and at this point most people have full dance cards when it comes to their time. They don't have any more. They are working the longest hours that are humanly possible, and yet the demand in their lives is continuing to rise. So time, within the context of increased demands on our capacity and the increasing complexity of the world we live in, just won't cut it. We need some other way to be able to meet the demands — the question is how?

Energy is something that can be expanded. From the perspective of physics, energy is not something you can get more of, but it is actually something that you can convert from one source to another.

We can convert the glucose that we ingest or the increased cardio-vascular capacity we create or the greater resilience we cultivate emotionally or the increased focus that we get when we get more control of our attention into more energy. We can then use that energy to get more things done and arguably to get them done at a higher level of quality. So energy in the human system is something we can increase.

Second of all, it is something we can renew. We can refuel. Time is like a train driving off into the distance. Once it's gone, it's gone forever, but energy is something that you can refuel. You can rest and renew and rejuvenate and have more energy, but you aren't going to get the time back again.

The third aspect of energy that makes it powerful is that we can get more efficient in the way we use the energy we have. We aren't nearly as efficient in using the energy as we could be and so we end up squandering a lot of energy. So basically, energy is an internal resource for us as individuals, and, for organizations, it is a resource that has been poorly managed and underutilized.

So how does someone identify their own personal energy deficits?

One way is through something we've created called an 'energy audit'. The idea of an energy audit is really to understand that energy for human beings, unlike energy for a car or refrigerator, is multi-dimensional, and there are four dimensions of energy: the physical, which is quantity of energy, the emotional, which is quality of energy, the mental, which is focus of energy, and the spiritual, which is the purpose to which you put your energy. Each of those components has the potential to be higher or lower in any given human being. So what we do first of all is help people become more aware of what their levels of energy are in each of those four dimensions. Next, we begin to think about what the costs are of these levels not being as high as they could be, and finally what people can do to address their deficits.

What are the triggers of low energy awareness? Feeling run down or that you have a shorter fuse?

There are four obvious triggers – or four obvious 'signs'– during a personal energy crisis. The first one, on the physical level, is fatigue. For example, hunger would be a good sign that you have an energy deficit, but the most significant one in the physical dimension is fatigue. The most powerful one in the emotional dimension is negative emotions. The most prevailing one in the mental dimension is distraction or distractibility, and the most obvious sign in the spiritual dimension is an absence of motivation.

What are the four forgotten needs that energize great performance? How are they connected?

When you meet your energy needs, what you do is free yourself to use your energy not to fill deficits, but to create value. So those needs you feel are actually energy needs, and the energy need in the physical dimension is for sustainability. The energy need in the emotional dimension is for emotional security and to feel valued for who you are. The need in the mental dimension is for self-expression. In the spiritual dimension it is for significance – in other words, for the sense that what you do matters. When you feel that what you do matters, you bring much more energy to it, more focus, more perseverance, more excitement.

Some would argue that it is not a company's responsibility or concern to nourish the physical, emotional, mental, and spiritual needs of their employees. Acknowledging such needs seems like quite a new concept in most corporations. Do you believe that executives are prepared to embrace the notion that rest and renewal for their employees and themselves will yield improved performance and sustainable productivity?

It's not a company's responsibility? This isn't an ethical question. This is a performance-based issue. It's a productivity issue, meaning that a profit-making company's primary responsibility is to earn money, and, in the case of public companies, to earn money for its shareholders. If that's the case, then what you want to do is put people in a position to perform at the highest level that they're capable of. As long as their capacity exceeds the demand placed on them, that's not an issue. They can deliver, and you don't have to do anything but ask them to show up and deliver on the capacity that they already have in the system, because the demand has not overtaxed it. We are no longer in this state in the world. Now the equation is flipped, and for many, many people, capacity is beginning to be overwhelmed by demand. So the question is how do you put your employees in a position where they are not spending their time and energy trying to fill their own needs at the expense of generating value for the company? To the extent that organizations make it important to help employees meet those needs, they are serving their bottom line. It's just a practical response to a changed environment.

Change often occurs, unfortunately, in the face of pain. That's true at the individual level as well as at the organizational level. Typically, people don't change, because they think it would be a good idea to change. They change because the pain of staying the way they are exceeds the pain of changing, which is considerable.

It's hard to change. We get very stuck. We get habituated to the way we are, even when it's not serving us well. People have to get to a point where pain is very high, before they begin to think they'll do things in different ways, much less in radically different ways. Talking about the idea that rest and renewal are a critical component of high performance is a transformational change. That is not a concept that organizations have lived by at any point since the industrial revolution. We have been in a so-called free-market world in which the ethic is that 'more, bigger, faster' is always better.

We are at an inflection point now because of this shift in the relationship between demand and capacity where the pain is getting very, very high, and organizations are in a position where they have to ask themselves the question, 'What do I need to do to make sure my employees can continue to be more productive?' So there is an openness, born of pain, to solutions that is much higher today than it was only ten years ago. I think that what makes the notion of rest and renewal – which can be regarded as the core aspect of what needs to change – more palatable to organizations is the degree to which we can make the case for it.

There is a significant body of science and research which demonstrates that, if you build in renewal in skillful ways, what you will get at the end of the day is more productivity rather than less. It's a pretty dramatic shift for organizations to go from valuing people for the number of hours they put in during any given day to valuing them instead for the amount of work they generate during the day, however they generate it.

Organizations are beginning to dip their toes in this water. The water is cold, and they sometimes pull their toes out, but more and more we are finding that, when they begin to experiment with the principles and also the practices that we teach, the results they get are sufficiently positive that they dip the toe in a little further. It's not unlike a toddler who begins to separate from his mother and goes out exploring and then runs back. They survive that first quest and go out again a little bit further and further each time.

The more forward-thinking, progressive organizations are experimenting with some of these principles and practices and finding that they are solving a lot of the problems that they have found no other way to address.

Has there been a shift in the workplace? Is all this prompting companies to change the way they work?

Yes, a radical shift. Generically speaking, it's about demand. There's a level of hunger and openness that companies have to these ideas that's greater than it was, much greater. In a more specific sense, I think there are two factors that have super-accelerated this over the last two or three years. The first one is the world of technology, or the digital world, which has increased both the amount of information that is so readily available to all of us and also the number of ways that people can communicate. There's an overload of incoming demand and data that has inundated people. I feel as if we have reached a sort of tipping point, and there are an awful lot of people at very high levels in a company who tell us that it's just not sustainable any more. They say things like: 'I can't do it and our people can't do it. We just can't keep up.'

The second factor that has really influenced this shift over the last couple of years is the economy. This tremendous recession that we have all had to live through has led to lay-offs. Those people who have been lucky enough to survive job cuts have often had to take on more work. They were already overtaxed, but now they're often doing the work of two or three people with no end in sight. Again the pressure on any given employee in any given company is as great as it has ever been, and there comes a point when even the most demanding boss has to look at reality and say, 'We need some answers.'

You have often said the counter-intuitive secret to sustainable great performance is to live like a sprinter. Can you explain this?

Most of us actually live like marathon runners. We are not really consciously aware that we live like marathoners, because it feels like we're going unbelievably fast. When you think of a marathon, there's no finish line in sight, so you have to conserve energy along the way if you want to be able to go on toward the finish line. What happens is that we are not fully engaging in most of what we do. We're not sprinting. We're not pushing ourselves to our limits because, if we did, we would collapse.

So we need to find ways to avoid fully engaging, so we can keep at it. The ability to fully engage, to get deeply absorbed, fully focused, to bring all your excitement to the table, to push yourself as hard as you can —continuously — obviously means you would be more productive. The difference between a marathoner and a sprinter is that a sprinter has a visible finish line, and it's not far away. The sprinter can see the finish line. Sprinters know that even if they throw themselves into the race with everything they've got, within a relatively short period of time they're going to be able to rest and refuel, and that's exactly what sprinters do.

A true sprinter might do multiple heats during the day, but each one is separated by a period of recovery. That's really what we're suggesting. When you're engaged, you should be fully engaged. You need to operate like a sprinter, but you make that possible by doing what a sprinter does which is to recover at the finish line each time.

The difference between the sprinter on a track and the sprinter in life is that in life we have lost our finish lines. They have all been pulled away from us by technology and by multiple demands in our lives. So in order to sprint, we have to reinstate intermittent finish lines, points at which we consciously and intentionally stop in order to renew and recover. This is an act of consciousness that you must build into your life if you're going to do things in a different way. Otherwise, everything in the culture pulls you towards a continuous expenditure of energy. Which means you will eventually run out of energy. Even before you run out of energy, you'll have less of it as the day wears on. I just want to give a concluding illustration of this notion. Let's say you have two people of equal ability and you set one of them on a task and tell them, 'It's 8:00 in the morning. Go at this continuously until 6:00.' Then, you take the other person and you say, 'It's 8:00 in the morning. Go at this for 90 minutes with everything you've got, and then take a 15 to 20 minute break and truly chill out, have something to eat, hang out with a friend, sit and breathe, listen to music, do something that renews you, then come back and do your work in 90 minute increments all the way through the day with breaks in between.' Then ask yourself in the eighth or ninth hour, who is doing better? Who is more efficient? Who is doing a higher quality of work? Who can focus better? Clearly, this is a no-brainer.

The answer is that we think we are meant to operate like computers. Computers can operate at high speeds continuously for long periods of time, but human beings can't, so why do we try?

Ninety minutes is the magical 'maximum' number. You have to work ninety minutes continuously. There is a rhythm in our body that we first learned about in terms of sleep called the basic rest/activity cycle that is essentially a ninety minute rhythm during which, at night, you move from light sleep into deep sleep and then back again towards waking through something called REM sleep. If you go through those five stages, you get a good cycle of quality sleep. In the daytime, the same pattern, called the ultradian rhythm, recapitulates itself, but instead of going from light sleep to deep sleep, you go from high alertness into fatigue. At the end of ninety minutes, the body, if you have pushed it to its relative limits, is screaming at you to give it a break, but we override this because we have ways to override it: caffeine and sugar and your own stress hormones – adrenaline and noradrenaline and cortisol – all those things that we can use to keep ourselves up and going, even when our body wants us to rest and renew.

So if you follow the pattern of the body, you get more done during the periods you are working and you refuel during the periods you are not. I like to refer to the Aesop fable about the tortoise and the hare, because it turns out it is wrong. The tortoise doesn't win the race. The reason the tortoise doesn't win the race is because the tortoise is continuously expending energy, maybe not fully expending it, but expending it. Somewhere in the race that tortoise is beginning to get fatigued. But the hare sprints and recovers, sprints and recovers, sprints and recovers, and finishes the race, while the tortoise is still out there, chugging along, feeling exhausted.

In the "Harvard Business Review" blog entry called "Six Keys to Being Excellent at Anything", you stress the importance of creating rituals and the quote is, "Ritualize practice. Will and discipline are wildly overrated. As the researcher Roy Baumeister has found, none of us have very much of it. The best way to ensure you will take on difficult tasks is to ritualize them. Build specific, inviolable times at which you do them, so that over time you do them without having to squander energy thinking about them." Why is it important to establish rituals in our lives and how do they differ from habits?

Typically, a habit is something that happens to you. Hence the phrase 'I fell into the habit of...'. Smoking is an example of a habit that people can fall into. It is usually something that occurs not by conscious intention, but by simply having done something repetitively. We define a ritual as a highly specific behavior done at a very precise time, over and over intentionally, until it becomes automatic so that you don't have to think about it anymore. There's power in a ritual. The reason we need rituals is indeed what Baumeister has demonstrated, which is that we have one reservoir of energy. It's not like we have multiple reservoirs. So each time we use will to get something done, that reservoir of will is diminished. The best way to think about this is to liken it to when you're on a diet or you're trying to resist eating. Over the course of a day, let's imagine that you keep walking by various potential sources of food that can attract you, particularly when they're really appealing foods like sugars and simple carbs and that kind of thing, foods you want to eat because they taste good. What happens is that your will gets broken down. Anybody who has been on a diet knows that it's much easier to resist something the first time than it is the fourth, and if it's the seventh or the tenth or the thirteenth, it becomes virtually impossible.

The way to circumvent this is not to build your life around things you resist, it's to build your life instead around things that you do. So if it's a question of food, the reason Weight Watchers works better than most diets is because it defines what you will eat rather than put you in a position where you have to resist eating. This is true of any ritual. When you define a particular behavior and you do it at a designated time, you reduce the amount of will and discipline necessary to get it done, and at a certain point you habitualize it in the more reptilian parts of the brain. The brain begins to fire the neurons that serve that particular behavior in a more predictable way. It becomes the equivalent of a habit, but it's a positive habit and you feel remorse when you don't do it.

Let's say you're somebody who gets into a ritual of working out regularly at a specific time. When you don't work out, it weighs on you and you feel uncomfortable and you think about it. You are pulled towards it. That's proof that you have ritualized the behavior. The less energy you can use to adopt a behavior, the more likely the new behavior will become a positive habit.

Isn't there a magic number associated with this, like 21 days or 28 days?

To be honest, I consider it a bit of an urban myth. I have seen no compelling evidence that there are a specific number of days within which a given behavior gets ritualized or habitualized, and part of the reason for this is that some behaviors are easier to ritualize than others.

When you have a complex behavior, to think that you can get it in place in a matter of weeks may be overly optimistic. It's one thing to get a workout ritual in place, which is not all that complicated, or a ritual like, 'I'll take my vitamins every morning before breakfast.' These are rituals that you could achieve in a reasonably short time.

Let's say, as an example, that you are somebody who sees the world as a pessimist, viewing the world through dark lenses, and that your instinct is to always imagine the worst. If you wanted to build a ritual, every time you started imagining the worst, you could try to build a ritual around another equally plausible story you could tell yourself, one that is more optimistic and empowering. You would know that the ritual was in place when you started to have that negative feeling about something and immediately, without having told yourself to do it, you summoned up an alternative, more positive scenario.

Most psychologists will say to you that it can't happen, that, when it comes to temperament, people don't change. So the person who sees the cup half empty will always see the cup half empty, and I'm here to tell you: 'Nonsense'.

Any behavior can be treated the same way a muscle is. You subject it to stress, you push it beyond its comfort zone, you give it a chance to recover, and over time, whatever that muscle is or whatever that behavior is will get stronger. It may take longer than a workout ritual, but it's definitely possible.

Don't these rituals that you employ take will and discipline to implement and to stick to?

They do and that's why you want to take your limited reservoir of will and discipline and use it as parsimoniously and as strategically as you possibly can in the service of a single behavior that you're trying to influence until you don't need it any more. You can't assume that a ritual can be put into place without some amount of will or discipline, but what you don't want to do is squander that will and discipline on lots of different things such that it gets burned down, before you can get one behavior in place.

Do you think it's best to focus on only one specific behavior that you want to change?

I'm a big believer in the fact that, the more you can concentrate your attention, the more likely it is that a certain behavior gets that intense amount of discipline focused on it. Sometimes you'll find behaviors that you can put in place or rituals you can put in place that are linked. You can get a 'two-for' sort of. You might have a ritual that says you're going to take a break every ninety minutes throughout the day, and part of that ritual is for you to eat something either every time you take the break or every other time you take it. Those two get linked, which means you've taken care of a nutritional need and you've taken care of a more generalized recovery need, but it's all part of the same ritual. So there is the possibility of doing more than one behavior, but as a rule one at a time is best.

Are there renewal activities that can be easily implemented to revive energy throughout the day?

Renewal is something that makes you feel renewed; for some people that could be smoking a cigarette.

Of course, many people reading this will be shocked. Well, they may be, and guess what? In the years since it became illegal to smoke inside buildings, the people who were addicted to nicotine and therefore had to go outside to get a break, got a short-term source of renewal that the people inside didn't get. The only problem is that this thing that was providing the renewal in the short term was going to kill them in the long term. It's a bad cost: benefit ratio.

But it's really fair to say that a cigarette is the pretext, because you could go outside the way a cigarette smoker does and just do the same things without smoking, i.e. go outside and take a break or a walk as a form of renewal. What you are always looking for is the highest octane renewal, meaning what is going to put the most fuel back in your system so that you can be fully engaged when you go back to work. It might be listening to music, it might be taking a walk, it might be calling someone you love and having a conversation about something other than work, or it might be taking a nap. By the way, it also could be active renewal. It could be taking a run, it could be yoga. Certain renewal activities expend physical energy, but they renew mental and emotional energy.

Here is the interesting thing about recovery. The better you get at it, the faster it happens. It's a skill that you can develop.

How do you get skillful at recovery?

The first thing is that you make it important. You train at it just as you would train at any other skill. So if it was a case of breathing and the idea was to quiet the mind, you would use focusing techniques that allowed you through practice to get more focused or actually quieter in the mind. In any given activity, whether it be a renewal activity or an energy-spending activity, there is a spectrum from unskilled to skilled. The most critical thing is to take renewal seriously. Most people don't. For most people, when you say it's time to take a break in a workplace, what do you think the first thing they do is? They check their e-mail. They think that's a break. Well, it isn't. It's a form of break, but it's a very low octane break.

It's like saying junk food is a source of nutrition. It is, but it's not a very good source of nutrition.

Our human side comes before the business side.
~ *Michael Tompkins, General Manager, Miraval Spa*

Miraval Magic: An Interview with Michael Tompkins

Michael Tompkins, says that, to become truly mindful, one must venture into "the valley within". This is the core philosophy of Arizona's Miraval Spa. "Everything we do encourages our guests to live in the present moment, conscious of the unique intersection of mind, body, and spirit," says Tompkins. "Miraval can be your catalyst for a healthy lifestyle change, your escape and support through challenging times, or simply somewhere to rest, reflect, and re-energize, as you begin the next chapter in your life story. For most of our guests, the experience is nothing less than a life-changing and life re-affirming moment."

Have you personally incorporated mindfulness practices into your own life?

I have so many things going on each day that it's a challenge to actually be able to stop and think clearly about what's going on at any particular time, whether it be meeting with one of my directors or meeting with a guest concerning a health or stay issue. But I'm able to access the tools that can enable me to put everything that is coming at me out of my mind, so that I can focus and be clear. I do that through a series of breath-work techniques that I can do at my desk. Oftentimes, I can be in meetings and nobody will know that I'm doing it, but it's a way that I can bring myself back to being in the moment. We help impart those skills to our guests so that they can live a better life.

What happens when you begin to live mindfully and integrate these positive changes into your life?

Well, it's interesting. I was in the business rat race, very successful in my career, Vice President of a billion-dollar company in the casino industry, under very high stress. I came to Miraval at 305 pounds, burned out, with a relationship that was probably in the worst place it was going to be, and not happy. I thought that money and personal success were going to bring me happiness.

What mindfulness has done for me is help me think about every single thing I'm doing. It doesn't necessarily have to be about the relationship that I have with other people. It could be my relationship with food. It could be my relationship with stress. Incorporating mindfulness has given me the most significant gift of my life. I've lost over 70 pounds since coming to Miraval and essentially I've done nothing different but be aware of the things I'm eating, and why I'm eating them. I simply need to ask myself, 'Am I really hungry? Is it because I am trying to fight stress?'

Beyond that, my relationship is the strongest that it has ever been. I can put down my cell phone. I can put away the computer and not have to deal with e-mails so that I can focus my attention on the relationship that I'm in and not all of the work-related issues that I have to worry about. So my partner feels that I'm an active participant in our relationship.

From a leadership perspective, I learned through the interactions with the horses in our Equine Experience that I had sort of separated myself. I've been able to step back and look at how I behave, not only with myself, but also with the people I interact with, whether they be strangers, friends, co-workers, peers, or subordinates. The fact that I now understand my behavior has been a tremendous learning experience for me as a leader at Miraval.

The upshot of this is that I love what I do. How many people get up every single day and love going to work? I do.

Tell us how you've incorporated mindfulness into your own workplace.

There are many practices related to mindfulness, and we try to instill them in whatever way we can. Being conscious of other people's time is huge for us. Nowadays, when people are so time stressed, that can become an issue. Our culture here lives by that. It's respectful of other people. Beyond that, our no cell phone policy is significant, as this helps maintain a sense of peace and calm. No staff or guest can use cell phones on the property. We have a cell phone area that guests can use, or they can use them out on the patios of their rooms. But in the public spaces we don't allow it. I think that creates a wonderful environment.

Beyond that, we live by the motto that we always try to do what's right. We live by that imperative with regard to serving our guests, the aspect of sustainability, our relationship to the sacredness of nature that surrounds us, and our many charitable endeavors.

Our human side comes before the business side.

TRY THIS

Through relaxation and mindful breathing techniques, Michael Tompkins is able to reduce stress, even with a full schedule. Through a consultation with the Andrew Weil Integrative Wellness Program at Miraval, he learned techniques involving the senses to help him become more "grounded" and in the present moment. These techniques can be used at your desk, in a board meeting, on a plane, or anywhere when stress takes hold.

Tell us more about your mindful breathing technique:

There are two things I do in this technique.

First I use my vision. I will look at something 15 to 20 feet away and just focus on one very small aspect of it. I will hold that in my vision and then blur my vision and then come back to having the vision in focus again. If you do that with the same object three or four times, it takes hold of you and grounds you.

It's at that time that I normally start this breathing exercise. It's actually quite simple. It's four inhalations very quickly through your nose, then four exhalations very quickly out of your mouth. You don't have to make a sound with it.

When the two above techniques aren't enough for you of themselves, as you do the breathing technique, take your thumb and touch your index finger, your middle finger, your ring finger, and your pinky at the same time that you're exhaling. Then you get the sense of touch, which will completely ground you. It literally takes three minutes, and if you do it once an hour or once every two hours, it's amazing how much it will lower your blood pressure. I try to do the breathing in and out about 20 times in a row.

Dr Weil's 4-7-8 Breath for Relaxation

Place the tip of your tongue against the ridge of tissue just behind your upper front teeth, and keep it there through the entire exercise. You will be exhaling through your mouth around your tongue. Try pursing your lips slightly if this seems awkward.

First take a deep cleansing breath, exhaling completely through your mouth while making an audible "whooshing" sound.

Then close your mouth and inhale quietly through your nose to a count of four, hold your breath for a count of seven, and then exhale completely through your mouth (again with an audible "whoosh") for a count of eight.

This counts as one breath. Repeat the cycle three more times for a total of four breaths.

Ancient Zen masters in China and Japan used koans (meditation objects) to train and ultimately test the progress of the student. One ancient koan puzzle was for the student to "pull a five story pagoda out of a teapot." When the student was able to answer the question spontaneously, creatively, and without hesitation, then he/she had truly learned to act with freedom in any situation. He/she was fully awake in the present moment.

20

THE AGE OF IMAGINATION

"There is no use trying," said Alice. "One can't believe impossible things." "I daresay you haven't had much practice," said the Queen. "When I was your age, I always did it for half an hour a day. Why, sometimes I've believed as many as six impossible things before breakfast".

~ *Lewis Carroll*

Is creativity reserved for only the rarest of jewels, those lucky few embodying exceptional audacity, free-spirited thinking, and unbounded imagination?

Do you ever wonder how some people experience that creative "flow" almost at will, producing works of art, written masterpieces, and new ideas at the drop of a hat?

Letter from Paris blogger, award-winning writer, and pop culture diva Beth Arnold provides some insight into this mysterious essence that permeates our awareness and illuminates our spirit.

"Although it may come in different packages within us, we all have it. We use it every day," says Arnold. "Creators create for themselves and also so other people can see, read, experience, and connect with their work in some way – and be transformed by it."

"Some of us are in the business of being creative, and some are creative in our business. Some of us may not even understand that we're creative. We grieve this lack and wonder how we find that part of ourselves or how we can awaken it. In others, creativity sparkles on their surface and resonates as the deepest part of their identities. They live and breathe it. They must create or die," she says.

How can we unearth this elusive gift in ourselves?

Does creativity lie in wait somewhere deep in the shadows of the right brain, searching for a way to move furtively past the logical left brain to take hold of expression?

We may not be aware of it, but we could be compromising our creativity simply because of an overriding physiological constraint. In a recent article entitled "Left Brain, Right Brain", writer Dan Eden speculates that the left hemisphere of the brain dismisses the right hemisphere, the side that governs creativity and imagination, as our "flaky cranial twin".

"It appears that most people will never reach their maximum (creative) potential because of compromises that have been made between these two governing bodies. Sometimes skills which the right brain can perform better are routinely handled with less skill by the left brain", says Eden. "In most people, the left brain takes control, choosing logic, reasoning, and details over imagination, holistic thinking, and artistic talent."[77]

I saw the angel in the marble and carved until I set him free.
~ *Michelangelo*

So how do we break free from the left brain's dictatorship?

"We have to open up our consciousness to the idea that we can be creative," says author and coach Peggy McColl. McColl believes we must engage in the spirit of playful curiosity and allow our minds to wander a little when we are stuck.

When we are curious about something, our mind anticipates the creation of new ideas. Without curiosity, we miss the expansiveness of the moment and are not open to receiving the gift of an idea. Curiosity serves to feed the imagination for the further elaboration of a fundamental idea. But ideas that are born of creativity can, at times, be met with disappointment.

"Creative people fail a lot. They fail because they are willing to try things. Scary, inadvisable, evolutionary, unconventional things." says writer Judy Clement-Wall.

Creative people are willing to leap into unfamiliar territory, says Clement-Wall. They do that because, even if they fail, it is the only real place where learning takes place.

Five-time world record holder, author, peak performance coach, comedienne, adventurer and TV host Fran Capo says that creativity is what allows us to take what people consider impossible and make it happen.

"Creativity is what motivates us to create spectacular movies, new inventions, wonderful books, medical breakthroughs, and breathtaking art. It is what allows the stand up comic to look at life differently than everyone else and say, 'Hey did you ever notice...?'

"Creativity is limitless, and therefore it is essential that you learn how to tap into your own creative force. I just ask myself the same question over and over again. How can I make this bigger? How can I make this better? How can I do something no one else has done? The beauty of this simple process is that, if you ask your mind something, it sets the seed going in the unconscious and your mind has no choice but to work on it until it comes up with an answer. I have been called 'relentlessly relentless'. I prefer the word, 'persistent'.

"You have to allow creativity to flow with no judgment. It's what inspired me to break four world records. For example, when I was going to climb Kilimanjaro, I asked myself, 'How can I do something different than anyone else has ever done up there?' My answer was to do a book signing at the top of the world. When I was going down to the Titanic, I asked myself the same question; 'How can I make my journey exceptional?' My answer in this instance was to become an ordained minister and do the first ever memorial prayer down by the wreck site.

Being imaginative in this way makes life interesting, and the possibilities are endless."

So how do we nurture that connection to our creative self? Scientists say it begins very early in life. We are born creators. But as we move through the school system, our creativity quotient tends to drop like the proverbial stone. Why?

Acclaimed author and TED Talk phenomenon Sir Ken Robinson has a simple explanation: the fault lies in our educational system. The world- renowned creativity expert says, "We are educating people right out of their creativity." Robinson feels that, in fact, the educational system as it is today encourages children to become good workers rather creative thinkers.

For that reason, Robinson has championed a radical rethinking of the world's school systems to cultivate creativity in young minds and acknowledge multiple types of intelligence. This visionary leader's message has resonated around the world. Since its debut in 2006, Robinson's webcast TED Talk has been widely distributed and followed. The words "Everyone should watch this" frame all his popular blog posts.

In 1998, Robinson led the British government's advisory committee on creative and cultural education. The committee undertook a massive inquiry into the significance of creativity in the educational system and the economy. And, in 2003, Robinson was knighted for his achievements.

In his book, *The Element: How Finding Your Passion Changes Everything*, Robinson takes a deep look at human creativity and education. This new archetype, as Robinson portrays it, is the foundation of finding one's personal satisfaction in life. And as Robinson says, "It's available to every person who knows how to find it."

"The Element is the place where passion and skill meet. People find The Element when they engage in the thing that they love that they are also especially good at doing. This leads to more than just a sense of personal satisfaction. Being in The Element insulates people against unpredictable changes and leads to a more flexible and productive society.

"The world is changing faster than ever in our history. Our best hope for the future is to develop a new paradigm of human capacity to meet a new era of human existence. We need to evolve a new appreciation of the importance of nurturing human talent along with an understanding of how talent expresses itself differently in every individual. We need to create environments – in our schools, in our workplaces, and in our public offices – where every person is inspired to grow creatively. We need to make sure that all people have the chance to do what they should be doing, to discover the Element in themselves and in their own way."[78]

According to Robinson, our global educational system is based, for the most part, on the 19th century idea of teaching to meet the needs of industrialism. To that end, school subjects such as mathematics, science, reading, and the like are encouraged by teachers because they can help develop skills that land students jobs. Conversely, music, art, and other creative means of expression fall by the wayside. That truth has become all too evident today as arts programs are being slashed and eliminated to keep strapped school budgets afloat.

"If you think of it, the whole system of public education around the world is a protracted process of university entrance," says Sir Ken Robinson.

"The consequence is that many highly talented, brilliant, creative people think they're not, because the thing they were good at in school wasn't valued, or was actually stigmatized," he adds. "We can't afford to go on that way."

"Pigeon-holing and making people into soulless worker bees is tantamount to beating out the properties that make each of us unique," concurs Beth Arnold.

Like Robinson, Arnold believes that 21st century models that incorporate enriched arts programs should replace current teaching systems before we educate children out of their creativity.

"We have to be careful now that we use this gift of creativity wisely," says Arnold. When it comes to our children, "Our task is to educate their whole being, so they can face this future. We may not see this future, but they will. Our job is to help them make something of it."

"Robinson refers to this crisis of human resources as our 'second climate crisis' and asserts that we need to address it with the same urgency as global warming." Says Arnold, "Sir Ken is singing to the choir with me."

Corporate Vision
How important is creativity in the C-suite?

A new breed of CEO is emerging, one that holds new esteem for the expression of human creativity in the work place. And as Steven Tomasco, a manager at IBM Global Business Services says, "It is very interesting that coming off the worst economic conditions they'd ever seen, [CEOs] didn't fall back on management discipline, existing best practices, rigor, or operations. In fact, they [did] the opposite."

According to a new IBM study which polled over 1,500 corporate heads and public sector leaders across 60 nations and 33 industries, creativity is now considered the most important leadership quality for success in business, outweighing even integrity and global thinking.[79]

Creative leaders are also more prepared to break with the status quo of industry, enterprise, and revenue models which prompts another 81 per cent of those polled in the study to rate innovation as a "crucial capability."

"Everyone has the capacity to be creative and studies show that creative people are happier," says Marci Segal, president of Creativityland Inc., a Canadian consultancy that specializes in creativity training for businesses. By encouraging employee creativity, organizations can improve morale, increase motivation and enhance engagement, she says.

⊙✖⊙

You cannot use up creativity. The more you use, the more you have.
~ *Maya Angelou*

Nurturing Your Creative Nature: An Interview with Peggy McColl

Can you develop your creativity? For 25 years Peggy McColl has used her techniques to help professional athletes, organizations, and individuals rediscover their creativity and unleash their full potential. A successful author and entrepreneur, McColl has created an enviable career and personal life by using tools that improve her ever-increasing imagination, creative vision, insight, and inherent wisdom.

Despite her humble origins, Quebec native McColl is recognized today as one of the most internationally acclaimed experts in the area of destiny achievement. The author of *Your Destiny Switch: Master Your Key Emotions and Attract the Life of Your Dreams* started her career with just one goal. She wanted to make a positive contribution to the lives of others.

To that end, McColl founded Dynamic Destinies, Inc., an organization committed to promoting sound principles for the creation of lasting and positive change. I wanted to know more about this crucial concept of creativity.

Can creativity be developed or learned?

Yes, I really believe it can. There are some people who are extremely creative. While they may have been born with a degree of innate talent, they foster and develop creativity through specific practices. I brainstorm ideas regularly, and it has been one of my daily practices, a way to elicit ideas more swiftly and effectively. I believe creativity can be learned and developed, like a muscle of sorts.

Would you provide some tools and tips to unleash creativity and explore our full potential?

I think it starts by deciding that you are open to creativity. Our mind is an incredibly powerful force. We have to open up our consciousness to the idea that we can be creative. We need to be open and to engage in a state of curiosity. One way is to start to study other creative people and what they've done. We can also take courses or attend events to learn from others, their success and their failures. In this way, we can actually learn the skill of creativity. Where did they get that idea? Was it passion driven? What did they do with it, once they got that idea? Open up your consciousness to realizing that you are a creative being and engage in the emotion of curiosity, where you observe, gather, and study what others are doing.

There is currently an abundance of information and discussion supporting the idea that our thoughts and emotions create our reality. You summarize this sentiment in your book, "Your Destiny Switch", by the following quote: "You can achieve your destiny be using your creativity and your positive emotions because feeling any one such emotion will attract events, people, circumstances, and outcomes that resonate to its vibration." Please explain how we can discover our true destiny through this creative process.

What it comes down to is paying attention to your feelings. By truly connecting to what you are passionate about, you can make wonderful things happen. When we are connected to our passion and are out there following through on what it is that we feel guided to do, then we attract things into our life that we don't necessarily expect. I believe these things come to us out of a place called magic or more accurately, from clear intention.

Tell me more about intention and creativity in terms of success. Are there particular tools such as vision boards, meditation, or other helpful exercises that facilitate this process?

Yes. Successful people are using tools that are contributing to their success. And it's not one size fits all. Each person uses a different mode that works for them, their own "One Thing", which is also the title of one of my books. Personally, one of the most potent tools that I use is called the Power Life Script. The script is written in a very positive way. I record this script and listen to it on a daily basis. In the script I affirm the beliefs I have about what I'd like to create in my life in the future. It's 22 minutes and is a tool that I use to keep myself connected to the life that I choose to live. It keeps me on track, if I ever find that I'm in a low energy state or not feeling particularly wonderful. That might be my "one thing", but somebody else might use another technique like a vision board.

I will give you another example. I met a woman the other day who had been in one of my workshops, and she had a stack of these little index cards. Every day she writes down what her intentions are, writing them in the present tense. On one side of the card she declares her intention, such as, 'I am a successful business woman...', describing it in a statement. On the other side of the index card she writes down how that makes her feel: 'I am grateful to be successful. It comes easily to me. I am calm, happy, and I'm content.' She writes this every day! This may sound crazy to some people, but it's her way of getting focused and staying focused. I think it's quite extraordinary.

I really believe that you need to have daily disciplines in place in order to achieve your creative aspirations and goals.

Do you believe in the creation of an "ideal life" plan?

Yes, I'm definitely a planner, but I also tell people my middle name is flexible. That's a paradox to some people. I tell them to plan because it's important in order to create the life they want. But they have to be flexible. The reason for this is that things change. You have to be flexible, because life is full of defining moments brought about by change.

How can you feel bullish about your life plan when you are down on your luck?

When you're down, it's hard to get back up again. I heard an expression recently that children need love the most when they deserve it the least. You see a child behaving badly, and the last thing you feel like doing is loving them, but that's what they really need. We are like those children. When our bodies are beat and when we're not healthy or happy – that's when we really need to tap into our creative side and take care of ourselves. We may be in a situation where the choice of being really happy may not seem like the logical choice or the thing that we feel like doing. But we have to connect with our emotions and find our passion, in order to create something better.

In the book "Your Destiny Switch", you say that to remain in an overall positive, balanced state of emotions, you need to create habits that will nurture positivity. To do this, you must master the art of switching your emotions, a skill that involves a three-step process: observe, decide, and switch. Can you describe for us how each step of the process works?

It starts simply with just noticing what you're feeling. Step two is to decide whether you want to change that feeling or not. Believe it or not, it's an important step, because we have to question whether or not we are truly motivated to change our patterns. Step three is to just decide whether you want to switch it right now or not. If you're feeling anger or fear, observe it. If you want to switch, then ask the question, 'What do I want to experience?'

Let's say I want to experience the feeling of faith. I say to myself, 'What would that feel like?' I immediately get the answer, and the feeling flows right in my body as soon as I engage in that question. This is creatively using your imagination to change your negative emotions. We are emotional beings, and our emotions flow through us. For all of us, there will be times when we might feel sadness. Sometimes it's important just to stay there, experience it, and allow it to run its course. I would never tell anyone to put a lid on pain and sorrow and pretend that it's not there, as that's not going to help you either. But once you decide to switch, you must use your imagination to allow yourself to feel how you want to feel. Stay with the desired emotion and breathe through it.

It definitely takes practice, but, once it becomes a habit, then it's easy to go straight to the feeling the next time. After doing this repeatedly, it feels as though you've already achieved your goals. You relax and feel like your spirit is resonating on a higher scale. It's a muscle that needs to be developed and should be practiced as a daily discipline like physical exercise.

What does the phrase "creative consciousness" mean to you? Can a person deepen their relationship with creativity within the space of spiritual consciousness?

I love those two words together. Creative consciousness means to me that you get into a state where you're allowing your creativity to rise up and be playful and you're engaging in that experience. You're allowing it to unfold and reveal itself. Creative consciousness can be summarized as just sitting down and saying, 'Let's connect to that creative emotion or feeling or thought'. Creative consciousness is like a full body experience. Let's really use and really feel its palpable nature to gain some clarity, to set some direction for our lives and to use it in order to do some good in the world.

If you really want to do something, you can do it by fully engaging your emotions, your spirit, and your creativity.

Remember Nelson Mandela and Marion Williamson have been pegged as writing that, 'You are a child of God. Who are you to be small in the world?'

Most of us have no idea of our real creative height. We are much more gifted than we know.
~ *Julia Cameron, author, The Artist's Way*

Finding the Artist's Way: An Interview with Julia Cameron

Julia Cameron has had a remarkable career as an award-winning playwright, filmmaker, poet, and writer of 30 books, including the crime novel *The Dark Room* and the recent drama *Mozart's Ghost*. But Cameron is best known for her hugely successful works on creativity.[80]

The Artist's Way, her most successful book, has sold more than two million copies worldwide. Her follow-up bestsellers, including *The Vein of Gold*, *Walking in this World*, and *The Right to Write* are also considered flagship books, renowned for their liberating theories. These powerful enablers of creativity are currently taught in universities, churches, human potential centers, and even in tiny clusters deep in the jungles of Panama.

"My books are not creative theory," says Cameron. "They spring straight out of my own creative practice. In a sense, I am the floor sample of my own tool kit. When we are unblocked, we can have remarkable and diverse adventures."

Is true creativity the possession of a relatively small percentage of the population?

No, absolutely not. We are all creative. Creativity is a natural life force that all can experience in one form or another. Just as blood is part of our physical body and is nothing we must invent, creativity is part of us, and we each can tap into the greater creative energies of the universe and pull from that vast, powerful, spiritual wellspring to amplify our own individual creativity.

As a culture, we tend to define creativity too narrowly and to think of it in elitist terms, as something belonging to a small, chosen tribe of 'real artists.' But in reality, everything we do requires making creative choices, although we seldom recognize that fact. The ways in which we dress, set up our homes, do our jobs, the movies we see, and even the people we involve ourselves with, these all are expressions of our creativity. It is our erroneous beliefs about creativity, our cultural mythology about artists ("All artists are broke, crazy, promiscuous, self-centered, single, or they have trust funds") that encourage us to leave our dreams unfulfilled. These myths most often involve matters of money, time, and other people's agendas for us. As we clear these blocks away, we can become more creative.

What factors keep people from being creative?

Conditioning. Family, friends, and educators may discourage us from pursuing an artist's career. There is the mythology that artists are somehow 'different,' and this mythology of difference inspires fear. If we have negative perceptions about what an artist is, we will feel less inclined to do the diligent work necessary to become one.

On a societal level, blocked creative energy manifests itself as self-destructive behavior. Many people who are engaged in self-defeating behaviors, such as addicts of alcohol, drugs, sex, or work, are really in the hands of this shadow side of the creative force. As we become more creative, these negative expressions of the creative force often abate.

How does your book, "The Artist's Way", free people to be creative?

The primary purpose and effect of *The Artist's Way* is to put people in touch with the power of their own internal creativity. The book frees people to be more creative in many different ways: First, it helps dismantle negative mythologies about artists. Second, it helps people discover their own creative force, access it, and express it more freely. Third, it provides people with awareness about their self-destructive behaviors and allows them to see more clearly what the impediments on their individual path might be. Finally, the book helps people identify and celebrate their desires and dreams and make the plans to accomplish them. It teaches people how to support and nurture themselves, as well as how to find others who will support them in fulfilling their dreams.

One of the central themes of "The Artist's Way" is the link between creativity and spirituality. How are they connected?

Creativity is a spiritual force. The force that drives the green fuse through the flower, as Dylan Thomas defined his idea of the life force, is the same urge that drives us toward creation. There is a central will to create that is part of our human heritage and potential. Because creation is always an act of faith, and faith is a spiritual issue, so is creativity. As we strive for our highest selves, our spiritual selves, we cannot help but be more aware, more proactive, and more creative.

Einstein, after years of fruitless calculations, suddenly had the solution to the general theory of relativity revealed in a dream: "Like a giant die making an indelible impress, a huge map of the universe outlined itself in one clear vision."[81]

The Spiritual Side of Creativity: An Interview with James Van Praagh

The extraordinary James Van Praagh's biography describes him as a spiritual medium, author, teacher, and television producer, all words that depict an interviewee who defies description.

Over the years, the world-renowned spiritual medium and creativity virtuoso James Van Praagh and his message of hope has touched a huge number of people due to his many appearances on such shows as *Oprah*, *Larry King Live*, *20/20*, *48 Hours*, and *Biography*. His unique paranormal experiences during the past twenty-five years have seen him author best-selling books, conceive intuitive meditation programming, create a successful state of the art website, conduct seminars to sold-out audiences, and produce successful television projects, including his most recent success, *Ghost Whisperer*, with Jennifer Love-Hewitt. Van Praagh has authored eight New York Times best-selling books: *Unfinished Business*, *Ghosts Among Us*, *Talking To Heaven*, *Reaching To Heaven*, *Healing Grief*, *Heaven and Earth*, *Looking Beyond: A Teen's Guide To The Spiritual World*, and *Meditations with James Van Praagh*.

Regarding his work as a medium, he states, "My greatest satisfaction in doing this work is witnessing an instantaneous change in people. When someone is alone and overwhelmed by grief, life seems over. But when I'm able to help teach someone to make contact with a loved one, their grief and loneliness disappear and proper closure can take place."

In your book "Talking To Heaven", you say that, "Fear is not only an illusion, but the largest block to personal growth and the potential of the human spirit to excel. By being 'in fear' we cannot live 'in love' and indirectly we say goodbye to a lifestyle rich in creativity and productiveness." How do we let go of the fear and allow creativity to shine through?

It's really a matter of learning about perspective and seeing yourself as a soul being. When you understand that you're a soul, with that comes the understanding that your natural state is one of love. You are God. God is love. When we come back to this 'illusionary' world many times, we will place ourselves in situations in which we are forced to go within and find answers, truth, ourselves. With the awareness that we are God and that God is limitless, we should see that fear is limiting. When we go in fear, we are not living from our truest selves. Once we free up the fear and see that there is only love and lessons of understanding, we will be free to be our creative God selves and create a life we choose.

Where does our source of creativity originate?

Creativity is the natural essence of God. We as light beings are free to use this God force in any way we choose. Hopefully the soul is advanced enough to use it only for good, but, as we look at this world, we see many who utilize this source in limited ways because they get caught up in the 'man power.' They use the force to take other lives, wage wars, make judgments and such.

Will developing our intuition (or sixth sense) enhance creative insight?

Intuition means 'into the soul' so that, in a way, it is listening to your true essence. The soul has been through many lifetimes in many dimensions and in many spaces and systems. As I said just before, the more you are 'in-tune' with your truth, the more you are in touch with God, the more you are able to explore the aspects of your being. God is of course that limitless creative force, always manifesting, growing, producing, so that it goes without saying that, the more you know God, the more you are open to using the creative force and expressing it effortlessly.

Do you believe that the creative process is fundamentally a spiritual one?

When you're being creative, you are closest to the true source of your being...your soul self. Creativity and Spirit are one. I think that, when we understand that we are 'spirits' having a 'physical experience' rather than the other way around, we open up the door to spiritual evolution and, in doing so, become aware of our creativity. So you can say that, as you become more spiritual, you become more creative.

Tell us about the influence of our dreams on creativity. In your book, "Looking Beyond: A Teen's Guide to the Spiritual World", you mention that some of the mind's best work is done in our dreams. Are these nocturnal stories a window into our creative source?

In the dream state we are freed from the limitations of the physical mind and open to the Universal Source. We are free and open to bring into our awareness all the positive creative things we can manifest in ideas. Recently I was remodeling a bathroom and I wasn't sure what the walls and cabinetry should look like, so I went to sleep that night with this on my mind. During the night I had a dream of walking into my bathroom and that it had beautiful yellow tiles and cherry looking cabinets. It spoke to my soul...or I should say it was an extension of my soul's energy. It was me. So in dreams we are more able to be in touch with our creativity.

TRY THIS

There are many ways to stir our sometimes-sleepy imaginations. James Van Praagh suggests the following techniques:

1. Get a pad and pen. Hold the pen in the hand opposite to the one you usually use and start drawing anything that comes to you on the pad.
2. Have a friend take out three different objects with different textures and scents, such as a fragrant flower, a lemon, a piece of rosemary, etc. Close your eyes and go to each object, holding them, smelling them. See what different reactions you have to each.
3. Look around your living room and pick a place on a wall that you see every day. Decide to use this wall as the "Doorway to your Creative Mind." Now on it place an object that represents something that you feel will open you up to that creative part of yourself when you set eyes on it. For me, I have a colorful painting of a garden of lavender, and anytime I see it, it opens up my creativity.
4. Make a list of five creative things you would like to do within the next year. Next to each one, write down a method you'll use to accomplish it.
5. Use your imagination and pretend you are a songwriter. Get out a piece of paper and say to your heart. 'What is it you want to say to me?' And write down the lyrics your heart wants to sing.

6. Walk around your neighborhood and pay close attention to the myriad forms of beauty. It can reside in objects, plants, trees, buildings, concrete. Just attune yourself to the beauty in everything. You may not think a roofline or a trash pile is beautiful, but they are. It all depends on how you look at it.

7. Have fun. Life is too short to ponder over. Just live it.

EPILOGUE

The deep inner prompting that drove me when I first conceived of this book was my abiding desire to give people a timely reminder of how vitally important it is that we should embrace life and all its wondrous, imponderable possibilities. All we need do is "come awake" before the new and unexplored pathways that life opens up to us each and every day. The key is to remain watchful. Only by cultivating these awakenings do we become more enlightened by the world around us and ultimately discover ourselves along the way.

How easy it is to get caught up heedlessly in the daily drama of life, the struggle to survive. How easy it is to forget that we are all connected at a much more profound level. The situation of our day presents a fascinating paradox. On the one hand, each of us is capable of assuming a role that is bigger than life and making an extraordinary impact on the world, as so many of the people discussed in this book have done. On the other hand, however, we are but one grain of sand among many millions. These are ostensibly opposed concepts: being humble and awestruck enough to know how seemingly insignificant we are, merely a spot on the globe, even while being big and bold and making a significant imprint on this world. But there is a deep and mysterious connection between these two ways of conceiving our role. It's when we truly embrace our own soul that we can't help but embrace our world.

In the face of all the life challenges that come our way, my hope has been to draw attention to the silver lining that embellishes the cloud. Through the material presented here I want to encourage people to harness the power of optimism. I want them to gain the abiding confidence that we control our destiny and that we alone can shape our experiences simply by re-aligning our intentions and the things we choose to focus on.

Life "happens" to us all, but it's how we choose to view these "happenings" that makes a quantum difference in our level of happiness.

The scientist Jonas Salk has stated that all species undergo significant crisis points in their evolution, whereby they become more interdependent and harmonious with their environment. These momentous shifts are necessary for survival. It is clear that we are in the shift age so eloquently described by David Houle in the first chapter of this book. I believe that the critical point of stress that besets us, characterized by the balance between human population growth and our earth's resources, is forcing us to re-center. It is, in fact, nature's way of moving us from a mentality of fragmented separateness to one of unitary connectedness.

We have reached the stage where, to survive, we simply have to depend on one another. The human species is one of very few that will help a fellow member from across the globe that they don't even know. We are also the only species that will run into a burning building to help another out of altruism. Surely, there is great hope and love here.

Of all the generations of humans that have lived, we have the opportunity to decide with conscious intent to participate in the great new shifting of our world towards a situation where hope and mutual care prevail. The desire to be ever climbing up the proverbial ladder and ever acquiring bigger and better things in the vain hope of achieving lasting happiness and personal gain becomes less and less meaningful in the light of this deeper longing to live a life of fuller significance, this striving to connect with others in a genuine and meaningful way.

These are my wishes. My great hope for us all.

~ Susan

NOTES AND SOURCES

To learn more about the author please visit: **www.steinbrecher.com**

Susan can be reached via email at steinbrecherinc@gmail.com or connect with her on Twitter: @SteinbrecherInc

Introduction

1 Dan Pink, "The Surprising Truth About What Motivates Us", www.youtube.com, 2010

Chapter 2

2 Kate Lister and Tom Harnish, *Undress for Success:The Naked Truth About Making Money From Home,* (Wiley, April 2009)
3 TeleworkResearchNetwork.com (Kate Lister and Tom Harnish, 2010) *Workshifting Benefits: The Bottom Line*
4 Ibid.
5 Ibid.
6 Ibid.
7 Ibid.
8 Ibid.

Chapter 3

9   Kiva.org

10 Harvard Business Review, "Why Sustainability Is Now the Key Driver of Innovation," by Ram Nidumolu, C, K, Prahalad, and M.R. Rangaswami, blogs.hbr.org

11 Business Wire, "Good News for Green Industry: Survey Finds Consumers Still Spending on Environmentally Responsible Products" June 30, 2010. www.businesswire.com

12 J. Manzoni, N. Nilekani, et al. "Tomorrow's Global Company: Challenges and Choices", report by 'Tomorrow's Company' (2007), www.tomorrowscompany.com

13 Greenbiz.com, "10 Things I've Learned About Building a Revolutionary, Responsible Company", Jeffrey Hollender, June 21, 2010. www.greenbiz.com

14 Tim Sanders, *Saving the World at Work: What Companies and Individuals Can Do To Go Beyond Making A Profit to Making A Difference* (DoubleDay, 2008)

Visit Tim at: www.TimSanders.com Author of the new book, *Today We Are Rich: Harnessing The Power Of Total Confidence*, April 2011, Tyndale House Publishing.

Chapter 4

15 Jonas Salk, "A Wise and Good Ancestor" interview with Richard D. Heffner on *The Open Mind* (11 May 1985)

Chapter 5

16 Kyle MacDonald, *One Red Paperclip: The Story of How One Man Changed his Life One Swap at a Time*, (Ebury Press, 2008)

17 Tony Hsieh, *Delivering Happiness :A Path to Profits, Passion and Purpose,*(Business Plus, June 7, 2010)

18 New York Times, "Recalculating Happiness in a Himalayan Kingdom", Seth Mydans, May 6, 2009, www.nytimes.com

Chapter 6

19 Huffington Post, "Consciousness and the End of the War Between Science and Religion", Deepak Chopra, June 25, 2010, http://www.huffingtonpost.com/deepak-chopra

20 The DNA Phantom Effect was first reported in Russia: P.P.Gariaev, K.V. Grigor'ev, A.A. Vasil'ev, V.P. Poponin, and V.A. Shcheglov, "Investigation of the Fluctuation Dynamics of DNA Solutions by Laser Correlation Spectroscopy," Bulletin of the Lebedev Physics Institute (1992), no. 11-12, p. 23-30, as cited by Vladimir Poponin in an online article "The DNA Phantom Effect: Direct Measurement of a New Field in the Vacuum Substructure" (Update on DNA Phantom Effect: March 19, 2002). The Weather Master website: www.twm.co.nz/DNAPhantom.htm (Source note from www.greggbradden.com)

21 Spirit of Maat, "Healing Hearts, Healing Nations: The Science of Peace and the Power of Prayer", Gregg Braden, November 18, 2001, www.spiritofmaat.com

22 Enlightennext Magazine,"The Science of Collective Consciousness", Robert Kenney, 2010, www.enlightennext.org

Chapter 7

23 Buddhist Parable, The Dhammapada translated by www.buddha.net

24 The Chronicle of Philanthropy, "Sex, Drugs and...Charity? Brain Study Finds New Links", Holly Hall, December 7, 2006, philanthropy.com

Chapter 8

[25] Buddhist Parable, The Dhammapada translated by www.buddha.net

[26] Jonathan Franzen, *The Oprah Show*, 2010

[27] CBS News, "American Debt Threatens Status as World Power: Can America Still be the World's Greatest Power, as the World's Greatest Borrower?", Lara Logan, April 8, 2010, www.cbsnews.com

[28] Marketing Charts, "Majority of US Workers Live Paycheck-to-Paycheck," June 10, 2009, www.marketingcharts.com

[29] Property Casualty 360, www.propertycasualty360.com

[30] Annie Leonard, *The Story of Stuff: How Our Obsession with Stuff is Trashing the Planet, Our Communities, and Our Health — and a Vision for Change* (Free Press: March 9, 2010)

[31] Ibid.

[32] Ibid.

[33] Ibid.

[34] Ibid.

Chapter 9

[35] USA Today, "Mindfulness meditation being used in hospitals and schools", Marilyn Elias, June 8, 2009, www.usatoday.com

[36] Opinionator, "Sitting Quietly, Doing Something", Daniel Goleman, July 16, 2009, www.opinionator.blogs.nytimes.com

[37] UCLA Newsroom, "How to Build a Bigger Brain", Mark Wheeler, May 12, 2009, www.newsroom.ucla.edu

[38] Dan Rather Reports, "Mind Science", Dan Rather, 2008, CBS

[39] Scientific American, "Michelangelo's secret message in the Sistine Chapel: A juxtaposition of God and the human brain", R.Douglas Fields, May 27, 2010, www.scientificamerican.com

Chapter 10

40 Buddhist Parable, The Dhammapada translated by www. buddha.net

41 Jeremy Rifkin, *The European Dream: How Europe's Vision of the Future is Quietly Eclipsing the American Dream* (New York: Penguin, 2004)

42 Think Global Green, "What makes Europe greener than the US?", Elisabeth Rosenthal, October 1, 2009, www.thinkglo balgreen.org

43 Centers for Disease Control and Prevention, "Halting the Epidemic by Making Health Easier: At A Glance 2010, December 17, 2009, www.cdc.gov

44 BBC, "Afternoon Nap is Good for the Heart", February 13, 2007, www.news.bbc.co.uk

45 Paul Krugman, "Learning From Europe", *Opinion*, New York Times, January 10, 2010, www.nytimes.com

46 Opinionator, "Hey America, Take the Day Off", Gail Collins and Timothy Egan, August 10, 2010. www.opinion ator.blogs.nytimes.com

47 Ibid

48 BBC, "Flexible working 'good for heart and soul'", February 17, 2010, www.news.bbc.co.uk

49 MSNBC, "Leaner nations bike, walk, use mass transit: Link found between 'active transportation' and less obesity in 17 countries, Associated Press, December 15, 2008, www. msnbc.msn.com

50 Habisch, Jonker, et al; *Corporate Responsibility Across Europe*, (Springer, Berlin, 2005)

51 CSR Europe, "CSR Europe's report on Biodiversity", www. csreurope.org

52 The New York Times, "Europeans Fear Crisis Threatens Liberal Benefits" Steven Erlanger, May 22, 2010, www.nytimes.com

Chapter 11

53   BBC News, "Toyota president says recall-hit firm 'grew too fast': Toyota's rapid expansion might have prompted safety issues which have led to 8.5 million vehicles being recalled, the carmaker's president has said", February 23, 2010, www.news.bbc.co,uk

Chapter 12

54   TNGG, The Next Great Generation, "The Interview: 12-year-old Orren Fox, @HappyChickens" by Edward Boches, December 14th, 2009, www.thenextgeneration.com

Chapter 13

55   Harvard Business Review, "How Social Networking Has Changed Business", Bill George, December 23, 2010, www.blogs.hbr.org
56   Shambhala Sun, "Did You Get The Message", Steve Silberman, March 2010, www.shambhalasun.com
57   The New York Times, "Growing Up Digital, Wired For Distraction", Matt Richtel, November 21, 2010, www.nytimes.com
58   Wieden+Kennedy, "Old Spice Case Study", July 30, 2010, www.brightcove.com

Chapter 14

59   Globe and Mail, "Take a grade-school approach to your grown-up", Mark Fenske, November, 18, 2010, www.theglobeandmail.com
60   Harvard Business Review, "Leadership on the Brain", David Rock, April 28, 2010, www.blogs.hbr.org

[61] Center for BrainHealth, "Are Our Brains Being Rewired by Technology?", Sandra Bond Chapman, Ph.D., January 31, 2011, www.brainhealth.utdallas.edu

[62] Reprinted with permission from: Posit Science, "Why Brain Fitness?", Michael Merzenich, Ph.D., 2010, www.posit science.com

Chapter 15

[63] Cinema Blend, "Gemma Arterton Gets A Nose Job In The First Tamara Drewe Trailer," Eric Eisenberg, August 26, 2010, www.cinemablend.com

[64] CNN, "Star makes documentary on paparazzi," Brooke Anderson's interview with Adrian Grenier on his documentary "Teenage Paparazzo", September 27, 2010, www.cnn.com

[65] MSNBC, "California Assembly Oks bill to send reckless paparazzi to jail: Photogs who break traffic laws to snap celebs face a year in prison and up to a $5,000 fine," Brent Lang, August 31, 2010, www.msnbc.msn.com

Chapter 17

[66] The Best Brain Possible, Debbie Hampton, www.thebest-brainpossible.blogspot.com

[67] The Heart of Healing, "The Seven Essentials of Healing" www.theheartofhealing.net

Chapter 18

[68] Buddhist Parable, The Dhammapada translated by www.buddha.net

[69] Unexplainable.net, "The Need for a Belief System ... a system of organization for your experiences!", Edward B. Toupin, March 24, 2005, www.unexplainable.net

70 For more information about Psych-K: www.psych-k.com

71 John Bradshaw, *Homecoming: Reclaiming and Championing Your Inner Child* (Bantam, 1990)

72 Bruce H. Lipton, *The Biology of Belief: Unleashing the Power of Consciousness, Matter and Miracle,* (First Hay House edition, September 2008)

Chapter 19

73 Buddhist Parable, The Dhammapada translated by www.buddha.net

74 Coaching 4 Wellness – Harvard University Study, Eysench 1988 study on Stress, www.coaching4wellness.net

75 American Psychological Association, "APA Poll Finds Women Bear Brunt of Nation's Stress, Financial Downturn: Annual Stress in America survey shows increasing stress takes toll on physical and emotional health,", 2008, www.apa.org

76 Department of Psychology, Stanford University, "Are you wondering what 'Mindfulness' is??", www.psych.stanford.edu

Chapter 20

77 View Zone, "Left Brain, Right Brain", Dan Eden, www.viewzone2.com

78 Ken Robinson, *The Element: How Finding Your Passion Changes Everything* (Viking Adult, January 8, 2009)

79 IBM, Capitalizing on Complexity, Insights from the 2010 Global CEO Study, May 2010, www.935.ibm.com/services/us/ceo/ceostudy2010/

80 Partial reprint of this interview courtesy of www.theartistsway.com

81 Wikipedia, "Creativity" (Brian, 1996, p. 159), www.wikipedia.org/wiki/Creativity

Made in the USA
Lexington, KY
29 June 2011